THE GUIDE TO
MYSTERIOUS ABERDEEN

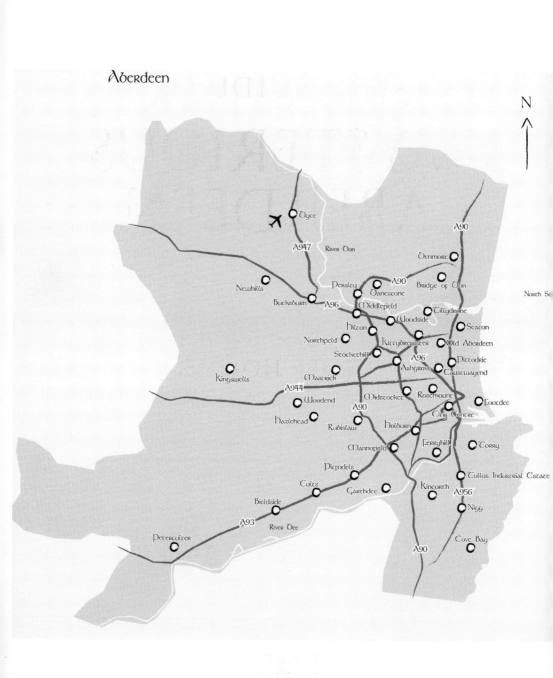

THE GUIDE TO
MYSTERIOUS ABERDEEN

GEOFF HOLDER

Frontispiece: Aberdeen. *(Jenni Wilson)*

To the terrible two, Slick and Shade, companions of the highest order.

First published 2010

The History Press
The Mill, Brimscombe Port
Stroud, Gloucestershire, GL5 2QG
www.thehistorypress.co.uk

British Library Cataloguing in Publication Data.
A catalogue record for this book is available from the British Library.

ISBN 978 0 7524 5659 1

Typesetting and origination by The History Press
Printed in Great Britain
Manufacturing managed by Jellyfish Print Solutions Ltd

CONTENTS

ACKNOWLEDGEMENTS AND PHOTO CREDITS

Many fine individuals and institutions have helped in the research for this book. I would particularly like to thank: Albert Thomson, First Master, Aberdeen Shoemakers' Incorporation; Andy Stewart, Store Manager, Primark Stores on Union Street; Judith Stones, Keeper of Archaeology, and Chris Croly, Assistant Keeper (Research), both of Education, Culture and Sport, Aberdeen City Council; Dr Arthur Winfield of the Mither Kirk Development Project at the Kirk of St Nicholas; Norman Adams, author; Dr Jennifer Downes, Curator (Science Collections) at the University of Aberdeen; Neil Curtis, Senior Curator, Marischal Museum; the ever-helpful staff at the Local Studies section of A.K. Bell Library, Perth, and the Reference Library of Aberdeen Central Library; Rachael Hayward and Al Hayes of East of Scotland Paranormal; the team at The History Press; Paul Revell at www.revellution.co.uk for website design; and, of course, the luminous Ségolène Dupuy for digital photography, driving, putting up with the cold and rain, and translating the relevant sections of a French book on UFOs.

The opinions and interpretations expressed in the book are of course my own.

The maps were splendidly produced by Jenni Wilson; the image of the victim of spontaneous human combustion on page 111 is courtesy of the Fortean Picture Library. Most of the other images are either by Ségolène Dupuy or the author, or from the author's collection, as indicated in the captions. The photographs on pages 141 and 142 are included by kind permission of the Deacon Convener of the Seven Incorporated Trades of Aberdeen.

All efforts have been made to trace the copyright owners of the images used. If anyone has knowledge of copyright on any of the images, please contact the publisher.

This book is part of an ongoing series of similar titles. If you would like to share any stories of the weird and wonderful, or wish to find more information, please visit www.geoffholder.co.uk.

INTRODUCTION

I cannot tell how the truth may be; I say the tale as t'was said to me.

Inscription on Downie's Cairn, Old Aberdeen

The man who died of fright ... the witch who never was ... a Pictish god standing in the reception of a council foyer ... alleged secret tunnels under ancient sites ... a talking statue ... giant frog submersibles ... wedding celebrations mistaken for an alien invasion fleet ... the lions that became a stone circle ... legends of William Wallace's dismembered limbs ... spontaneous human combustion ... sightings of river monsters and mermaids ... bodysnatching professors ... golf with giant skulls ...

Aberdeen is full of mysteries, marvels and strangeness, and this book is a comprehensive guide to them all. Within, you will encounter magic, witchcraft, folklore and superstitions; contemporary urban legends; gargoyles and graveyards; graverobbers and murderers; stone circles and prehistoric burial sites; UFOs and freak weather; and tales of horror, madness and dangerous porridge.

The Guide to Mysterious Aberdeen is organised geographically, with everything paranormal and odd described on a street-by-street or suburb-by-suburb pattern, ideal for exploration. The individual sections set out all the history, legends and associations of a particular place, along with descriptions of what can be seen now. A few stories do not fit into the geographical framework so are collected in this introduction, while witchcraft is such a major topic in Aberdeen it has its own interlude. Cross-references between locations are shown in SMALL CAPS. There is an emphasis on locations that can be visited, such as museums, cathedrals and public buildings. The degree of wheelchair access for these locations is described, along with opening hours and other visitor information. A good streetmap is recommended. Aberdeen traffic is notorious. If you can, take buses (day and weekly passes are available) or walk. With the exception of the link to Dyce there are now no suburban railways.

The book covers the entire area of the City of Aberdeen; exploring the arc of rural areas on the western fringe is best accomplished using the 1:25000 Ordnance Survey Explorer maps 406 and 421. National Grid References are given for hard-to-find sites. The county of Aberdeenshire is covered in my companion volume *The Guide to Mysterious Aberdeenshire*, published in 2009. Tales of ghosts and poltergeists are gathered together in another of my books, *Haunted Aberdeen* (2010).

A few words of caution. Aberdeen has the same problems as most major cities. Parts of the city centre (especially the 'underground city') are best explored in daylight, while the most advantageous time for visiting some cemeteries is in the morning, before the arrival of the alchoholically-enhanced.

THE TOP TEN

If you want to skip to the ten top 'mysterious' sights to visit, I would recommend:

1. St Nicholas Kirk and Kirkyard, and St Mary's Chapel (pages 65-76)
2. The Masonic Temple (pages 84-90)
3. St Machar's Cathedral and Graveyard (pages 172-7)
4. St Mary's Cathedral (pages 102-4)
5. Tyrebagger Stone Circle (page 163)
6. The Zoology Museum (pages 170-1)
7. St John's Church (pages 91-2)
8. The Tolbooth (pages 32-5)
9. The Winter Gardens at Duthie Park (pages 129-31)
10. Provost Skene's House (pages 49-54)

Two very different pairs of angels. St John's Church in St John's Place (above left) … and the Masonic Temple in Crown Street (above right). *(Both Ségolène Dupuy)*

USEFUL CONCEPTS FOR THE EXPLORER OF THE WEIRD

Water-spouting gargoyle in the Winter Gardens at Duthie Park. *(Ségolène Dupuy)*

Apotropaic – 'That which protects against evil.' Apotropaic actions and items are scattered throughout this book, from a cat buried beneath a hearth, to grave goods at ST NICHOLAS CHURCH, and the words spoken in various 'charms'.

Liminality – 'That which is betwixt and between,' a transition between one thing and another. Liminal times and places are crucial to magic – Hallowe'en, Midsummer and Rood Day all feature in the witchcraft episodes, as do doorways, thresholds and field boundaries – while liminal events such as the launching of a ship have their own special customs. In some ways the 'underground city' beneath Union Street is a liminal zone.

Magical Thinking – If you are buried close to the altar in a church, you will get to Heaven quicker (*see* ST NICHOLAS KIRK). If you drink water in which charmed bones have been washed, or that comes from a holy well blessed by a saint, the power of the bones or saint will transfer into the water and cure your illness (*see* the witch ISOBEL STRACHAN and the well at CHAPEL OF STONEYWOOD). If you point a 'killing bone' at someone, they will die (*see* MARISCHAL MUSEUM). Magical thinking is central to witchcraft, folk magic, superstition, and a great deal of ostensibly Christian practices.

Tradition and Truth – Who invents urban myths? Who first comes up with a notion that eventually transforms into a tradition, its origin apparently lost in the mists of time? Who mutates rumour into legend and and – when enough time has passed – into history? Who makes all this stuff up? Who believes it? The answer is ... me. And you. And everyone you know, and everyone you don't. We're all in this together. Some traditions are true. Some 'truths' are lies. This book might help you discriminate between fact, fiction, fable and folklore. Well, that's the rumour anyway.

PSYCHOGEOGRAPHY

(Most of the following paragraph appeared in my 2008 book *The Guide to Mysterious Glasgow*; as it applies equally to Aberdeen, I have included it here, with just a few changes to localise the description.) There are as many definitions of psychogeography as there are psychogeographers. For myself, it's about the way the physical environment has an unexpected, even spooky, effect on the mind.

It's something about the ways the power of place – of specific places – seeps into the parts of our brains that conjure fear, imagination, wonder, curiosity and the sense of the uncanny. It's about why certain places are haunted, and others are haunting. It's about memory and surprises. It's about seeking out places where extraordinary events once happened. It's about walking the streets of the city and accidentally spotting a winged monster on a metal drainpipe or finding a tree decorated with drinking mugs. It's about the surprising, the hidden, the obscure and the ignored – and the weird. It's about what this whole book is all about.

TIMELINE OF SIGNIFICANT EVENTS

11th century –	Earliest known church on site of St Nicholas Kirk.
1165 –	Completion of first cathedral (later St Machar's).
1179 –	Aberdeen becomes a Royal burgh, that is, an independent town with trading rights.
13th century –	Dominicans, Trinitarians and Carmelites set up friaries.
1308 –	Aberdeen Castle is destroyed.
1319 –	Robert the Bruce leases the Forest of Stocket to Aberdeen, a business deal that benefits both parties.
1320 –	The Brig o'Balgownie is built over the River Don.
1336 –	The forces of Edward III defeat the Scots at a battle by The Green. Death and destruction follow.
1411 –	The Battle of Harlaw; Aberdeen citizens join in the repulse of a Highland Army.
1489 –	'Old Aberdeen' becomes a burgh, independent of 'New Aberdeen'.
1495 –	King's College, Aberdeen's first university, is founded.
1527 –	The Bridge of Dee is built over the River Dee.
1529, 1538-9, 1545 –	Deadly epidemics, including plague.
1559-1560 –	The Reformation. Four monasteries and other buildings are ransacked but St Nicholas Kirk and St Machar's Cathedral survive.
1571 –	The Battle of Craibstone, a conflict between the Gordon and Forbes clans.
1593 –	Marischal College is founded.
1597 –	The principal year of the witchhunt.
1638 –	A sandbar blocks the harbour.
1639 –	A Covenanting army under the Marquis of Montrose defeat the Royalist defenders.
1644 –	The Battle of Justice Mills. A Royalist army under the Marquis of Montrose (the same one) defeat the Covenanting defenders. Death and destruction follow.
1650s –	Aberdeen is occupied by troops of Cromwell's army.
1671 –	An epidemic kills 1,700, a quarter of the population.

1740s –	Hundreds of children are kidnapped and sold as slaves in America.
1780–1832 –	Period of the bodysnatchers.
1801 –	Union Street is constructed, changing the face of the city.
1870s –	New harbour is constructed, creating a large and reliable port.
1891 –	Old Aberdeen becomes part of the City of Aberdeen.
1960s –	Oil is discovered in the North Sea.
2222 –	Montgomery Scott is born in Aberdeen (*see* page 98)

THE CONTEXT – ARCHAEOLOGY AND HISTORY

1. THE PHYSICAL ENVIRONMENT

Aberdeen today is a triumph of engineering in transforming the environment. Up until the eighteenth century the River Dee and its estuary flowed much further north than it does now. The railway station, Market Street, Union Square, not to mention most of the dockland area, was beneath a vast sheet of water. The town's geography was dominated by Castle Hill, St Katherine's Hill and the Gallowgate Hill, and limited by the ravine of the Denburn to the west and a loch to the north. The western approaches were beset with marshes and moors.

Then the Denburn was bridged and culverted, St Katherine's Hill was removed to make way for the Union Street thoroughfare, the river was tamed, the estuary reconfigured, the docks built, and large tracts of land drained. These days the modern road pattern obscures the topography, but beneath Union Street you can still see how the ground level slopes southward to the sea. The city to the east is bounded by an extensive beach facing onto the North Sea, and the River Don forms the northern physical boundary. Both the Dee and the Don are crucial in Aberdeen's story.

2. FROM PREHISTORY TO THE DARK AGES

In the Neolithic period (from around 3800 BC onwards) and the Bronze Age (from about 2500 BC onwards) farming communities constructed burial cairns (such as the ones near KINGSWELLS and TULLOS) and stone circles (for example, at MILLTIMBER and KIRKHILL FOREST). Many – but not all – of the single standing stones dotted around the city date from this era as well. The Romans left only one significant trace, at PETERCULTER. Little is known of Dark Age Aberdeen, although it would have been Christianised at some point, possibly even as early as the sixth century AD (*see* ST MACHAR'S CATHEDRAL).

3. THE MIDDLE AGES

Certain knowledge of the early medieval period is hard to come by, but we know that the town was ravaged in 1153 by a Viking named Eysteinn. There was a castle on CASTLEHILL (although some think an earlier version may have stood on St Katherine's Hill) and a community around THE GREEN and CASTLEGATE. Four monastic institutions (Trinitarians, Carmelites, Dominicans and the Grey

Friars) set up shop, and ST MACHAR'S CATHEDRAL and ST NICHOLAS KIRK rose to greatness. The citizens supported Robert the Bruce in his wars and leased valuable Stockethill lands from him. King's College was founded, the third University in Scotland. Plagues and epidemics ravaged the land. In 1411 the townspeople joined in the defence of Aberdeen at the bloody Battle of Harlaw, checking an army from the Highlands and Islands. This was seen as the definitive moment in the ongoing conflict between the warlords of Gaeldom and the Scots-speaking Lowlanders of prosperous Aberdeenshire.

4. THE REFORMATION

So much of Aberdeen's later history, and the various associated strange religious beliefs and actions, can only be understood by knowledge of the Reformation. By 1559 the Catholic Church, the former universal religion, was tottering in Scotland. A mob of 'Reformers' swept into Aberdeen from the south, destroying the monastic buildings and sweeping away 'idolatrous' images (not to mention pocketing some valuables during the looting). The following year Protestantism became the state religion, and Catholicism outlawed. The Reformation was not strong in the hearts of many Aberdonians, so wonderful buildings such as St Nicholas Kirk, St Machar's Cathedral and KING'S COLLEGE survived without too much damage, although their function and use had to change. MARISCHAL COLLEGE was founded as an explicitly Protestant alternative to King's, and Catholics were discriminated against. Catholic images were destroyed or mutilated, hence any survival from pre-Reformation times is historically rare and valuable.

The enmity between Catholics and Protestants has left traces in places such as PROVOST SKENE'S HOUSE and SNOW KIRK. Further religious conflict broke out in the seventeenth century, with the Episcopalians (supporters of a Church governed by king-appointed bishops, not surprisingly popular with troubled monarchs such as Charles I and II) warring with the Covenanters (extreme Presbyterians who denied the role of bishops and favoured 'bottom up' Church organisation). Aberdeen suffered badly in these conflicts, particularly at the BATTLE OF JUSTICE MILLS in 1644. Further religious persecution was meted out in the seventeenth century to the pacifistic Quakers, who were regarded as a dangerous alternative sect.

The Catholic Church had tolerated and encouraged many practices which the Reformed Church later regarded as 'superstitious', even occult. These included making pilgrimages to holy wells (such as the one at CHAPEL OF STONEYWOOD) to seek healing. The tolling of a hand-bell at funerals had several purposes, informing the populace that a coffin was passing by, and to show respect, and also to keep away evil spirits. In 1643 Aberdeen Council passed an edict prohibiting the ringing of bells because it was one of the 'superstitious rites used at funerals'.

5. THE EIGHTEENTH AND NINETEENTH CENTURIES

In 1661 Aberdeen had a population of about 5,000 stretched over some sixteen streets. A century later its footprint was still essentially the same, but its population had expanded enormously, creating a squalid, overcrowded urban rookery. Eventually the city fathers and the engineers broke the bounds of the convoluted medieval town, laying out straight roads, erecting bridges and viaducts, building new suburbs, and by 1800 had dragged Aberdeen kicking and screaming into the modern world. Union Street, a true marvel of civil engineering, cut straight as a die through history and topography. Local granite became the stone of choice for the neo-Classical architecture of the revitalised economy, creating the distinctive look of the Granite City. The railway came, as did a new harbour and new industries. The population boomed. Old Aberdeen, a separate town since the Middle Ages, finally amalgamated with its brasher neighbour in 1891.

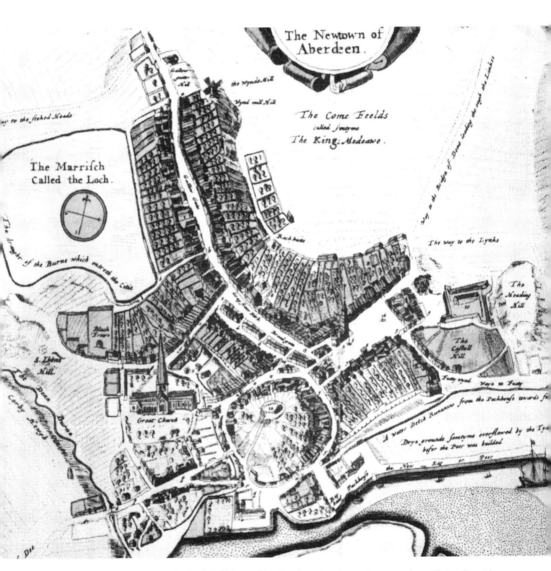

Aberdeen in 1661. St Katherine's Hill, lapped by the river, dominates the area where Union Street is now. The Denburn valley forms the boundary west of St Nicholas Kirk ('Great Church'). *(Author's Collection)*

The centre of Aberdeen, today. *(Jenni Wilson)*

THE DEEP

Strange things come from the North Sea, or are seen in its waters. In early 2002 a giant squid was washed ashore – and speedily conveyed to the National Maritime Aquarium in Plymouth, whose Kelvin Boot delightedly commented, 'I never believed I would see one in my lifetime. They really are the stuff of mythology' (*Independent*, 7 August 2002). A Great White Shark was seen in August 2008 (*Sun*, 9 September 2008). And, most bizarre of all, a boat fishing 32 miles (51.5km) offshore in early April 1982 found the floating carcass of an elephant (Janet and Colin Bord, *Modern Mysteries of Britain*).

In November 2000 a seabed scan 95 miles (153km) north-east of Aberdeen discovered an unidentified trawler 450ft (137m) below the surface. It was built between 1890 and 1930 and its hull was lying horizontally, indicating it had sunk 'flat'. The area, known as the Witch's Hole, was a 'pockmark', a piece of rugged terrain unlike the surrounding smooth seabed. All this led marine geologist Dr

Alan Judd of Sunderland University to conclude that the ship had been sunk by a giant bubble of methane.

The science of this rare and macabre phenomenon, as demonstrated experimentally in the laboratory, is that methane gas reduces the density of water; this means that ships can no longer float. The trawler would have sunk like a stone, possibly with no time to send a distress message. In addition, anyone jumping overboard in lifejackets would sink too. Judd had spoken to crews who had survived smaller gas emissions – their ships had temporarily lost some buoyancy and dropped a few feet in the water. Methane blow-outs from below the seabed were also thought to have sunk dozens of floating oil platforms. It was speculated that the phenomenon may be responsible for other shipping losses, such as those reported in the Bermuda Triangle. If the gas blow-outs reached the surface, they may even have taken out any aircraft flying above. The initial report was in *New Scientist*, quickly picked up by many newspapers, such as the *Daily Telegraph* on 30 November 2000. Dr Judd returned to the site in 2002 to make a documentary for the *Savage Planet* television series.

More extreme marine conditions hit a helicopter on 28 February 2002. The aircraft was severely buffeted by winds caused by a waterspout, the oceanic equivalent of a tornado, with a vortex of water reaching from the clouds down to the surface of the sea. The Super Puma helicopter was damaged but the pilots managed to regain control, and none of the eighteen offshore workers onboard were hurt. The case was reported in the *Herald* on 7 August 2003, when the Air Accidents Investigation Branch released its analysis of the incident.

A different kind of strangeness can be found in the cases of 'mystery coastal flares'. There have been several examples along the east coast of Britain of sightings of what seem to be distress flares, but when the search teams or lifeboatmen reach the area, nothing is found. These reports go back to the nineteenth century, and are so similar in form they may suggest some kind of rare aerial/marine phenomenon (perhaps the ignition of methane bubbles?). A typical example occurred on 20 November 1963. The coal-ship *Thrift* left Aberdeen bound for Blyth, Northumberland and was opposite Girdleness at 6 p.m. when the captain and three crew saw a pulsing red light around 15-30ft (4.5-9m) in the air, about a mile out to sea. When it was around three miles (4.8km) behind them the light suddenly went out. The *Thrift* turned back and searched the area for two hours, but found nothing. (The report is in *The Taming of the Thunderbolts* by Maxwell Cade and Delphine Davis.) On 20 March 1989 the Aberdeen coastguard put to sea after reports of red flares, but again there was no obvious source; the lights may have been caused by satellite debris falling that night, as there were many reports of lights, flashes and smoke trails along the north-east coast (*Press & Journal*, 21 March 1989).

UFOS AND STRANGE THINGS IN THE SKY

The mystery flares may be related to other aerial phenomena reported around Aberdeen, then again, they may not. UFO-spotting is something of a local pastime, possibly inadvertently encouraged by the large numbers of helicopters flying to and from the rigs and the proximity of Aberdeen airport and RAF bases, and definitely influenced by the current fondness for releasing small armadas of aerial fire lanterns at celebrations. The various online UFO forums are clogged with reports of silent orange lights floating in groups above the city. Great excitement is caused when the lights suddenly go out or appear to disintegrate. The lanterns are fragile paper spheres that rise because the flame at their centre heats the enclosed air. Sometimes they catch fire and fall apart, but usually the fuel simply runs out and the lanterns 'wink out' and fall to the ground. They are beautiful, but they are not mysterious. Reports of them are so common that one of the UK's most respected UFO organisations has simply stopped logging sightings of them. That being said, some genuinely odd things have been seen.

On 19 March 1719 the people of Aberdeen witnessed:

> … a great Lightning amongst the Clouds, which were of divers Colours, as Red, Yellow, Green, &c. And there was great Fire amongst the Clouds, which issued out from them like Sheets enfolding one another. The People thought that the Cloud touched the Earth, and Came down with a great Noise, which made many of the beholders run into their Houses, for fear the Fire should have devoured them.

The report was in a single-sheet broadside entitled 'Strange and Wonderful Apparitions'. A report in the *Statistical Account of Scotland* stated that in November and December 1792 'many of the country people observed very uncommon phenomena in the air (which they call Dragons) of a red fiery colour, appearing in the North, and flying rapidly towards the East.' And on 8 Aberdeen 1850 a dark red object with a yellow-orange plume ejected a small object that was seen to travel at right angles to the original course. A similar red object trailing sparks and dropping a dark mass was seen on the same day over the Cote d'Azur in France; presumably it was a meteor shedding parts of itself as it burnt up in the atmosphere (*La Chronique des OVNI* by Michel Bougard).

More recent sightings are perhaps more problematical, because the 'extraterrestrial hypothesis' is now so much part of our culture that when some people see odd things in the sky they automatically conclude that an alien craft is responsible, when meteorology, military activity, modern technology or misperception are more likely to be the cause. In 1966 the magazine *Flying Saucer Review* reported that eleven people had seen three unidentified craft in Aberdeen on 5 August 1948. In July 2006 the website www.ufoevidence.org had an eyewitness report from a man who as a boy had seen a large (100ft/30.5m diameter) orange-red sphere floating above the city centre in 1977. The report stated that there had also been a 'mass sighting' of a similar object in 1998, but I have not been able to track any report of this. Another website, www.ufocasebook.com, logged sightings over Aberdeen on 23 October 1998 (two shiny silver spheres), and 3 and 4 April 2001 (red, blue and green twinkling star-like object).

SPONTANEOUS ATHEISTICAL COMBUSTION!

An Aberdeen man attempted an incestuous relationship with his sister, then, rebuffed by her objections based on Christian morals, proceeded to denounce God, the Devil, Heaven and Hell as nothing but fictions designed to cow the weak and easily-led. No sooner had he uttered the blasphemous words than he was consumed by a great fire that, over two hours, burned him slowly to death, so that he suffered the torments of the damned in the very pit of Hell.

This, at least, is the event described in a ballad from around 1600, entitled *A wonderful Example of God's Justice shewed upon one Jasper Conningham, a Gentleman born in Scotland, who was of opinion that there was neither God nor Devil.* The title gives the game away – this is a typical example of a seventeenth-century moral tract inveigling against the evils of atheism. And very gorily the ballad makes its point too. Having bewailed his fate and – at great and poetic length, considering he is being consumed by fire – Jasper finally admits the existence of the Supreme Being and the Adversary:

> …with these speeches,
> his eyes fell from his head,
> And by the strings hung dangling
> below his chin stark dead.

Even with his eyes plucked out, Jasper can still keep up a commentary:

> See how the devils then he said,
> have pluck't my eyes out quite,
> That always was unworthy
> to view the heavenly light.

Finally Jasper has nothing more to say:

> Then from his mouth there fell
> his foul blasphemous tongue,
> In very ugly manner
> it most pitteously it hung.
> And there away it rotted
> in all the peoples sight,
> By lice and filthy vermine,
> it was consumed quite.

The end is not over. The fire ceases when Jasper dies, but his corpse smells so badly that no one will bury him, so it is left above ground to decay, the garden where the event having taken place being securely locked. So denying God gets you burned, tortured, mutilated, killed, and then left to rot.

It is possible the story was prompted by a genuine case where an Aberdeen gentleman tried to force himself on his sister, but I suspect it is pointless looking for 'Jasper Conningham' in the Aberdeen records. The ballad is a finger-wagging fable, warning good Christians not to stray from the precepts of a Godly society lest they suffer Mr Satan's barbecue sauce.

I found a copy of the ballad in James Maidment's *Scotish* [yes, one 't'] *Ballads and Songs*, published in 1849, and a superb commentary on the ideology of seventeenth-century religious ballads by Michael Goss in *Fortean Studies Volume 1* (1994). Mr Goss deserves some kind of prize for inventing the brilliant descriptive phrase re-used in the title here, 'Spontaneous Atheistical Combustion'. (For an example of Spontaneous Human Combustion, see CONSTITUTION STREET.)

A FOE TO THE EVIL ONE

'One day, during a snowstorm, the Revd George More was riding from Aberdeen to a village in the vicinity of that town. He was enveloped in a Spanish cloak, and had a shawl tied round his neck and shoulders. These loose garments, covered with snow, and waving in the blast, startled the horse of a "bagman", who chanced to ride past. The alarmed steed plunged, and very nearly threw its rider, who exclaimed – "Why sir, you would frighten the very devil!"

"I'm glad to hear that," said Mr More, "for it's just my trade."' (*The Book of Scottish Anecdote*, 1883).

CATS V. WITCHES

Sometime around the 1920s or early 1930s a workman renovating a 400-year-old property in Aberdeen lifted a massively heavy granite hearthstone to find the skeleton of a cat. The creature would have been deliberately buried as an apotropaic act to prevent witches and fairies coming down the chimney. The discovery is reported in Fenton Wyness' *Spots from the Leopard*, but no location is given. Where was this cat found and what happened to it?

URBAN LEGENDS AND 'FRIEND-OF-A-FRIEND' STORIES

'North-East Man Lost At Sea.' This is the classic joke of Aberdeen parochialism, a staple of journalistic barbs and after-dinner stories. The joke being, of course, that this was how a local newspaper reported the sinking of the *Titanic*. But although the story is much-loved, it is completely untrue. In April 2005 Sandy Hobbs investigated 'The Titanic Headline' in *Foaftale News*, the newsletter of the International Society for Contemporary Legend Research. He found numerous recent allusions to, and variations on, the story, but no evidence from the actual period. On 4 June 2004 the newspaper supposedly guilty of the *faux pas*, the *Press & Journal*, categorically denied it had printed the headline. And the proof is in *First Daily, The history of the P & J* by Norman Harper (1997). Harper reproduces the very page from

16 April 1912; The headline reads 'Mid-Atlantic Disaster: *Titanic* Sunk By Iceberg. 1,683 Lives Lost; 675 Saved. Liners Race to Rescue'. Not very parochial, then.

An Aberdeen newspaper did slip up in 1962, however. The *Evening Express* accidentally captioned Prime Minister Alec Douglas-Home as Mr Vass, a local bailie. The satirical magazine *Private Eye* thereafter maintained that Douglas-Home was an impostor, unmasked by the fearless investigators of the *Express*. For more than thirty years the magazine maintained this position, always referring to the former prime minister as Bailie Vass.

In 1993 Rob Adams wrote an article for the *Huddersfield Daily Examiner* in which he brought up two Aberdonian stories. The first, which he knew to be apocryphal because it was also told of Forfar and Edinburgh, was that many years ago a proposal was put before the council to attract tourists to the boating pond in one of the city parks by purchasing a dozen gondolas. One of the councillors objected on the grounds of economy: 'Wouldn't it make more sense just to buy two and see if they'll breed?'

The second tale, from 1987, Adams said he had on good authority. The council were discussing the city's first arts festival when one member suggested booking Louis Armstrong. There was a pause. 'But he's dead,' someone said. 'That's your opinion,' retorted the councillor, angry that the great jazzman was thought to be 'behind the times'. 'No, he's really dead,' came the reply, Mr Armstrong having passed away sixteen years previously.

In *Essays of Travel* (published in 1905, written some years earlier) Robert Louis Stevenson described how a man fell from a housetop in Aberdeen, and when being treated in hospital for broken bones, said he earned a living as a 'tapper'. The doctors did not know this work, so asked him to explain. When some slaters fancied bunking off work for a pint or two, their unskilled substitute would sit on the roof 'tapping' away with mallets to keep up the illusion that work was progressing. The slaters paid him out of their own pockets. Stevenson cautiously noted, 'I give the story as it was told me, and it was told me for a fact.'

According to the *Mail on Sunday* for 27 December 1998, an Aberdeen DIY store put up a notice about choosing the right paint because they were fed up with men returning colours their wives didn't like. The notice included reference to 'A poxy resin.'

SNAKES IN A DRAIN

In July 1997 seventeen-year-old Joss Clark was descaling his pet python Winston when the 6ft (1.83m) snake did a runner (well, a slither) down the toilet, re-appearing in the lavatory bowl of his neighbour two floors down. Not surprisingly the woman flushed it away, but Winston survived his U-bend adventure and was safely recovered. (*Daily Telegraph*, 4 December 1998.)

HAIR-RAISING

Advertisement in the *Aberdeen Free Press*, some time before the First World War: 'A really acceptable present for a lady is a nice piece of artificial hair, as, when not absolutely necessary, it is always useful and ornamental.'

SOURCES

All books, articles, newspapers and websites referred to in the text are listed in the Bibliography. Writing a new work on Aberdeen is a nerve-wracking experience for an author – possibly even an exercise in hubris – for so many good books on the city already exist. In particular I have made use of the output of Norman Adams (*Blood and Granite, Hangman's Brae, Scottish Bodysnatchers* and others), Robert Smith (including *The Granite City, Aberdeen Curiosities* and *The Hidden City*), Diane Morgan (*Lost Aberdeen* and *The Granite Mile*) and Fenton Wyness (*City By the Grey North Sea, Spots from the Leopard* and many more works). In terms of more antique contributions there are several dozen that deserve to be honoured, but pride of place must go to Aberdeen's first historian John Spalding, for *The History of the Troubles and Memorable Transactions in Scotland, from the Year 1624 to 1645*. Spalding not only recorded the history of his time, he also filled his work with omens, spirits, legends, monsters and other wonders. Here is a fine example of his style, a detailed description of a man with a parasitic twin growing from his chest:

> There came to Aberdeen an Italian monster of a man, about twenty-four years of age, having a birth growing from his breast upward, face to face as it were, a creature having head and long hair of the colour of a man's, the head still drooping backwards and downwards; he had eyes, but not open; he had ears, two arms, two hands, three fingers on each hand, a body, a leg, and foot with six toes, the other leg within the flesh, inclining to the left side. It had some signs of virility, it had a kind of life and feeling, but void of all other senses; fed with man's nourishment, and evacuated the same way as his. This great work of God was admired of by many in Aberdeen, and through the countries where he travelled; yet such was the goodness of God, that he could go and walk where he pleased, carrying this birth without any pain, yea, or unespied when his clothes were on. When he came to town he had two servants waiting on him, who, with himself, were well clad. His portraiture was drawn and hung up at his lodging to the view of the people; the one servant had a trumpet which sounded at such time as the people should come and see this monster, who flocked abundantly to his lodging.

1

THE CITY CENTRE – THE CASTLEGATE AREA

MERCAT CROSS – CASTLEHILL – JUSTICE STREET – THE TOLBOOTH

The annals of criminal jurisprudence exhibit human nature in variety of positions, at once the most striking, interesting and affecting. They present tragedies of real life, often heightened in their effect by the grossness of the injustice and the malignity of the prejudices which accompanied them. At the same time real culprits, as original characters, stand forward on the canvas of humanity as prominent objects for our special study.

Edmund Burke

CASTLE STREET

Also known as Castlegate, this pedestrianised area has been at the very heart of Aberdeen life since records began, having been the market square, public gathering space, the main fulcrum of the roads system, and the site of proclamations, executions and witches' meetings. In medieval times all the entrances and exits from the square were controlled by lockable gates called ports. Aberdeen's brief-lived castle once lay on Castlehill just to the east, where the tower blocks of Virginia Court and Marischal Court now stand, while St Katherine's Hill (now gone) once formed the urban boundary to the west. City life was administered and justice dispensed at the Tolbooth (now across the road), and the current Council's Town House, plus the Sheriff Court and Police Headquarters, continue to operate from the same area, a remarkable continuity of use stretching back centuries on the same site. When Marischal Street, Union Street and King Street were laid out, cutting orderly straight lines through the spaghetti tangle of medieval chaos, Castlegate was the hinge from which they sprung.

The striking hexagonal Mercat Cross is the finest of its kind in Scotland. Constructed in 1696, replacing a more ancient model, its decoration is enjoyably over the top, with gargoyles of dogs and monsters, Green Men, grotesque faces, foliaceous birds, thistles, bunches of grapes, the royal arms of Scotland and the Aberdeen coat of arms, and an extraordinary set of royal portraits in stone – James

I, II, III, IV, V, VI and VII, Charles I and II, and Mary Queen of Scots. The 1696 sculpture was the work of John Montgomery, also responsible for several of the carved gravestones in the burial ground of the KIRK OF ST NICHOLAS and the truly amazing monument to Bishop Scourgal in ST MACHAR'S CATHEDRAL. The whole affair is surmounted by a tall Corinthian column topped by a wonderful white marble unicorn. The arches have also been used for market stalls and, for a brief period from 1822, as what must have been a very cramped post office.

The high quality of the carvings reflects the Cross's symbolic importance as a signifier of civic authority and status. Monarchs were proclaimed here, Acts of Parliament read out, and convicted criminals chained up, exhibited and branded. An excellent overview of the Cross's history appeared in *The Lone Shieling*, a miscellany of essays published in 1908 by G.M. Fraser, the city librarian. Among other fascinating snippets Fraser records several punishments at the Cross. In 1563 two Flemish sailors were sentenced to have their right hands cut off for severing the cable of a ship in the harbour; the sentence was commuted to a public repentance and the pair duly appeared at the Cross with the cut cable, confessing 'by holding up their right hand and giving praise to God and thanks to the Council for the favour that had been shown them.' There is nothing in the records to show what was going on behind the scenes, but this was only three years after the Reformation; I suspect the two Flemings were Catholic and their 'giving praise to God' involved a specifically Protestant prayer. Presumably they preferred apostasy to amputation. In 1617 a man insulted one of the bailies and paid by being exhibited at the Cross and banished from the town. In 1640 a woman convicted of 'unbecoming behaviour' was scourged and banished; she was 'drawn in a cart through the streets, bearing a paper crown on her head, the bellman going before proclaiming her offence.'

Some of Fraser's other anecdotes feature the great canker of Scottish (and Aberdonian) history, religious intolerance. As the year 1688 drew to a close Scotland and England gained a new monarch, the Protestant William of Orange, who along with his wife Mary (James' Protestant sister) replaced Catholic James VII in a bloodless coup known (to Protestants, anyway) as the Glorious Revolution. Religious feeling was running high and in January 1689 some students from Marischal College – which, unlike King's College in Old Aberdeen, was defiantly Protestant – gathered at the Cross and conducted a trial of the Pope. The Plaintiff was found guilty of

Three of the Green Men that decorate the seventeenth-century Mercat Cross, Castlegate. *(Geoff Holder)*

various crimes and was burned in effigy. Around the same time a prominent Catholic, Peter Gibb, poked some fun at Protestant fanaticism by naming his terriers Calvin and Luther. Gibb was publicly rebuked and the two poor dogs hanged at the Cross.

Fraser also pooh-poohed the popular and much-repeated story that on festive occasions wine was pumped into a central cistern within the Cross and poured out of the gargoyles. He examined the records minutely and concluded that the Council supplied only limited quantities of wine, and this was dispensed in glasses to a small number of privileged individuals standing round the Cross. So all images of couthy Aberdonians lying beneath geysers of wine erupting from the mouths of gargoyles should be dispelled from your mind.

With the various urban developments in this area, and part of the Castlegate open space being subsumed into the eastern end of Union Street, the Mercat Cross has moved from its original location opposite the Tolbooth. Its current location is near where the Fish Cross once stood, *the* place in medieval Aberdeen to buy freshly-caught herring or mussels. Several of the witches convicted in 1597 were said to have danced around the Fish Cross (*see* INTERLUDE: WITCHCRAFT IN ABERDEEN, below). Almost opposite where Lodge Walk now runs was the Flesh Cross, a platform (this one with a crucifix) marking the site of the 'shambles', where beasts were butchered and meat sold. Between them the Mercat, Flesh and Fish Crosses defined the Aberdeen supermarket experience until the eighteenth century.

Around 1752 a pavement 84ft by 57ft in size (25.6m x 17m) was laid on the west side of the Cross, and – being largely free of mud and dung – the 'Plainstones' soon became a popular area for citizens of standing to conduct business and take the air. It had other uses, of course. In 1763 two toffs, Abernethy of Mayen and Leith of Leith-hall, had a disagreement while drinking in the adjoining New Inn. The quarrel spilled outside and the two fought an impromptu duel with pistols on the Plainstones; Leith was shot through the head.

In 1881 Walter Gregor, writing in his classic work *Notes on the Folk-Lore of the North-East of Scotland*, recorded a story that one of the Dukes of Gordon, stung at the criticism of the traditional two-ox plough by a Provost of Aberdeen, stated that the hand-made implement was so strong it could tear up the 'plainstones' in Castlegate. The Provost accepted the challenge, and the Duke brought his best oxen, plough and 'goodman' from Huntly. With an eager crowd of onlookers hoping for some entertainment, it first appeared as if the Duke would lose his bet; but when an extra goad was applied to one of the beasts, the team surged forward, scattering the plainstones right and left. Gregor does not give a date for the event and describes it as a 'tradition': it may or may not have happened as described.

Aberdeen has had several sites of execution over the centuries. After 1776 the gibbet was moved from GALLOWS HILL (near Pittodrie) to just west of the current position of the Mercat Cross, opposite King Street, where it remained for about a decade. In September 1785 a vagrant named John McDonald was hanged here for fire-raising. He believed that if he ate enough meat in the days before he went to the gallows, the drop would not kill him; this belief proved to be unfounded. John Milne in his 1911 book *Topographical, Antiquarian, and Historical Papers on the City of Aberdeen* describes the method of execution: the felon was escorted to the gallows on a carriage or sledge belonging to the watermen, a fraternity who carried butts of water through the streets; apparently it was the duty of the youngest member of this society to perform the task, a rather grim initiation ritual. At the gallows the noose was adjusted and the carriage driven smartly off, so that 'the victim was left suspended by the neck, with his feet within a yard of the ground.' Under these circumstances the 'drop' was unlikely to have broken the neck, so most victims would have died of slow strangulation. Things improved slightly with the construction of new-style gallows in front of the Tolbooth in 1788.

Milne recorded more on ancient punishments. In 1320 the Cock or Cuckstool stood on the south-west of Castle Street. This was a long beam balanced on a fulcrum, with a rope attached to one end. The criminal was tied to a seat at the other end and was ducked in water as many times as the law required. Apparently the Cuckstool was frequently used to punish 'scolding women, brewsters of bad ale, and profane swearers.' There is now no permanent water source in Castlegate; either there was once a pond or water-trough in the area, or the ducking stool was simply stored here and moved to somewhere watery when required. Next to the Cross was a post bearing a set of jougs, an iron collar on a short chain; gossips were sentenced to stand chained up here.

In the south-east corner of the square is the Castlegate Well or Mannie Well, named for the lead statue of the youth it supports. Each of the four corners is carved with a grotesque head which is actually composed of three conjoined faces. The former waterspouts have animal features. This well, built in 1706 as a key element in the public water supply, has too been on its travels, having been moved from the Castlegate in 1840, rebuilt in The Green some years later, taken down as an impediment to traffic in 1958, and finally re-erected close to its original home in 1972.

The western gable of the Old Blackfriars pub, looking onto Marischal Street, has a blocked-up window filled in with a curious setting of pebbles in the form of what appears to be a tree.

In a 1988 essay architectural historian William Brogden aptly described the mock-baronial towers and turrets of the late-Victorian Salvation Army citadel as 'Tinkerbell's castle', and its Balmoral-style remains a fantasy echo of the medieval castle that once overlooked the town from the hill behind it. In July 2007 a seagull nicknamed Sam became a celebrity for shoplifting packets of crisps from the RS McColl newsagents in the square. The cheeky (and brand-loyal) bird would wait until the store was free of customers, walk in through the open door – and steal a packet of its favourite, cheese Doritos. The bird would then rip open the packet on the pavement outside. Sam's regular habits were broadcast to a wider audience when a member of staff filmed the sneak-thief on his mobile phone and the footage appeared on the BBC Scotland website.

Above left: One of the three-faced grotesque heads on the Mannie Well, Castlegate. *(Ségolène Dupuy)*

Above right: 'Tinkerbell's Castle': the Salvation Army Citadel towers above the roofs around Castlegate. *(Ségolène Dupuy)*

CASTLE TERRACE

The south-east exit from Castlegate was Futtie's Port, which led via Futtie Wynd around the base of Castlehill to Footdee. The hinge for the footgate can just be seen at No. 4 Castle Terrace. Futtie Wynd later became Castle Brae and was known colloquially as the Hangman's Brae because it was home to hangman Johnnie Milne. Milne was a criminal-turned-hangman, having been convicted of stealing beehives in 1806 and offered either a choice of transportation to the colonies, or a job executing others. Milne's residence clearly had an impact on the area – he lived in 'Hangman's Hoose', the bridge over the adjacent Aberdeen-Port Elphinstone canal was known as Hangman's Brig, and in 1830 an inn on the Brae boasted a sign depicting a hanged man on a gibbet. Port, Wynd and Brae have now vanished under urban redevelopment – Castle Terrace was laid out in 1857 – and sadly no one chose to resurrect Hangman's Brae as a street name, although Norman Adams used it for the title of his eponymous book on crime and punishment, from which many of these details are taken.

CASTLEHILL

This area, once so crucial to the old town, now requires a major feat of imagination to reconstruct. Castle Terrace leads to the south side of Castlehill, occupied by the 1960s monoliths of Virginia and Marischal Courts. Here a castle once dominated the landscape – a castle that, however, appears only fleetingly in the records. It was certainly built in stone by 1264, so was probably a wooden structure long before that. It was a Royal castle with a permanent garrison and a constable who held it in the name of the king. Edward I of England may have stayed there in 1296. In 1308, during the Scottish Wars of Independence, the castle, held by the English, was besieged by the forces of Robert the Bruce. Although there is no contemporary documentary evidence, the attack was presumably successful, because after this date the castle was no more, and even Aberdeen's earliest historians could find no physical trace of it. A useful starter on the site's history is a booklet written by Chris Croly and published by the Council, *Aberdeen's Castle*.

The longstanding tradition is that the Aberdonians assisted in the siege and destruction of the castle and on the night of the final assault the secret password among the attackers was 'Bon Accord', now the motto of the city. Actually this is not so much a tradition as a founding myth, one of the city's core stories. 'Bon Accord' is found everywhere in Aberdeen, from company names to municipal works. There is even a Bon Accord shopping centre. The reality, however, is far less clear, for here we enter the strange land where pseudo-history, civic pride and make-believe join together to create what 'everyone knows' about Aberdeen. The attractions of the story are obvious – the brave burghers of Aberdeen not only demonstrated their courage and patriotism at a time of deep cultural crisis, they also (a) became associated with a genuine national hero and (b) picked the winning side. A result all round.

If only the records were so obliging. Sadly there is no contemporary evidence for the involvement of Aberdonians in the siege, and it must be asked how many local merchants, craftsmen and politicians would join in an attack on a castle, garrison and mint on which so many would have depended financially. The term 'Bon Accord' first appears on the town seal in 1430, over 120 years after the siege, and there is no evidence showing why this wording was chosen. Aberdeen historians writing in the sixteenth and seventeenth centuries did not mention the password story – and if they had known it, they would not have failed to include such a rousing episode. It therefore appears that the story of the Bon Accord password was constructed without any evidence from the motto adopted in 1430, and was probably invented by an Aberdonian mythographer in the eighteenth century.

At some point in the 1500s a chapel dedicated to St Ninian was erected on Castlehill. It went through several uses and was enclosed by a four-pointed fort built by Cromwellian troops in 1651-2. This was partly dismantled seven years later and these days only the little-visited but substantial south-east wall of 'Cromwell's Bastion' survives beside the playground beneath the tower blocks. The chapel and most of the citadel was swept away, to be replaced, in response to the perceived threat from France in 1794-6, by a massive barracks designed to house 600 men. The garrison dominated life in the vicinity, eventually becoming a depot for the Gordon Highlanders in the 1930s and being demolished three decades later to make way for the tower blocks.

In medieval times it was believed that a corpse would bleed when touched by its murderer; there is a persistent story that in the eighteenth century, when the body of a batman was found in the barracks, the entire regiment was forced to march past and touch the body, which was displayed on Castle Street. The body did not bleed, and the killer was never found. Aberdeen crime writer Norman Adams has questioned whether the event ever actually happened. *The Black Kalendar of Aberdeen*, a catalogue of crimes and criminals compiled by James Bruce in the nineteenth century, mentions two cases where soldiers from the barracks were accused of bestiality.

Both Robert Begg in 1749 and Samuel Court in 1762 received not proven verdicts; if found guilty they would have faced the death penalty.

There is no more popular urban story than a secret tunnel, and Castlehill has a good one. In 1893-94 the contributors to *Scottish Notes and Queries* were exchanging their experiences of finding a 'concealed passage' under the hill. Mr William Home had found a brick-lined passage leading from a warehouse in Castle Street towards Castlehill. The opening was 5ft 6ins (1.67m) high by 4ft 6ins (1.37m) across, and swiftly narrowed to a semi-circular tunnel 3ft 9ins (1.14m) in height. One of Home's men attached himself to a rope and explored the wet and slippery route for about 50yds (45.7m), as far as the underneath of the site of the Salvation Army Citadel, whose construction had begun in 1893. At this point the light he carried started to flicker, and not wanting to suffocate in bad air, he returned. Mr G.A. of Aberdeen then recalled that over sixty years previously he had heard of a party of young men taking torches up a passage that started somewhere near where the former St Clement's Church now stands on St Clement Street in Footdee (which seems a very long way for someone to build a subterranean tunnel). The boys apparently walked so far that they arrived under the centre of Castlegate, where they found 'the round large stone into which was planted the gallows in old times.' Mr G.A. had not explored the passage himself but had seen the entrance, and thought it was a secret route to bring food from the harbour to the castle during times of siege.

Mr James Walker, then living in Melbourne, Australia, appeared to have been one of the youths mentioned by G.A. In his letter he remembered exploring the passage with some friends around 1829-1831, when he was ten or twelve years old. The entrance was 'a little to the east of the point where Hanover Street now joins Commerce Street and Castle Terrace,' which is much nearer Castlegate than Footdee and seems more realistic. With a candle to light their way they proceeded beneath Castlehill and arrived at what they believed to be the centre of Castlegate. There the passage turned to the right (north) and they thought it led to Marischal College, home of the dreaded bodysnatchers. Fearing capture, murder and dissection, they turned back. Both Messrs G.A. and Walker stated the eastern end of the passage had been closed up long before 1893. It is possible that the tunnel partially explored from the west by Mr Home's workman was the very same passage, and his light flickered because, with the far end blocked, the oxygen was running out.

Of the three reports Mr Home's is the most reliable, simply because he was reporting something in the very recent past. Both Mr G.A. and Mr Walker were recalling events from more than sixty years previously – memory may have been at fault and the stories may have grown in the telling. Mr G.A.'s is the least dependable of all, because he did not enter the passage and was merely repeating what he had been told by other boys. Mr Walker did go into the tunnel but there was no way that he and his companions could have accurately known they were under the centre of Castlegate – they could just as easily have been in a cellar on the southern edge of the square. Walker stated the stories of Burke and Hare and the recent destruction of the 'Burkin' House' on ST ANDREWS' STREET were very much in their minds, so this may well have led to the fear that the passage continued on to Bodysnatching HQ at

Marischal College. There is no evidence from any other sources that bodysnatchers made use of concealed tunnels. Walker's description of the location of the eastern entrance also seems more likely than G.A.'s – and he did actually go in.

So, if the reports are at least partially accurate and there was a real 'concealed passage' beneath Castlehill, what was it? The siege-supply idea can be dismissed, not least because the tunnel did not actually go to the castle itself. The obvious suggestion is that, being brick-lined and low, it was some kind of sewer. However in *The Granite City* Robert Smith claimed that it ran to the shore from the cellars of Robert Burnett's house in Burnett's Close on Castlegate. Presumably this was the 'warehouse' Home had been working on, as the Close was demolished in the 1890s. Burnett was a prominent merchant, so the inference was that this was a secret route to bring goods from the harbour to his stores, either to avoid paying tax or because the goods themselves were contraband. On the other hand, this area has seen some of the most intensive road and housing development in Aberdeen, and no one has reported a tunnel in the area; so if it ever existed, perhaps it has collapsed or is entirely filled in.

The strangest element in the saga of the Castlehill secret tunnel is a brief entry in Home's letter. Describing the observations of his workman in the passage, he wrote: 'About 20yds along the tunnel *a sword was found thrust into the roof up to the hilt*' (emphasis added). One would think that if there were indeed a sword embedded in the fabric, someone would have been sufficiently interested to have retrieved it. Possibly the man had misinterpreted some kind of metal device inserted into the vault to help support the weight. Or perhaps there really is a dark tunnel beneath the hill, hiding a sword thrust hilt-deep into the earth, like some kind of inverted Excalibur.

HEADING HILL

This mound, easily reached by a footbridge from Virginia Court over the canyon of the dual carriageway, was once a place of execution. Clearly no one in the twentieth century wanted 'Heading Hill' on their address, as the place name has entirely disappeared, and the street itself is incongruously (and wrongly) named Castlehill. Beheading was a fate reserved for those of high status; those of a lower station were merely hanged. In 1574 John Ewyne or Ewen, a burgess of the town, was convicted of coining (counterfeiting coins, or clipping them to re-use the metal for making new coins). Such offences against the currency of the realm were taken very seriously, as it was technically a form of treason; Ewen was half-hanged, cut down while still conscious, then beheaded with a sword. Murderers Adam Donaldson (1577) and Thomas Wright (1579) were similarly dispatched with a sword. As the century progressed the technology of execution advanced, with the introduction of the guillotine-like Maiden, which in the 1590s did for two miscreants named Douglas and Litster. When not in use the Maiden was kept in the Earl Marischal's house on Castlegate, and carrying it up here, then setting up the ropes, blocks and moving parts, must have been a real pain (its blade is in the TOLBOOTH MUSEUM). The Maiden was last wheeled out in 1615 to remove the head of Francis Hay, the murderer of Adam Gordon, brother of the Laird of Gight. All these sorry tales and more can be found in Norman Adams' catalogue of crime and punishment in Aberdeen, *Hangman's Brae*.

Heading Hill, or the hollow between it and Castlehill (now the dual carriageway of Commerce Street) was also used for the occasional witch burning (*see* INTERLUDE – WITCHCRAFT IN ABERDEEN, below).

JUSTICE STREET

This is the continuation of Castlegate to the north-east, and is named for the Justice Port, the town gate where the heads of executed criminals were nailed up. A booklet published by the North East Museums Partnership, *Crime & Punishment Trails in Aberdeen & Stonehaven*, notes that in 1588 James Paterson (aka Spaldeston) was executed for the murder of shoemaker James Wischart, and his head spiked on the Port; Paterson was despatched on his own gibbet, having been the town hangman at the time of the murder. A few years earlier, John Gordyne had been hanged and his body quartered; his head was put on the Port, as a warning to others.

It was common practice for the government to dismember individuals they thought especially dangerous, and to send the various body parts to different towns, where they were ordered to be prominently displayed with a notice stating the individual's crime (usually rebellion or treason). When the hero of the Wars of Independence, William Wallace, was executed in London, his limbs were consequently scattered around Scottish burghs. There is a persistent story that Aberdeen received Wallace's left foot, and several legends have grown up about what happened to it; Fenton Wyness, in *Royal Valley: The story of the Aberdeenshire Dee*, claims that the appendage was displayed on the Justice Port. There are conflicting claims that it (or Wallace's hand) is buried in either ST FITTICK'S CHURCH in Torry or ST MACHAR'S CATHEDRAL.

A more reliable tale of a severed limb is attached to James Graham, the 1st Marquis of Montrose. Montrose was one of the great figures of the Civil War period, a brilliant general who switched sides (from the Covenanters to the Royalists) and swept into Aberdeen in 1644, trouncing the defenders at the Battle of Justice Mills (*see* JUSTICE MILLS LANE), throwing open the cells of the Tolbooth, and, in a rare lapse of judgement, allowing his troops to plunder, rape and slaughter their way through the city. The terror that Montrose inspired made its way into the folklore of later generations, as recorded in 1851 by William Anderson in *Rhymes, Reveries, and Reminiscences*. Anderson recalled an old aunt singing him a nursery rhyme which contained the lines:

> Has he seen that terrible fellow Montrose –
> Wha has iron teeth wi' a nail on his nose?
> An' into his wallet wee laddies he throws?

In 1650 this particular bogeyman was betrayed and captured. At his execution in Edinburgh he was denied the axe – as should have been his right as a gentleman – and was hanged by the Covenanters as a common criminal. His head was mounted on the Edinburgh tolbooth and his arms and legs cut off, for despatch to Stirling, Glasgow, Perth and Aberdeen. The rest of his body was buried in the Edinburgh Burgh-muir (now The Meadows), the site where murderers and other hanged criminals were casually interred – even in death Montrose was denied his privileges. But that night the body was dug up by his supporters and the heart removed, to end up embalmed and treasured as a relic by Lady Elizabeth Erskine of Mar, the wife of Montrose's nephew. The execution, the disinterment and the actions of Montrose's followers seemed to have rattled the authorities, and in the confusion the severed limbs got mixed up. Aberdeen was supposed to have received a leg, but got an arm instead. This was duly impaled on one of the spikes of the Justice Port, and was seen and recorded by several visitors. Perhaps about two years later the arm was taken down and buried in Lord Huntly's aisle in St Mary's Chapel below ST NICHOLAS KIRK.

When Charles II returned to power Montrose was rehabilitated and the first Scottish Parliament of the Restoration ordered 'that his body, head, and other of his divided and scattered members may be gathered together and interred with all honour imaginable.' There is a note in the Aberdeen Council records that this order was complied with in 1661, and the arm was disinterred with civic honours accompanied by the firing of guns, temporarily relocated to the Town House, and then sent to Edinburgh for a state funeral at St Giles' Cathedral.

At this point it is time to bring in a paper presented to the Society of Antiquaries of Scotland in 1896 by J. W. Morkill, charmingly titled 'Notice of a Human Hand and Forearm, Pierced with Nail Holes …' In 1891 Mr Morkhill had purchased a preserved human arm that indeed had two holes that were consistent with it having been nailed up, 'one through the centre of the hand, and a second one through the fleshy part of the arm near the elbow.' He also had documentation, including wills and family papers, showing that the item had been passed down through several generations of well-to-do Yorkshire families – most of them ardent Jacobites – and that from the earliest records it was stated that this was the arm of the Marquis of Montrose.

Was this the Aberdeen arm that supposedly had been reburied in Edinburgh? How had it arrived in Yorkshire? Morkill embarked on a quest to find out, a piece of detective work that took several years. Presuming the arm had never actually been buried at St Giles', he surmised he had been taken south of the border by a Cromwellian soldier. He found a Captain Pickering who had been on active duty in Scotland before his retiral to his native Yorkshire, where he died in 1699. Pickering had been owed money by various Scottish gentlemen, and he had the same surname as the first recorded owner of the severed arm, a Dr Pickering who died in 1773. Morkhill speculated that Pickering had acquired the arm in lieu of a debt, and had passed it on to his descendants in Yorkshire.

Morkhill also had the arm analysed by a doctor, who concluded it had never been under the earth. This conflicted with the attested records that the

Aberdeen arm had been buried in St Mary's Chapel for at least eight years before being sent to Edinburgh. In the absence of any other evidence Morkhill tentatively concluded that the arm he owned had been the one impaled at Dundee, and that the Aberdeen one had indeed been reburied in Edinburgh. Unfortunately this cannot now be confirmed: a search

A marriage lintel inscription in Peacock's Close, off Castlegate. *(Ségolène Dupuy)*

that took place in 1891 in the crypt beneath the Chepman Aisle of St Giles', where the Marquis's remains were supposed to have been reburied in 1661, found no trace of the bones. The grandiose tomb is there, but it is empty.

Several narrow closes and wynds run off from Castlegate and Justice Street, and those that are accessible are often worth exploring for their vestiges of old-world Aberdeen – Peacock's Close, for example, has a blocked-up doorway and what is probably a marriage lintel inscribed 'AS IK 1710'. Many of these lanes once led to the gardens behind the houses lining the medieval centre, although the open spaces have long since been built over. One of the openings on the north side of Justice Street leads under an arch into the small and delightful Chapel Court. Here is squeezed St Peter's Chapel, on what is sometimes claimed to be the site of a house belonging to the Knights Templars (in reality, the Templars merely owned land here, and never put up any kind of building). Built in 1803, St Peter's was the first Catholic church in Aberdeen since the Reformation, although a Catholic chapel in a dwelling house existed here from 1771. This was the beat of Friar Charles Gordon, popularly known as 'Priest Gordon', a man so respected that when he died in 1855 after fifty years' service, the whole city turned out to his funeral and soldiers lined the streets. The priest's avuncular ghost has been reported in CONSTITUTION STREET. Apart from some fine stained glass the interior of St Peter's is relatively plain. The main item of interest resides at the Lady Altar – a replica of the statue of the Virgin Mary known as Our Lady of Bon Accord or Our Lady of Aberdeen (*see* ST MARY'S CATHEDRAL on HUNTLY STREET for the full story of the miracles and legends associated with the original statue).

THE JUNCTION OF KING STREET AND UNION STREET

This area, from the corner on the east to the junction with Broad Street on the west, is still effectively Castlegate, but heavy traffic and the road layout now makes it easier to consider separately.

The Archibald Simpson pub is one of Aberdeen's finest pieces of architecture, its columned and curved frontage topped by a painted terracotta figure of Ceres, the Goddess of Plenty, a suitable guardian for what used to be the North of Scotland

Bank (and more recently the Clydesdale Bank). Inside, the former banking hall is decorated with a gilded and miniature version of the Greek sculptures on the frieze of the Parthenon. The bank, built in 1839-42 by the eponymous Aberdeen architect-genius Archibald Simpson, replaced the celebrated New Inn, built by the Freemasons in 1755. The brethren had their Lodge on the upper floor, reached by a rear entrance and a linking lane, still called Lodge Walk (best explored when the nearby courts and holding cells are not decanting their recent customers).

THE TOLBOOTH MUSEUM OF CIVIC HISTORY

Entrance on Castle Street, next door to Lodge Walk. Typically open July-September Tuesday-Saturday 10 a.m.-5 p.m. (closed for lunch) and Sunday 12.30 p.m.-3.30 p.m. Check www.aberdeencity.gov.uk for exact times. Admission free. Numerous stairs, with wheelchair access only to the entrance area on the ground floor, and not to any of the cells or rooms (a video 'virtual tour' is available). Frequent themed events.

The museum currently called the Tolbooth is actually the Wardhouse or Jail of the seventeenth-century Tolbooth, the larger (and now lost) building where Council meetings, civic bureaucracy and the courts were based. The fabric, built between 1616 and 1629 on the site of an earlier Tolbooth, includes many of the original features of the prison as it was in the eighteenth century – spiral stair-cases, heavy doors, iron chains, manacles, leg fetters and barred windows. Words such as *confined*, *cramped*, *dingy* and *grim* come to mind. It is truly atmospheric. The various display cabinets, interpretation panels and tableaux tell the story of crime and punishment in Aberdeen, along with the physical and civic development of the burgh. As well as common criminals and debtors, the prison over the years held witches, Quakers and Jacobites, often in hideously crowded conditions. The Wardhouse continued in use until the Bridewell gaol was built in 1808.

The current Entrance Hall was originally the ground floor access to the shops and businesses that flourished beneath the Tolbooth; the former main entrance from an external forestair can be seen above the reception, and various blocked-up doorways and floor levels indicate the changes in use over the centuries. Here can be seen the seventeenth-century column and unicorn from the MERCAT CROSS, which was damaged and replaced in 1907. The passage passes over the site of the Thieves Hole, presumably a dungeon-type cell. Here too was kept an iron cage for imprisoning some of the children abducted to work as indentured labourers in America (*see* UNION BRIDGE for the full story); there is a record of a woman coming to the Tolbooth to buy back her legally kidnapped son, not once, but twice.

The Civic Room was built as a depository for the Council archives; on display is the drum that was beaten at the head of processions to the gallows, its beat marking the mournful passage of the convicted felons' last minutes on earth. The upper floor cell, dubbed the Crime and Punishment Room, holds the blade of the Maiden – the guillotine-like device used for executions on HEADING HILL –

along with restraints and a scold's bridle. Over the years several misconceptions, even myths, have grown up around the Tolbooth. One is that the large key on display in this room was once heated red-hot and used for branding prisoners; this never happened and it was just the ordinary Tolbooth key. Another is that the current Crime and Punishment Room was the 'condemned cell', where prisoners on 'death row' were held before being led out to the scaffold in front of the building. In truth those due to be executed were simply kept anywhere there was space, and no special room was allocated to them.

That being said, the Tolbooth has seen some strange sights. In 1562, when both Protestant and Catholic factions were tussling over control of Mary Queen of Scots. George Gordon, the 4th Earl of Huntly and the most powerful Catholic in the North-East, plotted to arrange a marriage between the Queen and his son John. This effectively would have been a Catholic coup, so the Protestant Lords reacted immediately. Father and son were outlawed, and the conflict came to a head in September at the Battle of Corrichie near the Hill of Fare in Aberdeenshire.

George Gordon had been encouraged in his venture because his wife, the Countess of Huntly, said to be a consulter of witches, had had a prophecy or vision. It was foretold that the earl would soon be lying in the Aberdeen Tolbooth without a wound. This was interpreted as meaning he would be sleeping in the most important building in the city, and hence that the Gordons would be victorious in battle. But prophecies and visions are notoriously ambiguous, as anyone from Macbeth to Harry Potter can tell you. At Corrichie the earl fell off his horse, possibly having suffered a heart attack, and the unmarked body was deposited at the Tolbooth for embalming. The corpse was then taken to Edinburgh to be put on trial for treason. Not surprisingly, the earl was found guilty – possibly because his performance under cross-examination must have been rather poor – and the preserved body was propped up to hear sentence pronounced upon it. As part of the same anti-Catholic strategy, Sir John Gordon, who had been captured at Corrichie, was beheaded in Aberdeen. The persistent story is that Mary – who may, or may not, have been romantically interested in Sir John – was forced to watch as several clumsy strokes with a sword finally hacked off his head.

From left to right: The Victorian Town House; the spire of the seventeenth-century Tolbooth; and the statue of Ceres, Goddess of Plenty, on the former North of Scotland Bank (now the Archibald Simpson pub). *(Ségolène Dupuy)*

The gallows drum that marked a criminal's last minutes on earth, on display in The Tolbooth. Note the leopards on the coat of arms. *(Ségolène Dupuy)*

The Black Kalendar of Aberdeen noted that on 9 January 1753 Alexander Martin of Westertown of Huntly was charged with stealing and killing an ox. Whilst imprisoned in the Tolbooth, 'he was wrapped in the ox-hide by way of a great-coat, with the horns properly placed.' One wonders how long he had to remain in his smelly costume, and whether he was forced to act like a pantomime cow. Displaying felons with the proof of their crime seems to have been commonplace. Two years previously, William Macdonald and his wife Elspet Grant were taken through the town on a cart with sheepskins pinned to their necks, showing that they had been convicted of sheep-stealing. And in 1752 child-killer Christian Phren was forced to carry the burnt remains of her murdered infant to GALLOWS HILL.

About 1788 or 1790 the gallows was removed from further east on the Castlegate to outside the door of the Tolbooth, although it was not a permanent fixture, and, rather like in a Wild West film, the carpenters and joiners built a new platform for each execution, their hammering keeping the condemned prisoners awake in the cells right next door. On 29 October 1790 James Henderson was hanged here for the murder of slater Alexander Gillespie. Executions were manna from Heaven to the producers of the single-page news-sheets called broadsides; while the memory of the execution was still fresh, hundreds of onepenny copies would be flogged to the sensation-hungry public. The printer of the broadside entitled 'The last Speech and dying declaration of James Henderson' had apparently interviewed Henderson just before his death: the condemned man maintained he had only attacked Gillespie because the man was breaking into his house. Amongst various conventional pieties in what may have been a 'speech' ghostwritten by the reporter, Henderson stated: 'To the keeper of the tolbooth and his servants I desire to return thanks for their humanity and attention to me; and I pray that there [*sic*] kindness may be returned to them sevenfold.'

Henderson's body was officially handed over to the surgeons to be dissected, a sentence also carried out on murderers John Young (1801), Robert Macleod (1823) and William Allan (1826). When seventeen-year-old James Ritchie was hanged for sheep stealing in 1818 his case attracted much sympathy because it was obvious he was the fall-guy for the real criminals, who escaped justice. *The Black Kalendar of Aberdeen* stated: 'a man who had been instrumental in his apprehension, afterwards came to ruin, and suffered deep domestic affliction; and the popular superstition was, that that the blood of this unfortunate boy had cried to Heaven against him.'

Ritchie's body was buried at sea, and later that same year housebreaker John Barnet was consigned to a similar fate; but the tides brought Barnett's ashore at the mouth of the Don and his waterlogged corpse was handed over for dissection.

Another dissectee was Margaret Davidson, who had poured vitriol (sulphuric acid) into her sleeping husband's mouth. This was in 1830, forty-five years since Aberdeen had seen the execution of a woman. Then, as now, female murderers attracted condemnation beyond that attached to men, and two separate broadsides survive to show how she was demonised. One, simply entitled 'Murder', is filled with the ambience of gas-lit horror:

> She perpetrated this crime in the most treacherous manner; while he was asleep, and his mouth open, she poured down his throat the deadly draught, which held him in the utmost torture, till death put an end to his sufferings. It fills the breast with the greatest horror, to think how deliberately she committed the crime; and every person of feeling shudders at the bare recital.

The broadside concludes with a description of the hanging:

> After shaking hands with every one around her, she mounted the fatal Drop; she was seen praying very earnestly for some time; she then dropt the signal and was launched into Eternity amidst an immense multitude of spectators from various parts of the country; her body, after hanging about half an hour, was cut down and delivered over to the Surgeons for Dissection. On this melancholy creature no one seemed to be sorry for her fate, but looked on at the awful spectacle with indifference, and shewed no marks of compassion.

A rival broadside entitled 'The Only True Account' repeated a piece from the *Caledonian Mercury* of 11 October 1830, in which the usual details of Davidson's confession and execution were supplemented with something tinged with the supernatural. As a child Davidson had attended the hanging of thief Jean Craig on 23 July 1784: 'on the body being cut down, the rope was, as was then usual, thrown among the crowd, when the knot struck her on the breast.' Since her arrest Davidson had told several people she believed this episode had cursed her, leading her through a life of sin to ultimately murder, and death on the end of a rope.

Several of the people accused of witchcraft in 1597 and at other times were held in the Wardhouse. Google for 'Tolbooth' and 'witch' and you will come across multiple entries for Janet Walker, the Fittie Witch. Supposedly she was the Tolbooth's 'most famous inmate'. Strange, then, that she never existed. The truth – as confirmed by Chris Croly, the historian responsible for the Tolbooth – is that Janet is a composite figure drawn from the biographies of several of the Aberdeen witches; she was invented by Chris and his colleagues for the purposes of a historical recreation event. Since then she has taken on 'real' existence in the virtual world, being referred to on Wikipedia and on the website of *Most Haunted*. I look forward to tales of mediums encountering the spirit of this entirely fictional individual.

The Aberdeen coat of arms
on the Town House. The cats
are clearly lions, not leopards.
(*Ségolène Dupuy*)

THE TOWN HOUSE

A titanic Flemish-style exercise in Victorian neo-medievalism, this landmark tower
dominates the area and forms a triumphant exclamation mark at the end of the
Tolbooth and Sheriff Court complex, a tribute to municipal grandeur inside and
out. Close scrutiny of the coat of arms above the balcony reveals that the flanking
heraldic animals are clearly lions, not – as virtually everywhere else in the city –
leopards. *Jack Webster's Aberdeen*, a splendid book written by a veteran North-East
journalist, states that the beasts on the original coat of arms were indeed lions, as
shown by their manes, but have become leopards through simple confusion.

UNION STREET

It is fitting to finish this chapter with an episode called 'The Strange Experience
of the Reverend Spencer Nairne', which appeared in *Lord Halifax's Ghost Book* in
1936, his lordship being Charles Lindley, Viscount Halifax. In terms of the provenance of the episode, the book's introduction states: 'This story was sent by *Mr.
Wilfrid Ward*, the well-know Roman Catholic writer, to *Lady Halifax*, in September,
1912. The account was evidently written by *Mr. Spencer Nairne* himself.' At 8.30 p.m.
on a summer's evening in 1859, the twenty-six-year-old Nairne was strolling along
Union Street before taking a ship to Norway when he saw an acquaintance of over
twenty years, a Miss Wallis, walking along with a gentleman on her arm. Nairne and
the woman recognised each other as they passed, but as Nairne turned round neither she nor her companion were visible. Nairne searched the street and the nearby
shops, with no success. Some months later, towards the end of September, Nairne
met Miss Wallis in London, where he learned that she had had the same experience
as he – as they passed in Union Street, she looked around to find that Nairne was
nowhere to be seen. Even stranger, Miss Wallis had recorded the meeting in her
journal, so she knew it had happened in July. Nairne's diary, however, showed that
it occurred on 31 May. Had the pair – who were not close – seen each other's dop-
pelganger on two different days?

INTERLUDE:
WITCHCRAFT IN ABERDEEN

We wad listen wi' wonder while he wad declare
He had seen Luckie W— transformed to a hare;
He had tried her wi' lead, an', though nae very rich,
Wi' an auld crookit saxpence he crippled the witch.

William Anderson, *Rhymes, Reveries, and Reminiscences* (1851)

Aberdeen has probably the best-preserved municipal records in Scotland, some of which contain detailed notes on the trials and executions of a number of people accused of witchcraft. Those accused were held in the TOLBOOTH (from Chapter 1) or ST MARY'S CHAPEL and the steeple of ST NICHOLAS KIRK (both in Chapter 2), while witch-meetings were held at CASTLEGATE (Chapter 1) and ST KATHERINE'S HILL and POCRA QUAY, Footdee (Chapter 3). This interlude explores the story of the Aberdeen witches, with insights into folk magic, magical murder, demons, spirits, fairies, and the base cruelty of people claiming to act in the name of Christianity.

Witch-hunting in Scotland was not a case of mob rule, with pitchfork-wielding peasants tying an unpopular old crone to a stake and setting fire to some hastily-gathered branches. In contrast, it was a legal affair, with trials, prosecutors, witnesses, judges, juries, and a code of practice established by legislation and enforced by higher courts (typically the Privy Council in Edinburgh). It was still brutal and manifestly unfair, but in procedural terms the process was (usually) carried out within the letter of the law.

Witchcraft became a capital crime in 1563, signed into law by Mary Queen of Scots at the behest of the Satan-obsessed Protestants now in power. The full majesty of the law, however, was only infrequently wielded up until the final decade of the sixteenth century (in 1569 Katharine Cultis was tried for witchcraft in Aberdeen by the Earl of Moray, but we do not know the outcome). Then in 1590 King James VI suffered what he considered to be an assassination attempt by the witches of North Berwick. Kings do not take kindly to attempts on their life. The North Berwick witches were interrogated and tortured – and executed. Witchcraft became the terrorism of the day, and slowly witch executions started to spread through other parts of Scotland.

One example was the execution of Barbara Keand (or Kaird or Card) on 20 June 1590, atop HEADING HILL. Barbara's confession in the Tolbooth throws some light on the way powerful people attempted to use witchcraft as another weapon (alongside scheming, bribes, threats, and direct violence) in family conflicts. In 1587 she had been approached by William Leslie of Crethie in Aberdeenshire, who wanted her to use her magic powers to curse his enemy, John Leslie, Laird of Boquhane, over a land dispute. Barbara refused, probably because she had some kinship link with John Leslie's family. William left, threatening to break every bone in Barbara's body if she blabbed. He then employed another witch, Janet Grant from Cromar, who made a wax image of the Laird and roasted it over the fire. Barbara found out and tried to warn her kinsman, but John Leslie ignored her and the spell made him ill and eventually killed him. Despite Barbara's innocence of the murder, and even trying to help the victim, she was condemned to death for witchcraft. To us this seems manifestly unfair, but probably something is missing from the records, something that made her obviously guilty to both those who tried her and those who attended the burning, who applauded this vengeance for the murder of John Leslie.

The following month the actual image-melter, Janet Grant, along with Janet Clerk and William Leslie's servant, Bessie Roy, were also put on trial for the magical murder, this time in Edinburgh. The first two were found guilty and burned, but Bessie, despite her obvious guilt, was acquitted, probably because the court was packed with William Leslie's very powerful supporters, including several lords and two earls. William Leslie himself was charged with murder and consulting witches; he was granted bail and ordered to appear at a trial in Aberdeen. There is no record of this trial ever having take place. (P.G. Maxwell-Stuart excavated the documents for all these trials in his 2001 book *Satan's Conspiracy: Magic and Witchcraft in Sixteenth-Century Scotland*.)

Things were relatively quiet for a time. In September 1596 John Gordon or Williamson, 'a manifest witch', was detained in the kirk vault (ST MARY'S CHAPEL in St Nicholas Kirk). Interestingly he had pretended to be mute – there are a small number of cases in Scottish witchcraft where the accused had faked being mute (and sometimes deaf as well), and in each example the fake condition conferred added prestige and popularity. In some records the term 'deaf and dumb' seems to be a synonym for 'magically gifted'.

In 1597 all hell broke loose. Members of Aberdeen's elite – the provost, magistrates, bailies and ministers – seemed to be infected by some kind of 'witchcraft panic virus'. In January witches were being interrogated by Kirk Sessions in Slains, Dyce and Fintray. Two names came up: Isobel Strachan (also known as Scudder), and Janet Wishart, the matriarch of what in modern tabloid terms would be dubbed 'the family from hell'. The church could investigate witchcraft but could not prosecute a capital crime, so the accused were handed over to the civil authorities. A Royal Commission was granted from Edinburgh to prosecute Janet Wishart and six of her family and associates, and trials took place over 17-23 February, leading to Wishart's execution. Like most Scottish witches she was sentenced to be tied to a stake, 'worriet' – strangled to death – and then burned.

Around about this time came the 'tipping point', when the relatively limited remit of the first commission snowballed into a major witch-hunt. Wishart's son, Thomas Leyis, confessed to making a pact with Satan – and, significantly, named several women as witches. The process of getting people to accuse others was underway, a process aided by the judicious application of sleep-deprivation and occasional torture, all legal and above board. Letters were sent post haste to Edinburgh, citing this terrific opportunity to clear out the stinking cesspool of North-East witchery, and on 4 March a new Royal Commission was duly granted to try not named individuals – as was usually the case – but *any* cases of witchcraft. And the Commission was not just valid for the typical few weeks or months, but for five years. This effectively gave the Aberdeen authorities *carte blanche* to do whatever they wanted, and all within the law.

The unfortunates named by Leyis were the first to be interrogated and burned. Then the rural areas were scoured. Perhaps a valid comparison would be the Gestapo rooting out resistance fighters in occupied Europe, or the Stasi's cruel operations in former East Germany. Accused witches were encouraged to give up names. Lairds and ministers were told to hand over any likely suspects; some were only too glad to do so, while others, knowing what fate awaited those found guilty, refused to rat their parishioners out. There were many executions in March and April, but by the end of May the mania had burned itself out. Perhaps the magistrates were looking forward to their summer holidays and slacked off a bit towards the end. Seventy-six people were caught up in the panic. Of these, twenty-seven were definitely executed, one committed suicide and another died of disease or neglect in the Tolbooth or St Nicholas Kirk. Another eight were convicted of lesser offences such as charming, while five were acquitted. The records are not clear on the remaining thirty-four: they may have been released, but some may have been executed.

A second, smaller witch-hunt took place in the autumn and winter, with one execution and three people acquitted. Thereafter things calmed down for a time. The catch-all general commission was still legally valid, and was brought back into use for a time in 1599. After this, Aberdonians seemed to have a rethink, or perhaps an attack of conscience. Numerous witches were persecuted and executed throughout Scotland during the following century, but in Aberdeen anti-magical operations were confined to the Kirk Sessions and Presbytery imposing relatively minor punishments on charmers, such as fines, and forced repentance dressed in sackcloth while confessing their sins before the entire congregation.

In 1603 the Marquess of Huntly demanded the Presbytery tell him the names of all the witches and consulters of witches that they knew of; the Presbytery duly circulated the request around all their ministers, but no results seem to have been forthcoming. Between 1606 and 1608 five people were served with 'acts of caution', telling them to appear at court, but none of these came to trial, and there are almost no details of the charges, other than a note that Janet Patersone of Kennay had 'witched' John Forbes of Lethinty, while Agnes Chapman was alleged to have bewitched Cristian Fraser, 'sometime Lady Meldrum'. In 1630 Marion Hardie from Elgin named six women from Peterhead whom she said stood with her at the blockhouse on Pocra Quay and threw stones into the sea to sink a fishing boat. The council resolved to apply for a commission to try the denounced women but there is nothing more in the records. The same year James Hall confessed to employing a charmer to cure his illness – he had to sit on the penitential stool in church as punishment – and Marjorie Mearns was forced to beg forgiveness from a widow named Margaret Mason for calling her a witch. Mearns had spat and 'cast fire' at Mason, presumably actions that kept witches away. Mearns was required to kneel in front of the congregation and repeat 'False tongue, ye lied!' And in 1639 Andrew Young hired a 'sorcerer' to cure Isobel Aiken, his wife. The charm did not work and Young found himself making repentance in church.

There are no records of witches being executed in Aberdeen after 1598. As the seventeenth century progressed the intellectual climate changed, and from the 1680s onward it was becoming harder and harder to find a judge willing to sanction a witch-burning. The last Scottish witch execution in Scotland was in 1722, in Sutherland, and in 1735 – to the great dismay and protest of the Church of Scotland – witchcraft ceased to be a capital offence.

The voluminous Aberdeen trial records were collected in *The Miscellany of the Spalding Club Vol I*, edited by John Stuart in 1841. More records can be found in another of Stuart's indispensable volumes, *Selections from the Records of the Kirk Session, Presbytery, and Synod of Aberdeen* (1846). Reading them gives both an insight into the world of magical thought in post-Reformation Scotland – and chills the blood.

Describing the trial of each of the witches would require an entire book (Janet Wishart alone was accused of thirty-three individual crimes, each of them given in lengthy detail) so here are what you might call the 'edited highlights', with a particular emphasis on magical operations and supernatural beliefs.

JANET WISHART (EXECUTED 17 FEBRUARY 1597)

Wishart had a magical career stretching back some twenty-five years. She was noted for frequently staying out all night, up to no good, or sitting up through the hours of darkness, casting 'cantrips' or spells in front of the fire. She appears to have been a formidable, even frightening figure. Bear in mind that at this time Aberdeen's population was less than 5,000: everyone must have known who she was and her reputation. Here are some of the charges against her:

- 1573 – Bewitching two schoolboys, John Leslie and Johnson, so that they drowned themselves. Earlier that day the lads had spotted Wishart stealing things from her neighbour in Schoolhill.
- 1581 – Casting a fever onto Malcolm Carr's wife, the sickness lasting six months.
- 1585 – Spoiling the entire stock of ale of brewer Katherine Rattray after Rattray had insulted her. Rattray's daughter, Katherine Ewin, persuaded Wishart to restore the ale, so Wishart instructed Ewin to visit the brewing house before dawn, without crossing herself, speaking, washing her hands,

passing over water or having her son sucking at her breast. Having avoided all these taboos Ewin had to say 'I to God, and thou to the devil!' three times to the brew, and throw a charm of green, red and blue threads onto the fire. This restored the ale, but when Ewin revealed the charm to others, Wishart immediately cursed the child suckling at her breast, and the boy died. Then Ewin's entire brew vanished from a locked room to which only she had the key. For twenty nights thereafter a cat visited Ewin and her husband Ambrose Gordon, preventing them sleeping and taking a great bite out of Ambrose's arm.

- 1591 – Consulting with the Devil at the military blockhouse on POCRA QUAY in Footdee.
- 1592 – Murdering weaver Andrew Ardes by casting a fever that took eight days to kill him. As with most of the similar cases, Wishart had pronounced a curse or spell on the victim just before he sickened.
- 1593 – Cursing the child of Walter Healing to death. The Castlegate merchant had refused to sell Wishart some wool.
- 1594 – Cursing her servant James Ailhows because he refused to continue working for her. The man was sick for six months, and had to pay another witch to cure him. This she did by washing him in south-running water and passing him through a girth (an animal's saddle-strap).
- 1594 – Casting a fever onto Bessie Schives in Broadgate, so that the woman was sick for eighteen weeks, 'the one half-day roasting as in a fiery furnace, with an extraordinary kind of drought, that she could not be slaked, and the other half-day in an extraordinary kind of sweating, melting, and consuming her body, as a white burning candle, which kind of sickness is a special point of witchcraft.'
- 1596 – Casting a six-month illness onto her son Thomas' lover, Elspeth Reid, so that she became 'like a dead senseless fool'. At 3 a.m. on Midsummer, Reid had entered her Wishart's house to find the matriarch naked by the fireside, 'sitting between the shoulders' of another naked woman. This may have been sexual, although Wishart told Reid she had been performing a charm. Whatever the truth Reid was clearly shocked, and her illness developed immediately after.

Other, undated, activities included:

- Running as fast as an arrow between sailor Alexander Thomson and the dawn sun and casting a spell that caused him to contract an extreme fever. This took place below Castlehill. Thomson's wife and Catherine Crawford threatened Wishart with burning, so Wishart supplied 'certain beer and other drugs to drink' which restored the man to health.
- Delaying the birth of a child and causing the baby to be stillborn.
- Standing naked in a field at harvest-time and throwing stones onto the ground. This is described as taking place on her own 'Goodman's Croft', the name given to a plot of untilled land farmers dedicated to the 'Goodman' or Devil, in the hope that no evil would befall their other crops. The casting of stones was probably Wishert demonstrating to the Dev that the ground would not be ploughed, and it was all his.

- Poisoning a child whom she had wanted to wetnurse.
- Poisoning John Collson, who survived and went on to became Provost.
- Cursing a neighbour's cow to produce poison instead of milk.
- Putting her witchcraft into a pair of sheets that caused Meryann Nasmith to lose her mind, and be 'bound hand and foot for three days'.
- Causing a dozen hens to fall from their roost, dead at her feet.
- Raising the wind to winnow malt barley in her house, by putting a piece of live coal at two doors. Her neighbours were unable to winnow for lack of wind.
- Coming through John Allan's window every night for five or six weeks 'in the likeness of a brown tyke (dog)' and assaulting him; Allan was Wishart's son-in-law and had beaten his wife.
- Impoverishing her neighbour, stabler John Club, by casting drugs such as 'old shoon' into his fire (I have no idea what 'old shoon' was). It is worth noting that Wishart's husband was also a stabler, so this may have been a way of taking out a business rival. Other stablers were victims of Wishart's wrath, such as John Pyet, and James Lowe and his wife and child, who died of magical fever.
- Visiting the gallows after midnight and cutting parts off the corpse hanging there (presumably hands or fingers, plus toes and possibly genitals). The parts would have been used in some kind of magical operations.

THOMAS LEYS OR LEYIS (EXECUTED 23 FEBRUARY 1597)

Leys was Wishert's son, and seems to have been a chip off the old block, helping his mother to bewitch a neighbour's property, and threatening Andrew Clark with death if he proceeded against Wishert in court. He told his lover Elspeth Reid to stand on the foot of a certain man (an elf or spirit, or possibly the Devil) and hold the fellow's ear. This may have been either a way of temporarily transferring second sight, or of participating in a Satanic pact. Reid refused to do it, probably already fearful of her boyfriend's growing reputation in the black arts. Leys also predicted Reid would give birth to a girl on the Sunday after Martinmas, even before she knew she was pregnant. On Hallowe'en 1596 he led a group of witches on a dance round the Mercat and Fish Crosses, the music supplied by the Devil in person. Either costumes were worn, or shapeshifting was going on, because the witches were arrayed 'some as hares, some as cats, some in other likenesses'. It was for leading this party that he was executed, although three of the jury found him not guilty.

JOHN LEYIS (JANET WISCHERT'S HUSBAND),
ELPSET LEYIS, JANET LEYIS, VIOLET LEYIS (HER DAUGHTERS).

Violet had been accused of helping her mother mutilate the corpse on the gallows, and the others were suspected, but in the end the entire family were simply branded on the cheek and banished from Aberdeen, to suffer execution if they returned.

ISOBEL COCKIE (EXECUTED 19 FEBRUARY 1597)

Cockie, from Kintore, worked a con with Helen Makkie, aka Suppok: Helen would curse someone and then Isobel would happen by, offering to unwitch them. Suppok later died in prison, of causes unspecified. Cockie seems to have been involved in endless disputes with her unfortunate neighbours, who as a consequence suffered loss of livelihood, plus sickness and death among their herds, destruction of crops, spoiling of milk, and personal illness and death. In the most extraordinary episode, Cockie was at the same Hallowe'en dance as Thomas Leyis at the Mercat and Fish Crosses, when she became fed up with the poor quality of the music supplied by the Devil. So she marched up to Satan, took the jew's harp straight out of his mouth, and struck up a tune herself. For some reason the King of Hell, the Prince of Pride, the Archduke of Arrogance, did not take umbrage at this. Perhaps because it was just some bloke in a devil costume?

BESSIE THOM (EXECUTED 9 MARCH 1597)

If tabloid newspapers had been around in the sixteenth century, Thom would have been described as 'the Poison Witch' or 'the Black Widow'. Among the accusations against her (all of which she denied) was the murder by poison not only of the husband of her client, Elspeth Jack, but also her own husband Patrick Coull. She also offered to get rid of Isobel Irving's husband for a fee of 40s and a quantity of beef. Thom had been with Thomas Leyis at the notorious Hallowe'en party, and had also attended an earlier convention at Rood Day (14 September, the former Catholic Festival of the Holy Cross). Before dawn she and several other witches had gathered at the ruined chapel on St Katherine's Hill (now ADELPHI LANE), riding on trees, dancing and partying to the sound of music supplied by the Devil.

CHRISTEN MITCHELL (EXECUTED 9 MARCH 1597)

Mitchell was tried and executed at the same time as Thom, and had attended the same two dances as her. She was another poisoner, accused of murdering her son and daughter-in-law. On one occasion the Devil appeared to her as 'a little crippled man'. While she agreed to join the Devil's band, she stated she did not want to be a permanent member; the Devil immediately hit her so hard she was bedridden for several weeks.

ISOBELL STRAUTHAQUHIN OR STRACHAN, ALIAS SCUDDER (EXECUTED 21 MARCH 1597)

Scudder, from Dyce or Fintray, had inherited her magical knowledge from her mother, who learned it from an 'elf man' she had slept with. At one level she was there to fulfil female desires: she hid a charm in Walter Ronaldson's barn to make him stop beating his wife, and manufactured love charms from coins and red wax wrapped in cloth (the woman had to use it to strike the face of the man she fancied, who would thereafter be compelled to marry her). As part of her job as a matchmaker she caused a man to marry 'beneath himself' – the resulting marriage was emotionally and financially disastrous, which was blamed on Scudder's love spell. She also used magic to kill a new-born baby, cast sickness onto humans and animals, and bewitched doors and thresholds so that the first person to pass through them would take ill and die. She bewitched the mill at Caskieben so it ceased to work, and cured an invalid by giving him water in which she had washed human bones (taken from a graveyard or a corpse on a gibbet?). When the bones were afterwards thrown into the River Don, the water boiled. Scudder's daughter Elspeth Murry was also investigated, but not prosecuted.

MARGARET BANE OR CLERK (EXECUTED 25 MARCH 1597)

Bane, from Lumphanan, was one of those caught up in the sweep through rural Aberdeenshire. She had a magical record stretching back thirty years. Her execution was the Beatlemania of the day, with the large numbers of attendees breaking two of the wooden crowd-control barriers (costs for their repair are in the council records).

MARION GRANT (EXECUTED 15 APRIL 1597)

Grant, from Methlick, had several encounters with two spirits or demons. One she called 'Our Ladye', a gentlewoman clad in a white wyliecoat (a woollen or flannel undergarment); there is no hint in the record that either Grant or the court thought the spirit was the famous 'Our Lady', the Blessed Virgin Mary. The other more conventional devil was a tall man called Christsonday or Christonday, dressed in silk and carrying a white candle. Grant danced with both spirits and had sex with Christsonday. He taught Grant magical healing skills in exchange for her kissing his buttocks, worshipping him on her knees, and accepting his token and a 'a vehement nip in the thick of her hand at the shackle bone'. Her magical abilities included healing people and cattle using south-running water and prayers (which usually included reference to both the Holy Trinity, and Christsonday), and charming a sword so that its owner would be protected from harm. It is possible 'Our Ladye' may be the same as the spirit called the Queen of Elfland by Andro Man, who also knew Christsonday (see below).

AGNES WOBSTER (EXECUTED 24 APRIL 1597)

Wobster was from Longside. Around 1582 the Devil had appeared to her in the form of a lamb or calf, and she had agreed to be his servant. One of her magical skills was the ability to breathe fire.

ELLEN GRAY (EXECUTED 27 APRIL 1597)

Gray met the Devil in the form of an old, bearded man wearing a white gown. Apart from the usual claims (spoiling milk, cursing neighbours after disputes) she was accused of giving a man a permanent erection, which later killed him.

ANDRO MAN (EXECUTED 20 JANUARY 1598)

In many ways Man's case is the most fascinating because of the sheer quantity and variety of supernatural and magical detail, and the mixing of demonology and fairylore. Having read a great many witch-trial transcripts, I can honestly say that Man's is the weirdest I have seen. He was around seventy years old when brought to trial, and said that when he was a boy the Queen of Elfland came to his mother's house and was delivered of a child. Over the years Man had a long-term relationship with the Queen, who gave him his magical abilities – he was promised knowledge of all things, and the ability to heal every disease, but not to raise the dead. He was also told he would be a poor man all his life. He knew the elves, and at a fairy conclave he met the ghosts of James IV and Thomas the Rhymer, the latter the subject of a famous tradition that he too was the lover of the Queen of Elfland. Man was in service to a spirit who appeared like an angel, clad all in white and who went by the name Christsonday (the same as Marion Grant's spirit). Christsonday gave Man a mark, biting him on the third finger of his right hand. The interrogators insisted that Christsonday was the Devil, and the Queen of Elfland was another avatar of Satan.

The details of the Queen of Elfland are quite astonishing. According to his testimony, Man started a relationship with the Queen around 1565, when he would have been in the region of thirty-eight years old, and she bore him several children, which he saw but did not have any hand in raising. She could appear young or old as she wished, lay with any man she fancied, and 'makes any king whom she pleases', which probably means she raised humans to positions of power, just on a whim. In one intriguing sentence, it is stated that 'The Queen has a grip of all the craft, but Christsonday is the gudeman [husband, or landlord, or boss] and has all power under God.' The implication here *may* be that the Queen controlled the witches, or the world of Faery, as a kind of Governor beholden to Christsonday, and that the male spirit was the Demiurge, the supreme evil spirit set above humanity to rule the Earth. The interrogators were not happy at the statement that Christsonday had 'all power under God', especially when the spirit also claimed to be God's son-in-law.

Christsonday also 'revealed' much more conventional glimpses of the Christian apocalypse to Andro Man. On the Day of Judgment, 'the fire will burn the water and the earth and make all plain' and Christsonday will be at the gates of Hell with a record of sins for every individual, and 'each man will have his own dittay (indictment) written in his own book to accuse himself'. When the godly have been severed from the wicked, Christsonday will be cast into the flames.

Christsonday also knew the secrets of nature and the future – he told Man that crows brought stones from another district to make their young hatch, and that while 1598 would be hard on everyone, the following fourteen years would be far better.

In an extraordinary section, Man (according to the record) saw Christsonday come out of the snow in the shape of a stag. It was Rood Day, 14 September 1597, and also present were the Queen and a party of elves riding white horses. The location was the Binhill, and Binloch, their usual place of gathering (possibly Binghill near MILLTIMBER). All those attending, including Man, kissed Christsonday and the Queen on the buttocks. The elves looked and dressed like humans, enjoyed eating, dancing and partying, and were described as 'shadows' but also stronger than men. Christsonday had sex with the elves and spent much of the rest of his time on horseback. There were also some human men present, in thrall to the Queen; these may have been the spirits of the dead, imprisoned in the Realm of Faery – a surprisingly common theme in Scottish witchcraft lore. Man frequently visited the fairies, and knew that after he had feasted in their fine hall he would wake up in the morning in a moss, with dead grass and straw that were the true appearance of the fine furnishings and swords he had admired the night before. But this illusion did not bother him, and he would have attended the next fairy revel, on Hallowe'en, but by that time he was under arrest.

In some cases the true meaning of the content in the testimony is now obscure to us. Man could summon Christsonday by speaking the word *Benedicite*, a Latin word that had been incorporated into the everyday speech of the learned to mean something like 'Bless you!' or a similar exclamation of surprise. Elite magicians (those with educations and big books) considered Latin to be a suitable tongue in which to address demons and pronounce incantations, and perhaps Man had picked something of this up. However, when Man wanted to dismiss his spirit, things got a bit strange. According to his confession, Man had to place a dog under his left armpit, throw the animal into the spirit's mouth, and pronounce the word *Maikpeblis*. No one has been able to make sense of *Maikpeblis*, and the whole thing with the dog is odd. Was it a sacrifice? Did Christsonday eat the dog? Did the word 'dog' mean something else?

In terms of Man's more mundane magical practices, he typically operated in the field of agricultural protection. He placed four charm-stones at the corners of a field to protect the cattle from lungsaucht (a lung disease) and all other afflictions, a protection that would remain in place as long as the land remained unploughed. He dipped a plough-iron in lax water (salmon water) to prevent the oxen running away. He pronounced a charm nine times before the start of ploughing, to ensure a good harvest (he could also take the 'goodness' of the crop away, by throwing straw into the corn and saying nine times the charm 'The dirt to thee, and the crops to me'). He also cured a man by moving him nine times through a hank of unwashed yarn, and a cat the same number of times in the opposite direction; this cast the disease on the cat. And he did a bit of palm-reading as well. Interestingly, Man was apparently not charged with any *malefices* or 'evil acts', in contrast to some of the more unpleasant individuals mentioned above.

Once on trial in October 1597, Man must have thought he had found a way out of his predicament by confessing everything and volunteering to identify other witches. He was duly taken around Aberdeenshire, confronting suspects with the details of their magical crimes. He confronted Jonet Leask in Portsoy and Gilbert Fidlar of Auchmacoy, but after a complicated case involving a family dispute, both were set free. Man also denounced Elspet Graye, a man called Moress and his wife, a second woman named Gray, and Maige Saythe, whom Man averred had attended meetings with elves and Christsonday for six years, but none of these came to trial. After a time the authorities got fed up with the expense of maintaining Man for no result, and he was executed in January 1598.

SHOW ME THE MONEY

Aberdeen is unique in that not only have many of the testimonies of the witch trials survived, but also the financial accounts, all set out in the council's registers alongside other costs for couriers, poor relief and councillors' dinners. There are sums for peats, coals, tar-barrels, ropes and the other essentials for burning a human being. There is the fee for John Justice the executioner, which varied depending on how many witches were burned in a day (typically 13s 4d – around £100 in today's terms – for two witches, with a bit more if he hanged some thieves or other miscreants at the same time in the same place). Justice also received 6s 4d for branding the four members of the Leyis family on the cheek and banishing them from Aberdeen. There is a cost for a blacksmith to fashion two pairs of shackles for the steeple of St Nicholas Kirk. A sum is handed out in recompense for a halbert, the weapon having been broken while trying to control the crowds at an execution. There are also costs for dragging the body of Manteith, the witch who hanged herself in prison, through the streets. The total cost of the 1597 trials and executions was a substantial £1,771 17s 4d (very approximately, over £200,000 today).

On 21 September 1597, the provost, bailies, and council showed their appreciation of the work of Dean of Guild William Dunn, in part for 'his extraordinary pains in the burning of a great number of witches'. He was granted an honorarium of £47 3s 4d (about £6,000 in modern terms)

THE MODERN WORLD

On 16 April 2000 'Tony' from Aberdeen wrote to the *News of the World*'s psychic, Ruth Urquhart, about his girlfriend. She was attractive and sexy, but also 'into witchcraft in a big way'. Tony was worried she had put a spell on him, and was having nightmares about her, as well as losing his appetite and ability to function when she wasn't around. The thirty-something man was advised to light seven white candles, look out from a south-facing window at midnight and ask his guardian angel to break the curse. No comment.

2

THE CITY CENTRE – NORTH OF UNION STREET

PROVOST SKENE'S HOUSE – MARISCHAL COLLEGE – GALLOWGATE – ST NICHOLAS KIRK

Burnt and erased to the ground, in consequence of the sagacity of a Dog.

Broadside (1831)

KING STREET

The slender tower of the Arts Centre at No. 31 is an architectural reference to the Tower of the Winds in Athens. There are several recent reports of apparitions being seen in different parts of the building, which was formerly the North Church, built in 1830. In 1889 a prehistoric cist or stone-lined grave containing a beaker was uncovered at the south end of King Street; as we will see elsewhere, large parts of Aberdeen are built on the dead.

QUEEN STREET

The modern police headquarters is built on the site of the East Prison, Aberdeen's third after the TOLBOOTH (Wardhouse) and Bridewell. Several felons were buried in the prison grounds after being executed, including James Burnett in 1849 and John Booth in 1857, the last of the burials. The prison was closed in 1891 and demolished. Grampian Police maintain a 'museum' of gruesome crime-related artefacts, although there is no actual building. Some of the items are rotated through the display cabinets in the building. In late 2009, for example, one could see the axe used by George Stephen to kill his married lover Anne Forbes in 1864, along with a wax cast of the victim's skull proving that Stephen's woodsman's axe was the murder weapon. The cast was Aberdeen's earliest forensic 'production', as such items produced in evidence in court are termed in Scotland. Viewing the displays is possible upon application to the museum curator, via the force's website www.grampian.police.uk.

Someone between Queen Street and LODGE WALK was the Methodist Meeting House, site of the prank in 1763 involving a murderer's skeleton (*see* GALLOWS HILL).

BROAD STREET

Guestrow, the western strip of Broad Street beside the Illicit Still pub, may be the only place name in Aberdeen that has a direct reference to the supernatural; there again, it may all be a big mistake. The key turns on the interpretation of medieval documents, a fine art that can be endlessly argued over. A plaque on one of the houses states Guestrow is 'a name unique to Aberdeen but its origin is obscure.' Before twentieth-century redevelopment Guestrow was a substantial street in its own right, boasting several prestigious properties including PROVOST SKENE'S HOUSE. A charter of 1439 gives the street's name as Vicus Lemurum, which if the Latin is correct, translates as 'the Street of the Spectres or Ghosts'. From this, seventeenth-century writers, and others who followed them, suggested the medieval Scots original of the Latin phrase was Ghaist-row, 'Ghost Row', later corrupted into the modern 'Guestrow'. Certainly Alexander Keith, in *A Thousand Years of Aberdeen* (1972) mentions a document from 1450 which mentions the *vicus dict le Gastrow* ('the street called the Gastrow').

If 'Guestrow' is 'Ghost-row', which particular ghosts are being referred to in the place name? In 1904 G.M. Fraser, author of *Historical Aberdeen*, thought he knew the answer. He surmised that the street once overlooked the graveyard of ST NICHOLAS KIRK, a place which to superstitious medieval types would bring to mind unquiet spirits walking abroad. This ingenious argument falters on two points: firstly, there are hundreds of streets throughout Scotland with views onto graveyards, and none of them have the word 'ghost', 'ghaist' or any similar derivation in their names. And second – as pointed out by Edward Meldrum in an article for the Society of Antiquaries of Scotland in 1959 – even if you take away all the modern buildings, the inhabitants of Guestrow would have a fine view of the spire of the kirk – but not of its kirkyard. It therefore seems highly unlikely that 'Guestrow' refers to ghosts in its name. The cause of all the argument is of course the 1439 reference to *Vicus Lemurum*. One possibility is that *Lemurum* is a medieval Latinisation of an older word, possibly a corruption of a Gaelic place name. In which case, the original meaning is lost, and the only ghostly street name in Aberdeen is a mere phantom.

PROVOST SKENE'S HOUSE

Open Monday-Saturday 10 a.m.-5 p.m., closed Sunday. Entrance free. Guidebook available. Disabled access only to café on the ground floor, within the vaulted former cellar. This splendid restored period house is one of the few sixteenth-century properties to have survived urban redevelopment. The history is given in the interpretation sheets, panels and guidebook, so here the concentration will be on the more unusual aspects of the building.

THE EXTERIOR

The best view of the house is from the courtyard to the south, with its 1960s bronze sculpture ('Sea Fantasy') of a woman and child dancing in the water pool. Almost hidden round the south-western corner is one of the best sights in Aberdeen – a grotesque, grimacing bearded head. It has no direct connection with Provost Skene's House, as it used to hang on No. 35 Ragg's Lane. When the building – and Ragg's Lane itself – was demolished in 1959, the head was transferred to its current location. Inevitably such a carving has generated theories as to what the head actually represents, and Bernard Maitland Balfour's *Secrets, Stories, Skeletons and Stones* ably sums up the key stories. Version 1: Baillie Alexander Ragg erected it on the lane that bore his name (Ragg died in 1719). Version 2: the shop at No. 35 was a bookseller that sold Classical works, and the head is Homer, author of *The Iliad* and *The Odyssey*. The eyes have no pupils because Homer was said to be blind. (The Scottish Book Trade Index at the National Library of Scotland notes that Alexander Smith was running a bookselling business at No. 2 Ragg's Lane in 1847; in 1841 John Avery was operating as a printer and stationer at No. 1, while Alexander Russel had a bookshop close by at No. 7 Netherkirkgate from 1824-1832.) Version 3 (the favourite): George Russell or Russel (1810-1899) owned a bakery at No. 35. He fell out with his neighbours and when the Council closed the business because it was near a sewer, he blamed ironmonger Alexander Stephen for ratting him out. Russell therefore sculpted a caricature of Stephen and hung it where the ironmonger would have to pass every day. It is possible this is actually true.

Moving west along the southern front of the building, there is a seventeenth-century double-face sundial high up on the east stair tower, and then the entrance arch with an escutcheon marked 'AT AD 1673' and decorated with two grotesque faces. A modern plaque states that the archway was erected by Sheriff-Depute Andrew Thomson and his wife Agnes Divie at their house in Guestrow in 1637 (which is probably meant to read 1673); when the building was demolished in the 1950s the arch was set up in Union Terrace Gardens and then in 1970 relocated here, close to its original site. Looking upwards to the left of the arch, there is an elaborate coat of arms above the upper window. Dated 1626, the heraldry – which incorporates two wolves' heads – is marked M.M.L

Yaa-boo, sucks to you! The neighbour-annoying head on the south-east corner of Provost Skene's House. *(Geoff Holder)*

(Maister Matthew Lumsden) and E.A. (his wife Elizabeth Aberdour). Lumsden was a wealthy merchant and may – or may not – have commissioned the famous painted ceiling (see below). Binoculars reveal that the sculptor responsible for carving the work has signed it with his own mason's mark. More intricate carving – motifs of thistle-and-rose and grape-and-vine-leaf – can be found around the decorative doorway of the actual entry into the building, with its massive wooden studded door and deadshot lock.

The museum is set out as a series of rooms fitted out in the style of various periods. It should be emphasised that as the building went through many changes of ownership and use – including a twentieth-century doss-house – nothing is known about the exact use to which the rooms were put. So although the period detail is glorious, little of it – with the exception of the wonderful seventeenth-century plaster ceilings – is 'authentic' to the rooms, or even to the building. This includes the furniture, much of which is on long-term loan from the Victoria & Albert Museum in London. Whether this 'inauthenticity' has any relevance to the various accounts of ghosts within the building, I am unable to say. Certainly there have been numerous reports of haunting-type phenomena, as catalogued in Graeme Milne's *The Haunted North*, and noted room-by-room below. For example, in September 2006 heavy footsteps were frequently heard from several rooms that appeared to be empty, the noises coming at all times of the day. Those of a sceptical bent will note that the building is several centuries old and creaks with its age; wooden doors and fittings expand and contract with the weather; many of the rooms are dark and the staircases are confusing and tiring; and sound can carry through the labyrinth of passages and rooms in unexpected ways – all classic situations that can promote suggestion, especially in a building with an existing reputation. Nevertheless, the sheer quantity and variety of spooky experiences collected by Milne make a case that *something* might be going on.

THE TOWER
Staff locking up at night have reported hearing footsteps on the old stone staircase and feeling a sense of presence.

FIRST FLOOR
Having passed through the Georgian Dining Room you reach the so-called Great Hall, the first of three rooms set out in seventeenth-century style. Above the fireplace is the wooden coat of arms of Provost Sir George Skene, with three wolves' heads impaled on dirks. The associated story is that, out hunting in the Stocket Forest, Skene killed a wolf that was threatening the King – despatching would-be monarch-munching mammals is a sure way to personal advancement. Opposite is a massive oak cupboard carved with four Biblical scenes, and the heads of humans, animals, angels and demons; although appearing to be from the 1600s, it is in fact a fake from two centuries later. A portrait in The Parlour of Patrick Dune shows the good doctor posing with a human skull.

SECOND FLOOR

The Painted Gallery holds one of the more mysterious sights in Aberdeen – a cycle of religious paintings, commissioned from an unknown artist by persons unknown for reasons unknown at a date unknown. The room has ten flat and angled ceiling panels painted in a very naive style, showing the Life of Christ from the Annunciation and the Adoration of the Shepherds to the Crucifixion, the Resurrection and the Ascension. The artwork is rich in explicitly Catholic imagery, including representations of the Five Sacred Wounds of Christ – the heart, pierced hands and pierced feet – and the sacred monograms I.H.S. (the Latin form of the abbreviation of Jesus Christ) and X.P.E. (the equivalent in Greek). Images of the Five Wounds were the focus of a late-medieval devotional cult and are also found in the Aberdeenshire castles of Craig, Gight and Towie, all owned by families who remained staunchly Roman Catholic after the Reformation (they are also on the font in St John's Church on ST JOHN'S PLACE).

In 1959 Edward Meldrum, writing in the *Proceedings of the Society of Antiquaries of Scotland*, identified numerous images on the flat ceiling as the Instruments of the Passion, the objects associated with the arrest, trial and crucifixion of Jesus, and themselves a keen focus of Catholic veneration. These include: the thirty pieces of silver; the torch and lantern used by the soldiers at Christ's arrest; the sword wielded by St Peter to cut off the ear of Malchus at the arrest; the cock which crowed at Peter's denial; Pilate's ewer and basin, in which he washed his hands; the pillar against which Christ was bound during his flagellation; and the nails, hammer, ladder and pincers of the Crucifixion. The large panel displaying the Crucifixion itself shows the moon covering the sun, representing the eclipse that occurred during the Passion. Some of the work is poorly-executed, and occasionally eccentric: two of the men attending the Burial of Christ appear to be wearing kilts.

At some point several of the panels have been defaced or painted over, obscuring what was probably more explicitly Catholic iconography such as the Coronation of the Virgin Mary, images Protestants would have found particularly offensive. Once again, we do not know who erased these panels, or when. The entire imagery-set is Catholic, and the style is seventeenth-century. So we have a large, expensive and impossible-to-hide expression of Catholic faith being commissioned by a well-to-do citizen decades after the Reformation, when supposedly such 'superstitious Popish imagery' was anathema to the Protestant authorities. Who could have ordered this controversial work? Alongside the religious imagery is a coat of arms that resembles that of Matthew Lumsden (whose heraldry is carved on the exterior window). Could then Maister Lumsden, Baillie of Aberdeen, have hired an itinerant painter of religious scenes to decorate his house when he lived here from 1622 to 1644? Hardly – Lumsden was a hard-line anti-Catholic, a die-hard Covenanter, and indeed he did die for the cause when he was a member of the Covenanting army defeated by the Marquis of Montrose at the BATTLE OF JUSTICE MILLS in 1644. Perhaps the Lumsden heraldry is a red herring, or some kind of heraldic joke whose punchline is long lost. Or perhaps it wasn't Protestant Matthew who was the Catholic turncoat, but one of his family… perhaps his wife, Elizabeth Aberdour? Or another close relative? This enigmatic survival certainly has more secrets to give up.

Milne mentions that a visitor reported the door to the Painted Gallery resisted her, as if the room was full of people pressing back from the other side. When she forced the door open the gallery was empty. In 2009, during an investigation by the East of Scotland Paranormal group, a digital audio recorder picked up an anomalous sound that sounded like a human imitating an animal's growl. No one was near the machine when the EVP (Electronic Voice Phenomenon) was recorded and there was no other obvious source for this puzzling sound. Other examples of EVP were picked up in the staff-only attic room at the top of the building.

THE EIGHTEENTH- AND NINETEENTH-CENTURY ROOMS
More stairs take you to further period rooms. The Small Painted Gallery between the Eighteenth-Century Bedroom and the Regency Parlour is decorated with easy-to-miss miniature Classical figures and landscapes painted directly on and around the wainscoting. As Milne notes, this section of the building seems to attract the most reports of strange incidents, with accounts from the mid-1980s onward. The phenomena range from a sense of presence and a feeling of great sadness (felt by an electrician in the Parlour in March 2007) to physical force (several visitors say they have been shoved) and apparitions. In December 2006 a visitor standing in the Small Painted Gallery saw a woman sitting on the yellow silk sofa in the Parlour, dressed in a long dark dress and lace cap. A member of staff saw in a dark-haired woman wearing old-fashioned clothes in the same location; the solid-looking apparition seemed to notice the employee, and then vanished. And a worker from the café saw a figure in a bonnet and old-style dress on the staff-only staircase leading down from the parlour to the old kitchen next to the Cellar café; this apparition also disappeared. From these reports it seems the witnesses may have all seen the same apparition, a woman wearing clothing from the nineteenth century.

THE CELLAR
The popular café in the vaulted cellar gives access to the old kitchen, which contains a variety of domestic bric-a-brac all framed by the truly enormous fireplace (the location for the appearance and disappearance of the female apparition mentioned above). Edward Meldrum's 1959 article mentions a small underground wine-cellar reached through the floor of the main vault. The existence of this brick-arched space and its associated steps had either given rise to, or reinforced, rumours of a secret passage leading from the house to the harbour. Meldrum thought the tradition – which, like the vast majority of secret tunnels, is entirely without foundation – was prompted by building works uncovering a medieval sewer or the underground culverted burn that ran between Broad Street and Guestrow.

Perhaps the oddest mystery connected with Provost Skene's House is the so-called 'fertility charm' shown in the illustration. It is a bronze human figure with one hand on its chest, the other on its lower body. It appeared in a book called *City by the Grey North Sea: Aberdeen* written by the well-known Aberdeen architect and author, Fenton Wyness in 1965. Wyness re-used the image in his 1971 book *Spots from the Leopard*. In both books Wyness stated that the item had been found a few years previously in the city centre – either on St Katherine's Hill, or in a property on Shiprow – and was on display in Provost Skene's House.

Here the mystery starts, because there is no record of this item ever being at Provost Skene's House, or indeed anywhere in the city's archaeological collections. This has been confirmed by Judith Stone, the Council's Keeper of Archaeology, who herself has unsuccessfully tried to find any record of the object. It is not known whether the item was ever on display – perhaps as a loaned item – in Provost Skene's House, or even whether it actually is a fertility charm. There is no indication within either of the Wyness books about where the photograph was taken, or the size of the object. As far as I can tell, both Alex P. Reid, who published *City by the Grey North Sea*, and Impulse Books, the publishers of *Spots from the Leopard*, have gone out of business, so that line of enquiry is closed. An appeal in the local press generated no leads. If anyone has any information on this mystery I would be very appreciative if they could contact me via the publishers.

The utterly mysterious, and possibly lost, so-called 'fertility charm', from Fenton Wyness' *City by the Grey North Sea*.

NETHERKIRKGATE

Now very much part of the Aberdeen retail-mania, this was the site of the sixteenth-century tower named Benholm's Lodging or the Wallace Tower, demolished in 1964 to make way for Marks & Spencer and re-erected on TILLYDRONE ROAD in Old Aberdeen. As with Correction Wynd (see below), the lane scuttles beneath Union Street at the rear of Marks & Spencer, emerging onto the Green via an underground tunnel which is not the healthiest of places at night.

UPPERKIRKGATE

In 1886 a hoard of over 12,000 silver coins were found here in a bronze cauldron. A second hoard, this time of 3,000 silver pennies, turned up during the construction of the St Nicholas Centre in 1983. Both had probably been hidden for safekeeping during the Second War of Scottish Independence in the 1330s, when Edward III was rampaging around Scotland. In 1336 Edward's man Sir Thomas Roscelyn attacked Aberdeen and after a battle at THE GREEN his men burned the city and slaughtered many of its inhabitants.

MARISCHAL COLLEGE

A fairytale fiesta of finialed and fretted granite Gothic, the College's architectural peers are the Houses of Parliament – and Hogwarts. Currently being swept clean of several centuries of university usage, it will reopen in 2011 as the new Aberdeen Council headquarters, replacing the redundant monolith of ST NICHOLAS HOUSE opposite. Until then there is no public access. Marischal College was founded on the site of the Franciscan Friary in 1593 as a distinctively Protestant rival to the older KING'S COLLEGE in Old Aberdeen, around which the slight aroma of Catholic incense still lingered. The two colleges were united in 1860 as the University of Aberdeen. The current, almost pathologically extravagant façade dates to the rebuilding of 1895-1906, which created the second largest granite building in the world (the Escorial Palace in Madrid takes first place). Look out for carvings of the heads of eagles, boars and wolves on the wooden doors of Greyfriars, the church that occupies the south-west angle of the complex.

Binoculars or very keen eyesight will reveal two pairs of grinning gargoyles on each of the four upper faces of Mitchell Tower, at 235ft (71.6m) the tallest part of the complex. In 1931 the tower gained a little more height, in the form of a mock skeleton wearing a top hat. The pranksters had been medical students Donald Dawson and Charles Ludwig, who, as the *Press & Journal* for 9 December revealed, had carried up 'a weird pyjama-clad effigy crowned by a human skull and wearing a lum hat.' Ludwig in particular was a mountaineering daredevil who later crossed the wire hanging above the deep chasm of RUBISLAW QUARRY. After the seven-day wonder had entranced thousands, a pair of slaters climbed up and removed the grotesque figure, by now dubbed 'The Old Man of Marischal'. Ludwig had planned to meet the slaters on the spire dressed up as a skeleton, but his cunning plan was foiled when he found the trap door into the upper chamber of the tower locked. He qualified as a doctor, joined the RAF as a pilot when war broke out, and was killed in 1942. The best account of The Old Man of Marischal can be found in Robert Smith's highly recommended book *Aberdeen Curiosities*.

The west front of Marischal College in 2009, with building works for the new Council HQ. *(Geoff Holder)*

Whenever the records state that a criminal's body was 'given to the Surgeons for Dissection' what they generally meant that the corpse was taken by the academics at Marischal or King's College and there used as a teaching tool for the increasing numbers of medical students. Fresh corpses were essential so that students could find their way around a human body, identify organs and tissues, practice surgery – and therefore be more effective doctors. Unfortunately the demand for cadavers always outstripped supply, and most people looked on the practice of dissection as vile butchery, not to mention a violation of various half-formed religious taboos. William Gordon, seventeenth-century Professor of Medicine and Anatomy at King's College, could teach dissection using only bodies of animals until an Act was put into law in 1636 by the Privy Council, the most powerful legal body in the land. Gordon was granted permission to receive two bodies a year for dissection from the Sheriff and Magistrates of Aberdeen. This pioneering legislation made it clear who was intended for the slab:

> … notable malefactors, execute in their bonds, especially being rebels and outlaws … the bodies of the poorer sort, dying in hospitals; or abortive bairns, foundlings; or of those of no quality, who has died of their diseases, and has few friends or acquaintance that can take exception.

The legislation cautioned the university to act with 'moderation and discretion' and not to 'wrong any man of quality'. But two bodies a year, grudgingly delivered by the local authorities, was hardly going to meet demand. (The Act is reproduced in *The Miscellany of the Spalding Club*, edited by John Stuart in 1841.)

The supply of corpses improved a little after the Murder Act of 1751 laid down post-hanging dissection as an additional punishment for certain crimes, including suicide – so feared and despised was dissection that it was thought the threat of it might be a deterrent to those contemplating self-harm. In March 1765 the body of a boy named Clyne who had hanged himself became the first suicide to become the property of the surgeons. In 1821 Robert Mackintosh and William Gordon, convicted of separate murders, were ordered to be 'anatomised' after their executions. Mackintosh's aged father travelled to London in the hope of having that part of the sentence quashed; he failed, and his son not only died in agony because the noose was improperly fitted, he was dissected and his skeleton exhibited in the anatomical museum. *The Black Kalendar of Aberdeen* notes that Gordon maintained to the end that he had not killed his wife deliberately and seemed genuinely surprised to have found her dying. He may have assaulted her in a drunken dream or while in the grip of homicidal somnambulism, also known as sleepwalking murder.

In November of the same year a novelty was introduced into anatomical teaching at Aberdeen – Galvanism. The then-fashionable technique involved passing the new-fangled thing called electricity through the cadaver, to study how nerves and muscles worked. As noted in the *London Medical and Physical Journal* for that year, once George Thom had been hanged (for murdering his father with poison) he was taken by Drs Skene and Ewing: 'The upper part of the spinal cord and the sciatic nerve were immediately laid bare, and a Galvanic arc was then established ... when a general convulsive starting of the body was produced.' Further hook-ups caused contractions of the muscles of the arm and hand, the latter clenching so powerfully an assistant had difficulty opening it again. When it came to the face, the electrical inputs were seen to 'distort the countenance in a very singular manner. The eyelids were strongly contracted; and when the wire was applied directly to the ball of the eye, the iris contracted and dilated very sensibly.' The tongue was also made to move in all directions. After about seventy-five minutes the cooling body was less responsive and the experiment discontinued. One side-effect of the poorly-insulated Galvanic pile used was that 'every metallic substance about the table was highly charged.'

All the foregoing, of course, were legitimately-obtained corpses delivered under the letter of the law. But the cadavers were few and far between and a medical student could not graduate unless he had demonstrated surgical proficiency on a real body. There was thus a significant demand for fresh corpses that could not be satisfied through legal channels. And so the era of the bodysnatchers was born. As mourners left the side of a freshly-dug grave, the situation was being 'cased' by men who that night would return with pick and shovel, remove the earth, smash open the coffin and make off with the shroud-wrapped corpse. Most bodysnatchers were medical students – and sometimes their professors – while a few were 'professional' graverobbers who would deliver corpses to the college gate for cash in hand, no questions asked.

Much of the following is sourced from Norman Adams' surveys *Scottish Bodysnatchers: True Accounts* and *Dead and Buried – The Horrible History of Bodysnatching*. The Aberdeen Medico-Chirurgical Society was set up by students in 1789 and later became the Aberdeen Medical Society (although it could equally have changed its name to the Aberdeen Bodysnatching Society – but that might have given the game away). An entry in their minute book for March 1780 reveals the dire straits in which they found themselves: 'That week a plan for anatomical dissection was put in execution. A dog was dissected.' Four years later some former members wrote to the Society from London, urging action: 'We are sorry that dissections have been so long neglected at Aberdeen. We are certain that proper subjects might be easily had there and will certainly be unless students are wanting in themselves in spirited execution or in Common Prudence. Bodies are procured in London for dissection almost every day. We leave everyone to form their own opinion whether it would be not an easier affair at Aberdeen.' Not surprisingly, however, Aberdeen medical students found it hard to make the leap to actually violating a grave. Things had not improved by March 1797 when a former member noted that 'I am persuaded that a subject *now and then* might be procured in Aberdeen, and much knowledge might be acquired if the inspection of bodies at the hospital was more attended to.'

Perhaps the succeeding generation were less squeamish. The Society's minutes for 1806-8 reveal that each medical student had to take his turn 'watching' the city's graveyards for likely opportunities; dereliction of duty brought a fine as punishment, but a successful 'lift' was rewarded with a prize of half a guinea (10s 6d) and an extra shilling 'to warm the insides of their jackets'. On 12 November 1805 a minute noted that a body had been procured (probably from the graveyard at ST NICHOLAS) and was sequestered in the Anatomical Theatre, awaiting a teaching dissection by Dr Skene (he who later electrically worked on George Thom). The students responsible for the lifting hoped to galvanise their fellows into action: 'It is hoped that the exertions of the above will prove a stimulus to the rest of the members.' Over the next three decades the resurrectionists really got into their stride. Medical students could be seen roaming the city and rural areas in speedy two-wheeled horse-drawn cabs nicknamed 'Noddies' because of the way passengers were jerked around on uneven streets. All the city graveyards were 'hit', along with many rural sites such as Banchory-Devenick church just outside Aberdeen. Here was (briefly) buried 'Wiggie' Paterson, a schoolteacher well-known to the medical students because he lived close to Marischal College. His misfortune was to have knock knees, a condition not yet studied by the anatomists, so when he died in the 1820s he was quickly dug up, and his bowed bones ended up on display in the college's anatomical museum.

Another source was greedy relatives. In the early 1800s James Sangster, a night-watchman in Gallowgate, sold his own wife's corpse to the anatomists and then, in the words of *The Black Kalendar*, 'went about the town, with the tears in his eyes, crying out that the body had been stolen out of the Spital burying-ground.' Sangster was suspected of lifting several bodies from Spital graveyard (now TRINITY CEMETERY on King Street), and his character gave him the nickname of Satan. (*The Black Kalendar* on the 1840s adds: 'The name of *Satan* is one which is kept up in Aberdeen to this day. The present *Satan* is a most aged and venerable looking man. There have also been, since the memory of man, a K*ing of Hell* and a *Queen of Hell* in Aberdeen.')

As time went on local people took up defensive measures. Graveyards were guarded at night by men staying in purpose-built watchtowers; sometimes those men were armed. Mortsafes were introduced to make digging into a grave impossible. Coffins were stored in protected buildings. It became harder to extract bodies, so the snatchers travelled further afield – thus raising the risk of detection. There were fights in the graveyards between watchers and robbers, and a number of arrests. In 1815 two medical students were imprisoned and fined £100 for *crimen violati sepulcri* – violating a sepulchre. Bodysnatching became notorious, a crime everyone was talking about. Under such conditions rumours thrive. An angry mob assembled around Marischal College when a story went around that the companion of a doctor seen driving in through the gate on a gig had not been his lady-friend, but a corpse dressed up as such. Rural travelling folk developed a highly-developed mythology in which cold-blooded anatomists would murder any travelling people they came across, and whisk the bodies to dissection (and consequently damnation). These tales were still being repeated in the 1950s. In 1870 William Buchanan's *Glimpses of Olden Days in Aberdeen* described what the atmosphere was like at that time: 'If any person went home longer than usual they were sure to have been "Burked"…The hair-breadth escapes from sticking-plasters, and being pursued by doctors, that were retailed each morning were truly wonderful, and timid people were afraid to go out after dark.'

A key figure in the Aberdeen bodysnatching scandals was Dr Andrew Moir. Born in 1806, he became a brilliant student of anatomy at Marischal College, supplementing his meagre income by 'lifting' bodies from graveyards and selling them to other students. Following a sojourn in Paris – where the medical students were happily and legally supplied with uncountable numbers of bodies found drowned in the Seine – Moir returned to Aberdeen determined to improve the quality of anatomical teaching there. He first set up an anatomy school in Guestrow, across the road from and in direct competition to Marischal College, which is why the university academics labelled him 'a common resurrectionist' and 'dirty little Moir'. Being outside the mainstream medical establishment he had to obtain his corpses illegally, and organised the students who took his classes into 'lifting squads', with fines imposed on those who failed to participate. In 1829 a sack containing the limbless body of a man taken from New Deer churchyard was found abandoned near Moir's place, although there was no direct link with the doctor. In March of the same year a mob, inflamed by a rumour that a stolen corpse was being dissected in Moir's rooms, attacked the building and caused a great deal of damage. The police broke up the riot and arrested one man. Moir's work was temporarily put on hold but he bounced back, constructing a new anatomy school on ST ANDREW STREET (see below for what happened to that ill-fated building).

In a lighter vein, an amusing episode – which may be true, or may simply be a bodysnatching 'urban legend' – was related in a broadside entitled 'A New Way of Raising the Wind!' Quoting the original report in the *Fife Journal* of 26 February 1829, the onepenny sheet told how a multi-national group of sailors from an English ship *en route* from America spent a night's drinking in Aberdeen. Sailors were always keen to find ways to 'raise the wind', and in port often visited old crones who had a reputation for weather magic. This time, however, the merry band decided to provide the spirits of the winds with a mock sacrifice – and make some cash into the bargain. One of their number, a black man, was placed into a sack and carried to the address of a 'respectable Lecturer on Anatomy' (probably Dr Moir). There his comrades told a tale of woe, of how this poor man had died of apoplexy just before they put into port. The broadside described what happened next:

> Having got £3 in hand, with the promise of more next day, they carried the corpse down into the cellar, the lecturer and his servant coming along with them and locking the door. With as little delay as possible the black subject cut open the sack; and, with his knife in his hand, anxiously waited the return of the lecturer. He did not wait long, for, in a few minutes the lector came back to look at his purchase, when suddenly the dead man rushed upon him, which so much alarmed him, that he forthwith ran up the stairs, followed by the black subject, who, upon gaining the street door, lost no time in joining his messmates. A jovial bumper to the health of the Doctor and his subject concluded the spree; and the whole crew, 'gloriously fu',' returned to their vessel, which sailed next morning.

The scandals of the Burke and Hare murders in Edinburgh and the London Burkers finally forced the authorities to change the law, and in 1832 the Anatomy Act allowed licensed institutions to legally obtain any corpses if they were unclaimed after death, typically from the prison or workhouse. Bodies could also be donated, in exchange for the institution covering the burial fees. Overnight the resurrectionist trade vanished, and bodysnatching became history.

MARISCHAL MUSEUM

Unfortunately the building works at the College means that the Marischal Museum, the finest museum in Aberdeen and one of the best in Scotland, is closed for the foreseeable future. In the interim its treasures can be explored at www.abdn.ac.uk/virtualmuseum. Highlights include:

- Witch and charm stones
- Carved Neolithic stone balls of unknown purpose
- Sculptured Pictish symbol stones
- Ancient Egyptian mummies of humans, cats and crocodiles
- A pointing bone belonging to Aboriginal peoples of Australia – its twenty-three notches show how many people it has killed through its death magic (there is also an amulet bone used to counter such sorcery)
- The decorated skull of a revered ancestor from Melanesia
- South American dolls made from human foot bones
- Nuts used in folk magic rituals in Macedonia
- A seventeenth-century 'bog body' of a murder victim
- The kayak of a mysterious Arctic traveller who landed just north of Aberdeen in about 1700 but died soon after without anyone learning anything about him
- A slab from Mesopotamia inscribed with magical names in Greek
- Prehistoric beakers, skulls and grave goods found in Aberdeen burial cists
- A portrait (with accompanying skull) of Dr Andrew Moir, the infamous anatomist of ST ANDREW STREET

And hundreds of other items of interest from Scotland, Asia, the Pacific, the Arctic, Egypt, Australia, New Zealand and elsewhere.

In short, when the Marischal re-opens its doors those in search of magic, mysteries and marvels could spend days wandering around; it is a tragedy this superb museum is not open at present.

GALLOWGATE

Once a highway of great importance, this historic thoroughfare has degenerated into a strikingly brutal urbanscape that would not look out of place in some

Soviet-era backwater. The multi-storey flats on the east side of the street were erected over Quaker Close, site of the Quaker meeting house and burial ground. In *City by the Grey North Sea* Fenton Wyness states that although the graveyard was damaged by an enemy bomb in 1940, when the flats were constructed in 1962 the remains of some forty or so bodies were uncovered and scattered. The remainder still lie under the tower blocks.

The Quakers, or the Religious Society of Friends, were established during the ferment of the seventeenth-century Civil Wars, and in many ways their rise was due to the weariness many educated people felt with the extreme, fanatical fundamentalism displayed by many who supposedly followed the teachings of Jesus Christ, the Prince of Peace. Some of what follows is based on 'Quakerism in the North-East of Scotland', a paper presented by Delia Seager at a conference in 1997, and available from the Quakers Meeting House on Crown Street. The Quakers' core belief was in a personal, internal experience of God, termed the Inner Light. This direct contact with the divine did not need to be cluttered with the paraphernalia of organised Christianity, such as elaborate churches, ministers, sermons or hierarchies. Quakers were highly principled, refusing to pay church taxes, participate in military action or swear oaths – they maintained their word was sufficient. They thus defied all of the governing institutions – state, church and army – so perhaps it is not surprising they were brutally persecuted, with many imprisoned in the Tolbooth and, when space there ran out, in St Ninian's Chapel on Castlehill. Part of the fascinating history of Quakerism in Aberdeen is that many of its adherents were prominent citizens, including many wealthy merchants and even a former provost. In addition, Quakers had enlightened views on gender, and women were accorded equal status in finance and decision-making.

Quakers did not recognise the authority of the established church and so refused to bury their dead in churchyards. They therefore used their own graveyards, where, if there were any headstones at all, the style was of the simplest. Openly burying their dead in unconsecrated ground offended the righteously orthodox, so in 1671, when shoemaker Thomas Mill buried his infant child in the Friends' graveyard on Gallowgate, the magistrates acted. The walls of the burial ground were knocked down and the child was dug up and reburied in the kirkyard of St Nicholas. The following year another of Mill's children was exhumed, and in 1673 three more bodies, including two children, were forcibly removed for reburial. The worst of the persecution eased off after 1679, and when Elizabeth Goodall was laid to rest in the graveyard in 1692, the interment passed off peacefully.

Fenton Wyness' *Spots from the Leopard* recorded a strange tradition that grew up around Mary Bannerman, the prosperous widow of George Leslie, Laird of Findrassie. The rumour was that she had bequeathed her house on Guestrow to the Friends – provided they kept her embalmed body on the premises. This bizarre suggestion went against all the beliefs of the Quakers regarding simple funeral arrangements, and indeed Mary had made her desires known when she made her will in 1704, several years before her death: she was to be interred in the Gallowgate graveyard. In addition, 'I order that after my death my body is to be taken care of and wrapped in plain Grave-cloaths ... without any vain superfluous attire unsuitable to my profession. And that it be put in a plain Coffine without any mulloring, Carving or Collouring.' Nevertheless, the rumour persisted and when the house on Guestrow was demolished in the 1920s, expectation was high. Perhaps to the surprise of some present, a large stone coffin was uncovered. Quakers gathered as the coffin was opened ... and revealed to be empty. The mason present exclaimed, 'Yon's nae a coffin, it's a soo's troch! [pig's trough]' Quite what the 'coffin' actually was remains a mystery, as the object itself appears to be lost, and all trace of the Quakers of Gallowgate has been erased.

An otherwise ordinary wall alongside the alley of Seamount Place incorporates several inscribed stones from the eighteenth century. The most obvious is a lintel with an anchor in the centre flanked by the letters DF and EI. Below can be seen:

1777

WL   AM

HF

I have no idea whom these initials commemorate.

Above left: A modern 'stone circle' outside Porthill Court tower blocks, Gallowgate. The stones appear to have come from a demolished building. *(Geoff Holder)*

Above right: On the left are eighteenth-century inscriptions built into a wall off Seamount Road. Marischal College is in the background. *(Geoff Holder)*

Below: This way to the gallows. Street sign, Gallowgate. *(Ségolène Dupuy)*

Gallowgate is so named because it was the route from the city to the first permanent place of execution, a prominent ridge where Spring Garden now stands,
between West North Street and Gallowgate. The gallows was certainly in place by
1661, when it was shown on Parson Gordon's map of Aberdeen. The last person
hanged here, on 1 November 1776, was wife-murderer Alexander Morrison. By
this date the city had expanded and people could see the gallows – and the bodies
left hanging – from their houses, so the site was moved to the less populated GAL-
LOWS HILL to the east. Morrison's friends soon removed the body and threw away
the chains in which it had been hung. *The Black Kalendar* states that these chains
were thereafter stored in St Mary's Chapel of ST NICHOLAS KIRK, but when the
church was refurbished they were given to Mr Rainnie, the building contractor.
Unless Mr Rainnie's descendents still have these gibbet chains in an attic somewhere, they are long lost.

ST ANDREW STREET

Burking Shop Destroyed –
A particular Account of the Extraordinary Demolition of an Anatomical Theatre, at
Aberdeen, on Monday last, the 19th December 1831, which was Burnt and erased to
the ground, in consequence of the sagacity of a Dog.

Such was the title of another broadside, this one dealing with the most dramatic
event in the Aberdeen bodysnatching story. Dr Andrew Moir, having recovered
from the assault on his premises on GUESTROW (see above), had erected a purpose-
built anatomical theatre on Hospital Row, a now-vanished area near the west
end of St Andrew Street. His brilliance as a lecturer attracted many students, who
were also delighted to get 'hands-on' experience dissecting cadavers. Which, of
course, were largely obtained illegally from graveyards. Moir was already disliked
because of his suspected grave-robbing; this, combined with the murderous activities of Burke and Hare in Edinburgh, and the news of bodysnatchers at work in
London, had created a volatile situation.

The spark was provided by a dog, which dug up part of a carelessly-buried corpse
behind the theatre. Within minutes a mob gathered, forced their way into the
theatre, assaulted Moir and the students, and discovered three bodies prepared
for dissection. When the corpses were paraded outside, the sight of the mangled
remains sent the crowd into a frenzy. Fire, levers and impromptu battering-rams
were deployed, and within hours the substantial stone-built theatre had been
entirely demolished, an astonishing feat of logistics that demonstrates just how
motivated the mob were. Upwards of 10,000 people watched the final conflagra-
tion, with splinter groups chasing and attacking medical students and launching
a second assault on Moir's home at No. 63 Guestrow. Moir himself had fled
and, according to popular rumour, spent the night beneath a table-tomb in St
Nicholas' kirkyard. Official response to the destruction and disorder was inef-

fectual at best, and the magistrates and police seemed content to let the mob's fury run its course. Only three men were arrested, and come April 1832 were imprisoned for twelve months, while Moir won £235 damages from the Council.

After the Anatomy Act of 1832 legitimised the collection and dissection of cadavers, Moir rebuilt his career, and in 1839 he was finally fully incorporated into the medical establishment, being appointed lecturer in Anatomy at King's College, a post he filled for five years before dying from typhoid fever contracted from a patient. He was thirty-eight. Moir was one of the most capable and skilled medical practioners of his day, but because of the events of 1831 he will be forever associated with 'the Burking House'. Nothing marks its site these days; but nearby is a fitness shop called, ironically, Bodyworx.

GEORGE STREET

Merlin's Grove at No. 202 sells a wide range of magical items, from candles and crystals to witchcraft tools and pagan paraphernalia. They also act as a kind of informal occultural networking centre.

ROBERT GORDON'S COLLEGE

Fronted by the imposing figure of Gordon of Khartoum and sporting a statue of Robert Gordon himself in a toga, this attractive eighteenth-century establish-ment is situated partly on the site of the medieval Dominican Friary, destroyed by the Reformation mob in 1559. In 1833 a stone-lined grave was found here, containing the remains of two adults and one child, possibly a benefactor and his family, all buried inside the friary church. In 1883 another grave was found on the site of the Art Gallery next door, which may have been the location of the friary's main cemetery. Over a century previous, in 1777, many bones, including fourteen or sixteen skulls, were uncovered somewhere nearby. The *Old Statistical Account* described one of them as having 'long yellow hair, neatly wrapped round and plaited with an woollen fillet or string in form of a queue, which did not appear to be rotten'. No coffins were found, and the bodies had not been conventionally buried; possibly it was a mass grave of plague victims or those killed in a battle. All these human remains are now lost.

ABERDEEN ART GALLERY

No. 78 Schoolhill. Open Tuesday-Saturday 10 a.m.-5 p.m., Sunday 2 p.m.-5 p.m. Admission free. Good wheelchair access.

Entering through a doorway topped by a helmeted head and a bronze frieze featuring chubby naked children engaged in sculpting, painting and drawing, the gallery opens up into an impressive columned central space. A small number of paintings on the upper floors feature mythological or supernatural themes: Stanley Spencer's *Resurrection – Reunion* has the resurrected dead joyfully reunited with their loved ones on Judgment Day, while George Frederick's *Orpheus and Eurydice* powerfully explores the famous Greek myth of Orpheus' doomed quest through the Underworld to bring his wife Eurydice back from the land of the dead.

Attached to the gallery is the Cowdray Hall War Memorial, a striking, if austere, domed space lined with plastercasts of notable Classical and Renaissance sculptures, including a winged but headless Victory. (The exterior, dominating the corner of Schoolhill and Blackfriars Street, features a magnificent lion set in a colonnade that would not look out of place in imperial Rome.)

The court also has *Tombstone Bearing Symbols of the Evangelists*, a 1952 sculpture by James Hamilton with expressive carvings of the Bull, Angel, Ox and Eagle that symbolise the four writers of the Gospels. Another massive plastercast, this time of the Athena group of the Pergamon Frieze from Turkey known as the *Gigantomachy*, shows the battle of the Gods and Giants. The goddess Athena holds the serpent-entwined giant Alkyoneous by his hair, having plucked him from the grip of his mother Gaia, the Earth-spirit from whom he draws strength, while the winged figure of Nike looks on.

The most evocative pieces are found within the modern art collection on the ground floor. Ken Currie's *Gallowgate Lard* is a macabre portrait of a sickly-looking individual who might possibly be a vampire or zombie – the use of beeswax mixed with the paint increases the sense of deathly pallor. A collaboration between artist Damien Hirst and photographer David Bailey, *Jesus is Condemned to Die*, shows the head of Christ replaced by a cow skull bearing a 'crown of thorns' of barbed wire, while Christ himself is brandishing the pair of knives that will kill him; the disturbing imagery suggests that Jesus is implicit in, or accepting of, his own death. The best works, however, are by the young Scottish artist Charles Avery. *The August Snakes Stand Erect (As That Is How Their Beards May Best Be Admired)* is a superb sculpture of three life-size king cobras – each sporting a truly bizarre string-like beard, which makes them look like reptilian Chinese sages. And *Untitled (Men Leading Unridables)* manages to cross the Hebridean landscape of Avery's childhood with a *Star Wars*-like scene, in which a pair of nineteenth-century agricultural workers attempt to control a pair of two-clawed beasts that look like a science fiction elephant-horse hybrid, all against a backdrop of Egyptian pyramids and a Scottish bothy.

KIRK OF ST NICHOLAS

At present the church is open May–September 12 noon–4 p.m., Monday–Friday, and on Sunday morning for services. Check www.kirk-of-st-nicholas.org.uk for exact details. Admission is free. The graveyard is open from 8.30 a.m.–7 p.m. daily in summer and 8.30 a.m.–4.30 p.m. in the winter. Currently, only the transepts (Drum's Aisle and St John's Chapel) are accessible for wheelchair users, but this will change when the new complex is completed.

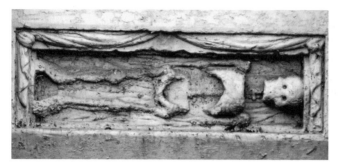

Above left: St Nicholas kirkyard: a skeleton lies in its silk-lined coffin. *(Ségolène Dupuy)*

Above right: St Nicholas kirkyard: a loinclothed angel blowing the trumpet of the Resurrection. *(Ségolène Dupuy)*

I suspect that few of the people who use the kirk's expansive graveyard as a shortcut between Schoolhill and Union Street, or who spend workday lunchtimes sunning on its benches, realise that St Nicholas is one of the Aberdeen's greatest treasure troves. There has been a church here since the eleventh century, and its central location means it has been at the heart of both the good and the bad in community life. Here can be found examples of medieval 'magic for the dead', a whole host of supernatural beliefs, and residues of witchcraft, not to mention gargoyles, elaborately carved grave monuments, exceptional (and quite strange) tapestries and woodwork, and an enigmatic stone sculpture of a rat. Oh, and the miracle-working original version of Santa Claus.

The cathedral-sized kirk has a complex history, having undergone centuries of rebuilding, destruction, reconstruction and changes in use. Cruciform in shape, the only medieval part still remaining forms the two transepts and the central crossing; after the Reformation the church was physically split into two, the Choir becoming the East Kirk and the Nave the West Kirk, a division which still stands. Following subsequent rebuilding, the West Kirk now dates from 1755, a Georgian masterpiece with an imposing atmosphere, while the East Kirk and steeple are largely Victorian Gothic. The East Kirk is currently closed while it is being gutted and an imaginative multi-storey community centre built within the shell. When the Mither Kirk Project comes to fruition the city will not only gain a superb central facility, but also, hopefully, the magnificence of the church will become more widely known.

THE GRAVEYARD

The grandiose entry through the granite colonnade on Union Street provides a fitting introduction to a graveyard that houses the dust of many of Aberdeen's great and good. The burial ground is crammed with memorials, many of them table-tombs, while Celtic crosses, statues, and quasi-Egyptian or neo-Greek styles are also much in evidence. An information panel at the north end locates the most interesting gravestones. Arranged against the western churchyard wall are some of the most elaborate structures. Two adjacent neo-Classical monuments of 1659 and 1663 are festooned with the symbols of both mortality – skulls and crossed bones, coffins, hourglasses, gravedigger's tools and mort-bells – and immortality, as represented by winged heads or souls. Another even more elaborate monument of 1696 has a carving of a complete skeleton in its silk-lined coffin flanked by the tools for digging the grave and guarded by a pair of very Scottish-looking angels carrying lamps, while thigh bones and skulls are linked by the thread of life and an hourglass flits by on wings ('time flies'). The whole thing is topped with a pair of Angels of the Resurrection lustily blowing on their corpse-awakening trumpets. Other memorials include one in the form of a tomb-recess, with crowns, more skulls, and a pair of curious birds, while one of the many gravestones used as paving slabs bears a heraldic panel from which flourishes a pair of sea monsters.

Two monuments in the north part of the kirkyard are of especial interest. One is a table-tomb that marks the last resting place of Dr Andrew Moir, the body-snatching owner of the 'Burking House' burnt down on ST ANDREW STREET who spent a night hiding from the mob under a similar tomb, while the other commemorates John Anderson, the 'Wizard of the North'. Anderson (1814-1874) was the premier stage magician of his day, a flamboyant character noted for his flair for publicity and his routines such as the Great Gun Trick, where he appeared to catch a bullet in his mouth. Once when he was staying in digs, his landlady handed him back his deposit and evicted him when she found out who he was, stating she could 'smell the brimstone on him'. When Harry Houdini visited Aberdeen in 1909 to perform a death-defying escape in the HARBOUR, he made a pilgrimage to Anderson's grave and arranged for its upkeep.

Contrary to popular belief, very few ghosts are reported from graveyards (far more are seen in houses, roadsides, pubs, castles and workplaces). The single known episode at St Nicholas is from a summer's afternoon in 1982, when a church elder was re-laying some of the old gravestones as paving flagstones. Both he and a companion saw a black-haired woman wearing a long white dress and white veil. Most remarkably, she was hovering 2ft (61cm) above the ground. The apparition glided about 25yds (22.8m) to the corner of the church, and then vanished. The encounter is related in Norman Adams' *Haunted Scotland*.

THE TRANSEPTS (DRUM AISLE AND ST JOHN'S CHAPEL)

The medieval stonework here is the oldest standing above ground in the kirk. When St Nicholas was split in two after the Reformation a wall was built closing off the two churches, although the congregations still used the transepts as common ground. The pre-Reformation church had held thirty-one altars, most used as 'chantries' – that is, priests were paid to engage in a daily round of prayer or chants for the deceased benefactors. This was believed to speed the soul's progress from Purgatory to Heaven, and hence used as a form of afterlife soul-insurance policy by the wealthy. The belief that the prayers of the living assisted the souls of the dead extended to distant ancestors – Robert Wilson, in *An Historical Account and Delineation of Aberdeen*, describes how the Incorporated Trade of Shoemakers paid for a chantry for Crispinus and Crispianus, two

Above left: St Nicholas Kirk: stained-glass window to the oil industry in St John's Chapel. Note the oil rigs, tankers and helicopter landing pad. *(Geoff Holder)*

Above right: St Nicholas Kirk: African sculpture marking the anniversary of the abolition of slavery. The European slave trader sits beneath a canopy, flanked by money and a shackled foot. *(Geoff Holder)*

Christian martyrs who were killed for their faith in AD 300. As both were cobblers by trade, they were regarded as the shoemakers' patron saints. Although if they were martyrs, surely they would have gone directly to Heaven, by-passing Purgatory altogether, and thus having no need of the intercessionary prayers of the living? The religious mindset of the medieval world was not always consistent. Similarly, the Hammermen dedicated a chantry to their tutelary patroness, St Helen.

The Reformers swept away all the chantries and altars, but a few remnants remain mortared into the walls, including a votive stone to an unnamed saint showing a woman and four of her children at prayer. There is also a votive ship hanging from the roof; such models of ships are common in northern European churches and typically signify an offering of thanks for a safe voyage or a successful maritime career. Other items of interest include heraldic stones, Baroque eighteenth-century memorials, elaborately-carved graveslabs in the floor, and various sculptured bits and pieces rescued over the centuries. Much more recent is a colourful wooden African sculpture commemorating the abolition of slavery. St Nicholas has seven beautifully-carved stone effigies, the largest collection of medieval effigies in Scotland. Three are in the north transept, formerly known as Holy Blood Aisle and Collison's Aisle. Two are of a husband and wife, while the third is often thought to be Provost Robert Davidson, although the dates of the sculpture (between 1430 and 1465) do not match the known facts of Davidson's death: he famously perished at the Battle of Harlaw in 1411, in which the Lowlanders of prosperous Aberdeenshire fought off an invading Highland army. The 'fighting Provost' was also a pirate, and in one court case was accused of pirating goods belonging to Richard Whittington, Lord Mayor of London, owner of the famous cat and future star of pantomime. In *A Thousand Years of Aberdeen* Alexander Keith claimed that during the rebuilding of 1740, Davidson's grave was opened and a silk skull-cap taken away.

The 'Davidson' tomb-recess has become an impromptu shrine by accident, because it is located in the marvelous and moving refurbished area devoted to commemorating all those who died in the Piper-Alpha disaster and others who lost their lives working in the North Sea oil and gas industry. Now known as St John's Chapel (named for the patron saint of oilmen), the furnishings – chairs, table and lectern, designed by Tim Stead in 1990 – are composed of layers of different coloured wood. The first letter of the name of each tree in the layers spell 'We Remember You' (although the 'You' is actually 'Yew'). The chapel is wonderfully illuminated by Shona McInnes' glorious stained glass telling the story of the oil industry; this is surely the only stained glass window in the country that features a helicopter landing pad.

THE SPIRE AND CARILLION

In 1351 Provost William Leith of Ruthrieston gifted two large bells named St Lawrence and St Mary to the kirk. This was no ordinary act of piety; Leith had murdered a man called Catanach, one of his bailies, at ASHGROVE and this was his way of saying sorry – and seeking expiation of his sin. Sadly these bells are no longer extant because in 1874 the medieval steeple caught fire and spectacularly crashed through the roof of the East Kirk, which had only been recently reconstructed in 1837. This also destroyed the area in the tower where some of the witches were imprisoned in 1597: 'Mantieth' hanged herself here while 'Suppok' died of unknown natural causes. There is a record of a blacksmith being paid to forge shackles for the witches in the steeple. Both the spire and the gutted East Kirk were rebuilt, and the forty-eight new bells form the largest Carillon in the world. The Carillon is open on special occasions such as Doors Open Day, and is worth the climb.

THE WEST KIRK

This opened in 1755 and is a magnificent reflection of Georgian Presbyterian sensibility, with a massive pulpit and sounding board, chairs carved with angels, numbered pews, a splendid clock, and heraldic panels scattered among the columns. There are more medieval effigies in the south passage. The foyer by the west door hosts a number of elaborate memorials and a collection of sculptured work, including armorial panels, grave furniture, ancient cross-marked stones and two cresset stones – boulders carved with numerous hollows used for early oil-lamps. It also houses, in rather awkward places, two major treasures – the Liddell brass and the Jamesone needlework panels. The former is an astonishingly detailed brass panel dedicated to Dr Duncan Liddell (1561-1613). The long Latin inscription translates as:

> Posthumous Fame, the never failing certifier of merit hath dedicated and conse-crated this monument to the eternal memory of D. Duncan Liddell MD, whom virtue took possession of at his birth, and as he grew up, profound skill in medicine and all departments of Philosophy and Mathematics adorned, and generosity dis-tinguished above his contemporaries. To him the public Professor of Mathematics in the College of Aberdeen owes his yearly Stipend, and Six Alumni of the same College their maintenance.

The memorial is more like a painted portrait than a conventional brass monu-ment. Liddel is shown writing at his desk, wearing the cap, tunic and fur-trimmed cloak of a Renaissance intellectual, surrounded by his books, scientific instru-ments, globe, letter-opener, inkwell, candle, personal seal, hourglass – and a human skull. Even his spectacles can be seen on the desk. This is a major work of art and deserves to be better known. A monument to Liddell stands near DYCE.

The four large tapestry-like needlework hangings by Mary Jamesone all portray Old Testament stories with the characters depicted in seventeenth-century cos-tumes – in *The Finding of Moses* it is amusing to see Pharaoh's daughter and her attendants dressed like ladies from the court of Charles I. The same panel shows that the bridge spanning the Nile is the Bridge of Dee, the buildings of Cairo are the houses of Aberdeen, and ten babies are floating down the river. *Jephthah and his Daughter* tells the horrifying story of Jephthah, a Jewish leader who, when fighting against the Ammonites, made a vow that if he was victorious, 'what-ever comes out of the doors of my house to meet me, when I return in peace from the people of Ammon, shall surely be the Lord's, and I will offer it up as a burnt offering' (Judges 11:31). The tapestry shows the moment when Jephthah's daughter rushes out with her musical instruments to welcome her father home, not realising that Jephthah will now have to sacrifice her to fulfill his rash vow. Many commentators have noted that human sacrifice was against both Jewish and God's law, and have queried this passage. Several scholars have suggested the original Hebrew reads '… shall surely be the Lord's, *or* I will offer it up as a burnt offering'. In other words, if it had been an animal, then it would have been sacrificed, but Jephthah's daughter was merely dedicated to the Lord, that is, she remained a virgin and the Jewish equivalent of a nun. The 'kill the first thing you meet' theme is a common one in other mythologies and in Scottish folklore.

The third panel depicts *Esther and Ahasuerus*, an everyday tale of palace intrigue and attempted genocide. Ahasuerus, King of Persia (usually identified with Xerxes) is holding out his golden sceptre to his beautiful queen, Esther, showing

Above left: St Nicholas Kirk: the Mary Jamesone tapestries. Pharaoh's daughter (in seventeenth-century costume); the River Nile crossed by the Bridge of Dee, its gate clearly visible; and the Egyptian city of Thebes, looking remarkably like Aberdeen. *(Ségolène Dupuy)*

Above right: Detail from the *Esther and Ahasuerus* tapestry: Haman the Persian being hanged on a Scottish gallows. *(Ségolène Dupuy)*

that she will not be punished for speaking to him without permission. Esther is secretly Jewish, and Ahasuerus' prime minister Haman has plotted to hang Esther's uncle Mordechai and murder all the Jews in Persia. In the background can be seen the gallows intended for Mordechai; as a result of Esther's intervention it is Haman who is executed instead – he is probably the figure hanging from the gallows. After all this violence, *Susanna and the Elders* is a bit of light relief, the popular story of voyeuristic old men playing Peeping Tom on a lovely young woman in her bath. The edges of the panels are alive with grotesque faces, crowned heads, and other seventeenth-century decorative motifs.

THE EAST KIRK

The decayed former medieval choir, partitioned off and reused as the East Kirk after the Reformation, was replaced in 1837, only to suffer destruction by fire in 1874 and hence a complete rebuilding in Victorian Gothic. The East Kirk is now to become a new community centre, and before construction began a major archaeological excavation took place in 2006. This threw up a truly amazing number of discoveries, many of which throw light on spiritual beliefs, rituals and funerary practices from the Middle Ages onward.

The foundations of the earliest stone church were uncovered, dating to probably the late eleventh century. Arranged in an arc around the semi-circular apse of the church were twenty burials of babies and children, one of which had been placed in a hollowed log. None of the others had coffins, but several had stones

The East Kirk following the 2006 excavation. The many gravecuts can clearly be seen. To the rear is the former external west wall of St Mary's Chapel, below the floor level of the Victorian church. *(Ségolène Dupuy)*

supporting their heads and feet. Some of the burials seem to pre-date the stone foundations, suggesting there was an earlier wooden church on the site. Other very young children were found buried in difficult-to-reach recesses of the fifteenth-century church, and many other graves were found inside all the different church structures down the centuries. Burial in church was theoretically forbidden after the Reformation, but St Nicholas, like many churches, conveniently overlooked this prohibition in the face of commercial reality: wealthy people were more than happy to pay for in-church burial, and the most expensive plots were near the altar. Again, this is a form of magical thinking in a Christian context: ending your days close to the holiest spot in the church increased your chances of an easy ride to Heaven.

Altogether 924 skeletons were unearthed, covering around 900 years of burial practices. In many cases graves were intercut by later burials, with the gravediggers simply scattering or randomly reburying bones as they came across them; a fifteenth-century wall cut through a number of earlier graves, neatly chopping off the skeletons at the ankles. One man in his early twenties had met a bloody death – he had lost his upper jaw and nose to an edged weapon, and other battle wounds were found around his skull and chest. Another skull had had its top cleanly removed, probably during an autopsy. A mother who had died in childbirth had been buried with the baby still in her pelvic girdle. In another grave, an old woman had been placed directly on top of a middle-aged man who had been buried decades earlier; it is tempting to think she was his widow. In this case the man's hair and skin were still well preserved. An older man was found interred face down with his left hand behind his back, a practice so aberrant it suggests he may have been 'punished' for something. Even stranger, a baby had later been buried near his feet.

'Magic for the Dead?', a 2008 article by Roberta Gilchrist in the journal *Medieval Archaeology*, examined 'The Archaeology of Magic in Later Medieval Burials' with particular reference to apotropaic objects found in graves at St Nicholas. Gilchrist argued that 'the placement of amulets with the dead was strategic to Christian belief, intended to transform or protect the corpse'. Wooden staffs or rods, apparently made especially for burial, may have been linked to pilgrimage and hence the soul's journeying through Purgatory to Heaven. A pewter Pièta badge, showing Mary holding the tortured body of her son Jesus after he was taken down from the Cross, was found on a middle-aged woman. PIètas were often purchased at pilgrimage sites but the style of this one suggested it had been made locally and was associated with the popular medieval cult of Our Lady of Pity, which is also the dedication of the fifteenth-century St Mary Chapel next door (see below). Women in particular were taken with the compassionate imagery of the Pièta and this individual suffered from severe osteomalacia (adult rickets); perhaps she had a special bond with St Mary of Pity, and if so this was probably a protective amulet.

Several scallop shells were found, these being symbols of a pilgrimage to the shrine of St James de Compostella in Spain. Two were on a skull, so were probably attached to a pilgrim's hat, while a third was found near the thigh-bone and so may have been in a bag suspended from the waist. The shells may simply have been buried because they were the treasured possessions of the deceased; equally they could have been designed to assist in the 'pilgrimage' into death and resurrection. Some bodies had single beads, which may have been amuletic in purpose, while others held coins in their hands, another item designed to bring good fortune in the afterlife. One individual was buried with a heart-shaped brooch, probably a love token, while one funeral involved the careful deposition of flowers and other plants around the corpse. In theory, 'grave goods' at a funeral were anathema to Protestant orthodoxy; in practice, the clergy clearly turned a blind eye to these tokens of grief and commemoration.

The post-excavation analysis of the finds is ongoing; a summary can be found in a booklet entitled *East Kirk of St Nicholas Project 2006*, available in the kirk, while the results are posted on the project's comprehensive website, www.aberdeencity.gov.uk/localhistory/loc/loc_archkirknicholas.asp.

ST MARY'S CHAPEL

This extraordinary hidden gem is currently accessed off Correction Wynd at the bottom of the graveyard, and is only rarely open on special occasions. Often called the crypt or undercroft because its position on a slope means it is below the level of the main church, it was built in the fifteenth century and dedicated to the cult of Our Lady of Pity, a dedication referenced in the Victorian stained glass depicting the Pièta. The chapel is T-shaped, with vaulting ceilings supported by corbels carved with numerous gargoyle-like grotesque faces. The most famous sculpture is the 'rat' on a corbel at the T-junction. Although to some eyes it resembles an otter, folklore has firmly established it as a rodent, and inevitably stories have been invented to explain its presence here. In one version, a heretic was chained up here and was eaten alive by rats; a second story is that the creature ran off with the church silver; and a third was put into verse by local writer William Anderson in his 1851 book *Rhymes, Reveries, and Reminiscences*. In the poem, the bishop of St Nicholas places a curse on the individual raiding his apple-trees:

Far left: One of
the many carved
heads in St Mary's
Chapel, underneath
St Nicholas Kirk.
(Ségolène Dupuy)

Left: The rat (or
otter?) carved on
one of the corbels
in St Mary's Chapel.
(Ségolène Dupuy)

> Such sacrilege merits
> The torments of hell,
> And I curse him with candle,
> With book, and with bell.
> May he lack, when alive,
> Both of water and bread,
> And conscience torment him
> Until he is dead.
> May his flesh and his sinews
> Be torn from his bones
> By rats, and may no one
> Hear his last dying groans.

A choirboy, Gregory Law, was found with the fruit, and was imprisoned in the vault:

> Lacking food three long days
> By a chain he was bound,
> And the fourth there was only
> A skeleton found.

But it turns out that Friar David is the real culprit, as he planted the stolen goods on the innocent lad. David confesses and is absolved. However:

> He in sanctity died, but
> They found in the morn,
> His flesh by the rats from
> His bones had been torn.

The clergy are now struck with fear that the curse may be 'on the loose', so the poem finishes with the raison d'être for the sculpture:

> And the bishop, to prove
> He the friar did assoil [absolve],

Placed a rat made of stone
On St- Mary's aisle.

Its qualities as literature aside, 'The Bishop's Curse; Or, The Rat of St Mary's Aisle' isn't exactly solid history: for a start, St Nicholas was never a bisphopric, and so never had a bishop. The reason for the insertion of the rat/otter/other tailed mammal in the chapel may remain forever mysterious. The opposite corbel to the 'rat' has another enigmatic carving, this time of what appears to be a man hitting a ball with an old-fashioned golf club. Another possible explanation that has been put forward is that the man is chasing the rat with a stick. Alternatively, its real meaning may be something else entirely.

More strangeness can be found on the bosses on the roof. Two are fairly ordinary – the city arms, and an angel holding three shields – but the badly-eroded central one depicts the reverse of the 1430 Seal of Aberdeen, showing St Nicholas restoring three children to life. Nicholas was a real person, the fourth-century bishop of Myra, in what is now Turkey. In legend he miraculously rescued some sailors caught in a storm, and hence became the patron saint of mariners. Aberdeen being a seafaring city, it was logical to choose Nicholas as its tutelary saint. The scene on the boss refers to the story of three little boys (or, depending on the version told, a trio of scholar-clerks) who were murdered by a butcher to be sold to his customers as joints of ham (or meat pies – shades of Sweeney Todd). Nicholas detected the crime and performed the astonishing miracle of bringing the three dismembered and salted bodies back to life. Even more famously, the saint saved three poor young women from a life of prostitution by secretly donating bags of gold to their family; in one version of the tale, the final bag was dropped down the chimney and plonked into one the girls' stockings, hung over the fire to dry. This gift-giving inevitably made Nicholas a popular saint; his name in Dutch migrated from Saint Nicklaas to Sinterklaas, from where it was a short step to the English version, Santa Claus. In recognition of the transmigration of a fourth-century saint into a universally-recognised symbol of consumerism, the Turkish town of Demre, next to the ruins of Myra, has recently erected a statue of a red-suited Santa Claus, swinging his bell, holding his sack of presents, and sweltering in the 40°C heat.

Other pleasures include the dozens of carved sixteenth- and seventeenth-century woodwork panels in the crypt, all rescued from different parts of the main church. Two feature representations of the Virtues Prudentia (Prudence, holding a serpent while only looking at it in a mirror, a clear reference to the Medusa) and Fortitudo (Fortitude, tightening her belt while clinging to a strong pillar), both decorated with marginal figures of grotesques and animal heads. Another has a strange horned winged head and two beasts that look like demonic cows. One set of panels, probably medieval Flemish, shows the three Magi adoring the infant Jesus (although Mary looks as if she is selling her child off to the highest bidder). The floor is packed with horizontal tombstones, including one with a skull and a motto that can be translated as 'Death, the best of blessings'. Another stone has a skull and two sets of crossed bones, a beast, and two figures which may be the children of the deceased. Diligent searching will turn up a slab carved with an axe or knife and a memorial to Burgesses Thomas and Andrew Burnet, two brothers who died at the BATTLE OF JUSTICE MILLS in 1644.

Following the Reformation the chapel underwent numerous changes of use over the centuries, from a soup kitchen to the store for the city gallows, as well as a plumbers shop and a prison. An iron ring on the west wall is said to be where witches were chained up in the 1590s. The chapel's current configuration is a legacy of the sympathetic restoration of 1898. All in all, if the opportunity ever arises to visit St Mary's, take it – it is probably Aberdeen's greatest hidden treasure.

Note: some of the information in the foregoing section has been taken from the small booklets 'Grave Slabs in the Kirk of St Nicholas' and 'St Mary's Chapel – A Brief Review', both published on behalf of the Mither Kirk Project, while I have also included information gleaned from a scholarly lecture in the chapel by James Stewart, which I was privileged to attend in 2009.

CORRECTION WYND

This was the site of the medieval St Thomas's Hospital, built over in the eighteenth century. Building works in 1902 uncovered bones from the hospital's burial ground. The atmospheric lane follows the natural slope to run under Union Street, clearly showing that the latter is a kind of flyover, leapfrogging over the wynds and dips of the old town in a series of arches, creating an underworld of shadows and tunnels. Under the right conditions (rain or mist, and an all-too-brief absence of noisy drunks) Aberdeen beneath Union Street can resemble *noir* Prague, or the subterranean Vienna of *The Third Man*.

BELMONT STREET

Slains Castle, a pub and restaurant housed in the converted South Church of 1830, is of course named for Slains Castle at Cruden Bay on the Aberdeenshire Coast, the site that inspired Bram Stoker in his creation of Castle Dracula. When the unusual themed venue (think *The Addams Family* meets Hammer Horror) opened in 1999 staff claimed to have seen the apparition of a man in a dark coat, which they interpreted as a minister. Nothing has been noticed recently and all the staff who witnessed the strange sights have now left. Nevertheless, with three floors of Gothic décor *in excelsis*, Slains is absolutely stuffed with the ideal accompaniments to a meal: skeletons in chains, gargoyles, bubbling flasks that would happily grace Dr Frankenstein's laboratory, magical and alchemical symbols, witchcraft items, suits of armour, demons, screaming heads, monstrous beasts, and portraits with the eyes cut out. It's a home from home.

3

THE CITY CENTRE – SOUTH OF UNION STREET

SHIPROW – TRINITY QUAY – THE GREEN – JUSTICE MILLS

Let us explore the ruined Abbey's Choir;
Its fretted roof and windows of rich Tracery,
The Sculptur'd Tombs o'ergrown with shrubs and brambles,
'Midst broken arches, graves and gloomy vaults

Francis Grose, *Antiquities of Scotland*, 1789

MARISCHAL STREET

On 18 July 1966 Mr G.E. was looking out of the open window of his top-floor flat at 5.30 a.m., waiting for the milk-van to arrive. It was a clear, bright morning. All of a sudden, 30ft (9.1m) above the window, there was a flying saucer. It was grey, silent, turning slowly clockwise, with a circumference of around 15ft (4.6m), and a flat lower surface. It headed straight towards the beach until it went out of sight. The account was in a letter written to the J. Allen Hynek Center for UFO Studies on 15 July 1983, and the address written on the letter was Brentwood in Essex (it was reproduced on the website www.waterufo.net). Other than the nature of the sighting itself, there are two unusual elements in the account. Firstly, the writer stated that the next day the local paper reported that at least a dozen people had seen an object falling into the sea, and from this he believed that the craft came from some underwater power. And secondly, he claimed the experience had changed his personality, from a bad-tempered and vicious atheist to a pious Christian. This is an example of a sub-genre of UFO literature where a close encounter engenders religious or quasi-religious beliefs.

In an example of the way the Cosmic Joker likes to toy with us, I was walking down Marischal Street, ruminating on this sighting, when I passed a sign for a hair-dressers saying 'Walk-Ins Welcome'. Walk-Ins is the term used in alien abduction circles for humans who have an alien that has 'walked in' to them and is living inside

Marischal Street. 'Walk-Ins' are (a) casual customers (b) people who have extraterrestrials living inside them. The first option probably applies here. *(Geoff Holder)*

their body. Because the alien is fragile, it needs to be protected by layers of flesh; 'Walk-Ins' are typically very obese.

SHIPROW

This winding and narrow uphill street was the main route into the city until the roadbuilding improvements of the eighteenth and nineteenth centuries. There was once a massive gate, Shiprow Port, at the southern end, but this was removed in the 1700s.

MARITIME MUSEUM

Open Tuesday-Saturday 10 a.m.-5 p.m., Sunday 12 noon-3 p.m. Closed Monday. Admission free. Wheelchair access to most parts of the building (not Provost Ross' House). This enjoyable museum incorporates three conjoined buildings – Provost Ross' House, built in 1593 and the residence of Provost (and ship-owner) John Ross of Arnage from 1702; the former Trinity Congregational Church of 1877; and a modern glass-fronted structure linking the two. Amidst the hands-on displays on the oil and gas industry, and other aspects of Aberdeen's association with the sea, there are a number of curiosities.

FIRST FLOOR
Introductory Display – a votive model of the *Agnes Oswald*, made in 1830 and gifted to the Gilcomston Chapel of Ease (now Denburn Parish Church). Although the leaving of votive objects in churches – particularly in thanks for healing – is essentially a Catholic practice, votive ships are widespread in Protestant seafaring nations bordering the North Sea and the Baltic. They were essentially offered as thanks for protection at sea or a successful career at sea, and were often crafted by retired seamen. They can also symbolise our 'navigation' from cradle to grave.

Picture Gallery – another votive ship, with the Dutch name *The Schip*. The model was made in 1688 and placed in the Seamen's Loft in ST NICHOLAS KIRK.

Fishing and Whaling – a whale tooth and eardrum, and an example of scrimshaw decoration on whalebone; the displays contains wonderful titbits of information such as the return of the whaler *Latona* in 1807 with a 'seahorse' (actually a walrus), and the *Neptune* bringing another prize from the Arctic six years previously, this time a 'unicorn' (in reality a narwhal).

PROVOST ROSS' HOUSE
Clippers Room – the wooden display case for the Aberdeen Line is carved with a pair of sea monsters.

THIRD FLOOR

The archaeology exhibits here include Mesolithic flints, Neolithic stone axes and their metal Bronze Age successors, a number of Roman coins, a Viking steatite cup, and a wooden medieval reliquary box designed to hold a personal holy object, probably hung from a belt.

TRINITY QUAY AND REGENT QUAY

John Milne's invaluable 1911 work *Topographical, Antiquarian, and Historical Papers on the City of Aberdeen* has a number of interesting snippets on this area. At James Street was a crane or 'cran' used for unloading heavy goods from ships. On occasions (such as in 1602 for Janet Scherar) it was pressed into use for some unusual punishments. Miscreants such as prostitutes, fornicators and blasphemers were sat on a ram's horn at one end and 'ducked' in the harbour. Of course, no authorities in the modern world would use water immersion as a form of torture, would they? There is a persistent belief that the cran was also used to 'swim' witches (if they survived the underwater ordeal they were guilty, if they drowned they were innocent). However, swimming witches was very rarely practiced in Scotland, and there is no record of it having occurred at Aberdeen.

What certainly did occur was execution by drowning. In the sixteenth century two men and four women were drowned in the deep pool called The Pottie, which was opposite Shore Brae. The men were convicted of murder, the women of child murder (typically of infants born outside marriage). The last case, on 27 March 1587, was Elspeth Mitchell, wife of burgess Patrick Maver.

Rather luckier was escapologist Harry Houdini, who jumped, fully chained and manacled, into the harbour on 1 July 1909, emerging triumphant from below the waves minutes after the large crowd thought his lungs must have burst.

The Moorings Bar has a fine pub sign displaying a mermaid in a traditional seminaked pose.

THE HARBOUR

If the creation of Union Street changed Aberdeen in 1801, the construction of the harbour in the 1870s ensured the city's success. For centuries the port was basically the estuary of the River Dee, a vital lifeline for trade, yet continually imperiled by shifting sandbars and the vagaries of the elements. Two examples can be found in a work by Aberdeen's first historian, John Spalding, *The History of the Troubles and Memorable Transactions in Scotland*. In October 1637 four ships at anchor were driven out to sea by a great wave of water coming down the Dee; one of the vessels was a military transport, and some ninety-two soldiers drowned or went missing. Spalding was always seeing omens and portents, usually ascribing

the consequent miseries to the wrath of a God provoked by the religious and
political turmoil of seventeenth-century Scotland. He concludes the episode of
the 'spate that smashed the ships' with one of his customary prognostications:
'This rain to continue so long together, the like was never seen in our age, and
came for no good token.'

More bad omens – 'fearful signs by water' and 'many monstrous high winds'
continued throughout 1638, culminating in the mouth of the harbour becoming
completely blocked by a sandbar on 26 December. Ships were stranded and at
low tide it was possible to walk dryfoot from one shore to the next:

> It amazed the haill people of Aberdeen, burgh and land; they fell to with fasting,
> praying, mourning, weeping all day and night; then they went out with spades and
> shovels in great numbers, young and old, to cast down this fearful bar, but all in vain;
> for as fast as they threw down at low water, it gathered again at full sea. Then the
> people gave it over, and became heartless, thinking our sea trade and salmon fish-
> ing was like to be gone, and noble Aberdeen brought to destruction … But while
> they are at the pain of despair, the Lord of his great mercy removed clean away this
> bar, and the water did keep its own course as before, to the great joy of the people
> of Aberdeen, and comfort of the people round about. But this bar came not for
> nought, but was a token of great troubles to fall upon both Aberdeens.

In one of the great engineering accomplishments of the Victorian era, the Dee
was diverted, the sandbanks cleared, the harbour area doubled, Albert Basin created, and vast tracts of land drained – everything south and east from the railway
station and Union Square was once underwater. Thomas White Ogilvie, in
The Book of Saint Fittick, tells the story of a maverick engineer named 'Davie
do a'thing' (David Anderson of Finzheuch) who removed the huge stone called
Knock Maitland or Craig Matellan which blocked the harbour mouth:

> David gathered together a lot of empty barrels, and fixed them securely, at low
> water, to the base of the obstructing rock, then, planting a flag on its summit, and
> seating himself as on a throne, he waited for his servant, the tide, which, in its due
> time came, and lifting Davie and the rock, buoyed on the bowies, carried them
> westwards, amid the acclamations of the citizens.

As with other industries, Aberdeen shipbuilding had its particular customs.
A Captain Shewan recorded one in *The Great Days of Sail*. As the ship left the slip:

> Two or more stalwart shipwrights took up positions at the waterside and, at the
> critical moment, seized any victims within reach, and plunged them head over heels
> into the recoiling wave thrown up by the vessel's passage into the water. They were
> ducked not once but three times, unless they were agile enough to escape: and I
> have been told by an old Aberdonian that he has seen unfortunate youths chased,
> dripping wet, half-way up the street, and when caught, brought back and ducked
> until it was deemed their baptism had been sufficiently thorough.

The passage was quoted in J.M. McPherson's classic work *Primitive Beliefs in the North-East of Scotland*, where McPherson thought the practice might have been an echo of human sacrifice to a god of the sea.

In 1896 the great Aberdeenshire folklorist Walter Gregor contributed a tale of a phantom ship to the French journal *Revue des Traditions Populaires*. Gregor had been told the story by a seventy-year-old sailor; it is not clear whether the man was a witness to the episode, or was passing on a legend he had been told. Two fishing boats left Broadsea bound for Aberdeen, but were separated by a storm. One was approaching Aberdeen harbour in the dark when the crew saw the other boat ahead. They followed their companion safely into the harbour but when tying-up could see no sign of it. It transpired that the first fishing boat had never made it to Aberdeen, and was presumed lost at sea.

In 1888 Robert Chambers published *The Book of Days*, a compendium of curiosities connected to specific dates. In it he resurrected a note in *Scottish Notes and Queries* for November 1858, in which the contributor claimed to have seen a publication called the *Aberdeen Almanac, or New Prognostications for the Year 1688*, which apparently contained the following passage:

> To conclude for this year 1688. Near the place where the famous Dee payeth his tribute to the German Ocean, *if curious observers of wonderful things in nature* will be pleased thither to resort the 1, 13, and 29 of May, and in divers other times in the ensuing summer, as also in the harvest time, to the 7 and 14 October, *they will undoubtedly see a pretty company of* MARMAIDS, creatures of admirable beauty, and likewise hear their charming sweet melodious voices in well tun'd measures and harmonious lays, extol their Maker and his bounty praise; 'That godly honest men, in everything, In quiet peace may live, GOD SAVE THE KING!'

I have been unable to track down an extant copy of this *Aberdeen Almanac* for 1688, and so have had to rely on the nineteenth-century reports. If it was a genuine publication, how did the writer know that 'mermaids' would turn up at the mouth of the Dee on the predicted dates? Or is it some kind of political allegory, relating to the events leading up to the Glorious Revolution of 1688? Chambers' own comment subtly indicates how much faith he had in the report: 'The piety and loyalty of these predicted mermaids are certainly remarkable characteristics.'

ADELPHI LANE

This cul-de-sac off Union Street can also be reached by a pedestrian route up from the Maritime Museum. When the fog is down on a dark night the Georgian buildings and enclosed spaces make one think of the London of Sherlock Holmes (or Spring-Heeled Jack …). The court is on the site of what was the crest of St Katherine's Hill, before the engineers sliced it off to make way for the topography-busting Union Street. The medieval St Katherine's Chapel here was in ruins by 1661; it was one of the meeting places of the Aberdeen witches in the 1590s, with pre-dawn dancing to music supplied by the Devil (*see* INTERLUDE: WITCH-CRAFT IN ABERDEEN). In the seventeenth century the first recorded building used by the Aberdeen Freemasons was somewhere near here.

UNION STREET

In her book on the history of Union Street, *The Granite Mile*, Diane Morgan relates an 'urban legend' she was told as a child. Some citizens were concerned that at 60ft (18.3m) the street would not be wide enough, so one dark night, by the light of flaming torches, they surreptitiously moved the alignment pegs another 10ft (3m) to the current width of 70ft (21.3m). Morgan found a reference in *Aberdeen Awa'* by George Walker (1897) that the width was actually changed when the New Streets Bill was going through Parliament, with an instruction issued to shift the deviation pegs *in the night time*, probably to make the work simpler. The sight of a work-gang moving the pegs at night prompted the rumour which eventually mutated into the 'secret changeover by citizens' legend.

In contrast to say Glasgow or Edinburgh, Aberdeen displays very few sculptures on its buildings. Along Union Street, you can find a bearded fellow on No. 62 at the corner of St Nicholas Street, and the head of a Native American (or First Canadian) chief on Canada House, No. 201.

THE GREEN

There is much debate among historians as to whether this open space was the original early medieval settlement of Aberdeen before the focus of population moved east to the Castlegate area. The suggestion is that the first wooden castle may have crowned the adjacent St Katherine's Hill. Whatever the exact sequence, The Green is certainly ancient. It must have already been urbanised when the Trinitarian Friars set up a monastery on the east side in around 1211, and with the establishment of the Carmelite Friary on the south side in 1273, and the existing St Nicholas Kirk to the north, this would have been the very locus of religious life in the Middle Ages. Both the friaries were eviscerated by the Reforming mob, with Brother Francis of the Trinitarians being stabbed and thrown into the flames in December 1559, making him the first Catholic casualty of the Reformation in Scotland. Nothing now remains of either establishment or their graveyards, although an outline of part of the excavated Carmelite church is built into the paving stones in the car park off Martin Lane and Rennie's Wynd, and the medieval street pattern established by the walled precinct of the Carmelites still persists.

In earlier days the Dee flowed close to The Green, as shown in the following case. In 1604 Helen Gibb was in trouble with the Kirk Session for performing some

Above left: A pair of winged griffons in the tiled entrance to Nos 136-138 Union Street. Griffons traditionally guarded valuables and places of importance. *(Ségolène Dupuy)*

Above right: The outline of the wall of the Carmelite Friary, marked in the stones of the car park off Martin Lane. This is the only trace of one of the most important buildings of medieval Aberdeen. *(Geoff Holder)*

kind of magical water charm on her beer, although the details are scant. On the Tuesday or Friday before St Bartholomew's Day (24 August) 1603 she took three drops of water from the spout at Nethermill then immediately filled her brewing cauldron from the river beside the Trinity kirkyard. She carefully mixed the collected drops of liquid with the river water, and commenced brewing. Presumably the drops of Nethermill water would, in some unknown manner, help her beer achieve the required quality. This sparsely-recorded case is in J.M. McPherson's *Primitive Beliefs in the North-East of Scotland.*

A 1914 work by Matthew Power, *The Protomartyr of Scotland, Father Francis of Aberdeen,* stated that, with the Trinitarians and Carmelites gone and no one maintaining the water defences, the river invaded the Trinity kirkyard and carried away some of the bodies, the ravaged graves and coffins being visible at low tide. In 1606 an Alexander Davidson obtained a license to build a ship in the kirkyard; obviously he knew he would have no difficulty launching it from there. In the seventeenth century the remains of the Trinitarian monastery were converted into the first Trinity Hall or Trades Hall of the Seven Incorporated Trades of Aberdeen. The Trades moved to their second base, on UNION BRIDGE, in the 1850s, when the last of the old buildings were demolished for the construction of the railway and Guild Street. Large quantities of human remains were found – the coffins crumbled to dust and the skulls fell to pieces when lifted. It bears repeating again: much of central Aberdeen is built over the remains of the dead.

CARMELITE STREET

Urban development in this area turned up human remains in 1879, 1904, 1908, 1924 and probably other times before and since. Organised excavations in the 1990s uncovered several hundred skeletons from the graveyard and church of the Carmelite Friary. The burials date from the end of the fourteenth century to the destruction of the friary at the Reformation. Inevitably all this has percolated into the urban legend-pot, and several sightings of monkish apparitions have been reported in this street and the general area of The Green.

STIRLING STREET

Two allegorical ladies perch on the balcony over the entrance to the Carmelite hotel, one carrying a sheaf of wheat and a sickle (presumably she represents Agriculture), the other a flower in each hand (Horticulture?). The former has a curious ear-like shape carved into her supporting stone, the meaning of which is utterly obscure. Inside there is a fine collection of Victorian stained-glass windows, and a series of themed upmarket suites: the Japanese Suite features a massive wooden head of Buddha and other Oriental ornamentation, while the decadent Cabanel Suite has a quasi-mythological ceiling painting of cherubs hovering above the bed; the winged heavenly beings are, of course, blindfolded. The Carmelite was originally the Imperial Hotel; during its later incarnation as the Grampian Hotel a man called Richie Tait had a number of 'strange occurrences' in one of the rooms in the unused part of the hotel, dubbed by the staff the Haunted Room. The report is in Dane Love's *Scottish Spectres*.

CROWN STREET

The Masonic Temple at No. 85 must be the finest purpose-built Masonic building in Scotland. Eleven Lodges and several Chapters of Freemasons hold their meetings in this massive neo-Classical complex. Freemasonry being, ahem, not a *secret society* but a *society with secrets*, the building is not usually open to the public except on special occasions such as Doors Open Day. The website of the oldest lodge in the building, Lodge Aberdeen No. 1 Ter, states that the first mention of a Masonic lodge in the town records is as far back as 1483, with further entries in 1527 and

1544. There was definitely a lodge operating in Aberdeen before 1670, as internal records stretch back to that year. Over the centuries Freemasons met in various locations, from an open-air assembly near GIRDLENESS, to ST KATHERINE'S HILL, then Gallowgate, the Links near Footdee, and the corner of Union Street and King Street at LODGE WALK. The present temple was built in 1910, and is quite possibly the single most decorated, symbol-rich and esoteric building in the whole of Aberdeen.

EXTERIOR
Even if you cannot get inside, the façade proclaims the nature of the building with a battery of occult symbolism. Prominent among the carvings are many of the classic symbols of Freemasonry:

- The Set-square and Compass (signifying moral virtues and the boundaries of appropriate behaviour) encompassing the letter 'G' (for God the Creator).
- The Six-pointed Star, long thought to be the seal of King Solomon – Masonic tradition is steeped in Solomonic references.

Left: The west façade of the Masonic Temple, with classic symbols of Freemasonry: the chequered Mosaic Pavement, the set-square and compass, and the abbreviated names of the three Grand Masters who built the Temple of Solomon. *(Ségolène Dupuy)*

Below left: The Temple foundation stone, showing not the date 1912 but the Masonic year 5912, using the *Anno Lucis* dating system. *(Ségolène Dupuy)*

Below right: The sundial on the south gable of the Temple. Once again, the date reads 5912 AL. *(Geoff Holder)*

- The abbreviations SKI (Solomon, King of Israel); HKT (Hiram, King of Tyre); and HAB (Hiram Abiff), the last being the master-builder also known as the Widow's Son. In Masonic lore these were the three Grand Masters involved in the building of Solomon's Temple
- The black-and-white Mosaic Pavement (supposedly the floor of the Temple of Solomon was decorated in this manner)
- The All-Seeing Eye, symbolising the Eye of God
- The Blazing Star, indicating Divine Providence, although there are several other interpretations
- The Sun, a marker of strength and wisdom or, again, Divine Providence – possibly derived from an Egyptian source. There is a spectacular golden sun on the sundial that dominates the southern gable of the building. The dial is based on Christopher Wren's design at Morden College in London, although the deeply moulded face of the Aberdeen sun is entirely Masonic. The Latin motto below the Sun is a quote from the Roman poet Horace and translates as 'I number none but the cloudless hours', an injunction to live well.
- And the tools of Freemasonry – the plumbline, the setting maul (the tool that knocks or sets stones into place), the trowel, and the hammer or gavel. At one level these are simply practical items used in construction, but of course deep symbolism has also been read into each of them. For example, the plumbline indicates Justness and Uprightness, the need for a man to walk and act in an upright manner in the sight of the Creator, the Grand Geometrician.

Added to these can be found non-Masonic carvings such as foliaceous lions, and winged heads. The strikingly large inscription AVDI VIDE TACE means 'hear, see, be silent', a standard Masonic injunction to observe both prudence and the fraternity's secrets. On the rear of the building is the foundation stone, with a Setsquare and Compass. Freemasons have the need to Masonicize everything, and so it is with dates; rather than use conventional dating, with the standard forms BC and AD, they reference the *Anno Lucis*, the Year of Light, which is 4000 BC. Hence the datestone is not marked 1912 AD, but *Anno Lucis* 5912, the twentieth century being the fifty-ninth century by Masonic counting. The inscription beneath the solar-headed sundial, CVIXII A.L. means the same. The whole *Anno Lucis* notion is, by the way, a nonsense, part of the urge of eighteenth-century Freemasons to invent a spurious antiquity for their creed.

MAIN ENTRANCE VESTIBULE
This is the first of the Temple's magnificently-appointed internal spaces. The floor is inset with a representation of the twelve signs of the Zodiac in marble, while an imposing mantelpiece holds statues representing Wisdom, Fidelity, Charity and Strength, and the legend *Sen Vord is Thrall And Thocht is Fre Keip Veill Thy Tonge I CoinSell The* ('Since word is thrall, and thought is free, Keep well thy tongue, I counsel thee'). The motto is generally attributed to King James I in his *Ballad of Good Counsel*, and appears incised on the 'advice stone' of the Abbott's House in Dunfermline; it was popularised by Sir Walter Scott in *The Fair Maid of Perth*.

Above left: The Temple vestibule, with the representations of Wisdom, Fidelity, Charity and Strength, a motto on prudent speech, and one of the wonderful painted plaster ceilings. *(Geoff Holder)*

Above right: The marble Zodiac set within the Mosaic Pavement of the vestibule. *(Geoff Holder)*

Above left: A full set of Masonic symbols on display in the Temple. *(Geoff Holder)*

Above right: Hiram Abiff, the architect of the Temple of Solomon; in Masonic lore, he was murdered for his knowledge. *(Ségolène Dupuy)*

The standard Masonic symbols adorn the walls, woodwork and the wonderful painted plaster ceilings, as they do throughout the building. Another symbol found on the floor (and elsewhere in the temple) is the triple Tau, which looks like two letters 'H' at right angles; it signifies the Temple at Jerusalem or 'A key to the treasure'.

THE GRAND PROVINCIAL HALL (GROUND FLOOR).

Strikingly dominated by its black-and-white Mosaic Pavement (actually a carpet), in this spacious room can be seen some of the standard layout of Masonic Lodges: the two globes on pillars, one of which is always recumbent (signifying Night) while the other (Day) is erect; the gavel of authority; the altar with the Holy Book (in this case, and as usual in Britain, the Bible); candlesticks; a desk in the form of an equilateral triangle; and the 'rough' and 'perfect' ashlars, two small blocks of stone symbolising the 'unmodified' man and the 'perfected' man who has become improved through spiritual disciplines. Here is also a chair dated 1710 and wonderfully carved with Masonic symbols.

CHAPTER HALL (GROUND FLOOR)

This is similar in layout to the Grand Provincial Hall, only here the mosaic pattern on the carpet is in red or blue. Above the entrance is a wooden statue of Hiram Abiff, the architect of the Temple of Solomon, identified by his acronym HAB. The several coloured curtains are the 'Veils' – passing through them symbolises the enlightenment that comes with progression through Freemasonry. The metal lectern for the Holy Book is cleverly wrought with multiple variations on

The Craft Hall. The 'perfect' ashlar block represents the man improved by spiritual disciplines, the plumb-line indicates Justness and Uprightness, and the recumbent globe signifies Night (an upright equivalent symbolises Day). *(Geoff Holder)*

Above left: The doorknocker for the Craft Hall, with a horned Medusa-like face encircled by snakes. *(Geoff Holder)*

Above right: The All-Seeing Eye, symbolising the Eye of God. *(Ségolène Dupuy)*

the Christian Cross. In the corner is a curious wooden box with a large circular access. This was used to determine whether an applicant was to be admitted to a lodge – members placed within the box white balls (for 'yes') or black balls ('no'). If the applicant received more of the latter than the former, he was not accepted (hence the origin of the term 'blackballed').

THE CRYPT
This extraordinary ritual space can be viewed through a grating in the floor of a vestibule on the ground floor. It consists of a narrow domed, cylindrical and win-dowless basement with a circular black-and-white pavement centred on an altar inscribed with an equilateral triangle and the four Hebrew letters for Yahweh or Jehovah. The marble walls are brightly decorated with more Hebrew lettering (the names of the Twelve Tribes of Israel), signs of the Zodiac, patterns, flowers, scenes of mounted horsemen, towers, and several seated figures whose exact sym-bolism escapes me; one is holding a trident. Circling the edge are the legends *Deo regi fratribus honor fidelitas benevolentia* ('For God, king and the brethren; honour, fidelity and benevolence') and *Talia si jungere possis sit tibi scire satis* ('If thou canst comprehend these things, thou knowest enough'). The whole awe-inspiring space breathes a powerful sense of High Ceremony.

THE LANDING
Display cases here hold Masonic memorabilia, such as regalia, ceremonial trowels and mauls, and snuff-mills and cut-throat razors inscribed with Masonic symbols. The most intriguing artefact on display is a copy of *The Laws and Constitution of the Grand Lodge of Scotland* from 1848. According to the accompanying interpreta-tion, it was found during building works in 2002, secreted in a space behind a wall in Talbots on Exchange Street. Quite why the book was deposited in this 'Masonic Kyst' remains a mystery.

Above left: 'G' (for God the Creator) above the Blazing Star (Divine Providence). *(Geoff Holder)*

Above right: One of the angels in the Craft Hall, her eyes lowered so she cannot witness the men-only rituals. *(Geoff Holder)*

MAIN TEMPLE OR CRAFT HALL (FIRST FLOOR)

Similar in apparel to the other halls, this is even more magnificent, by dint of its vast barrel-vaulted and painted ceiling supported by numerous polychrome angels (whose semi-nudity clearly demonstrates they are not genderless). All the angels have their eyes lowered; being female, they are not allowed to view the rituals of the male-only society. The amount of carved and painted symbols in the room is immense, with every piece of woodwork, including the organ and chairs, bearing some mark, and a painting absolutely packed with esoteric meaning hangs above the door. The brass doorknockers feature a horned being encompassed by entwined snakes biting on a decorated seed or pearl; below the knocker is a spyhole to check on who seeks admittance.

In complete contrast to the baroque excess of the Masonic Temple, the modest Quaker Meeting House opposite, at No. 98, is a model of plain simplicity. Here you can pick up information on the Society of Friends and the persecution of Quakers in Aberdeen (for more on Quakers, see GALLOWGATE).

ST JOHN'S PLACE

In terms of gargoyles and grotesques, most Aberdeen churches are almost entirely lacking, probably because sculpting in granite is not the easiest of tasks. This makes the Episcopal Church of St John the Evangelist even more striking. The exterior, reminiscent of an English parish church, abounds with dozens of heads of kings, queens, bishops and more ordinary folk in medieval headgear, while up on high a pair of praying angels robustly support an arch for the Cross. Within, there are more angels, beautifully painted, and a sixteenth-century font from Kinkell near Inverurie, with crisp carvings including a rose (symbolising the Virgin Mary), the crown of thorns, and the Five Wounds of Christ. The gold-plated reredos at the altar was designed by Sir Ninian Comper and features his trademark 'strawberry signature', included as a tribute to his father Revd John Comper, who collapsed and died handing out strawberries to poor children in Duthie Park. The Virgin Mary is writing in a book held by an angel; the inscriptions translate as 'For whom all things were made' and 'The Word was made flesh'. Among the superb Victorian stained glass, look out for St Cuthbert holding the crowned severed head of St Oswald of Northumbria – Oswald's head was interred within Cuthbert's coffin, so the two are always represented in this comic-horror manner.

The church also contains a genuine mystery, a perplexing puzzle that has already exercised the mind of Dr John Morrison, Senior Lecturer at the Department

Above left: The Five Wounds of Christ, on the sixteenth-century font in St John's Church. *(Geoff Holder)*

Above right: Detail of the altar in St John's. The Infant Jesus is holding Sir Ninian Comper's strawberry symbol. *(Geoff Holder)*

of History of Art, University of Aberdeen. In a 2002 lecture reproduced on the church's website, he discussed the huge mural painting that covers the chancel arch. This beautiful artwork depicts scenes from the Gospel of St John, including the miracle of the fisherman finding their nets filled with fish. At the focus of the painting is the heavenly host, with winged and haloed angels playing trumpets, harps and lutes, and singing the praises of the Creator. The winged heads of cherubs flit among their complete-body comrades.

The mystery comes not only from the fact that there is no record of who produced this immense work or when they did it, but also because it is painted using a technique called divisionism, developed by the Post-Impressionist French painter Georges Seurat in the 1880s. Divisionism was *avant-garde* for its day, and Post-Impressionism was not really known in Britain until 1910, when an exhibition appeared in London. Yet Morrison, piecing together the fragmentary records and drawing on the memories of the congregation, tentatively concluded that the mural was painted *before* 1910. So we have a mural skillfully executed by someone expert in the unusual technique of divisionism, yet apparently produced at a time when few British artists were familiar with Post-Impressionism, and the public not at all. Morrison speculated that it may have been a Scottish painter who had travelled in *fin-de-siècle* European artistic circles, but the identity of this paragon remains unknown. Hopefully more light will be brought to bear on this fascinating mystery. In the meantime, the mural remains a beautiful enigma.

AFFLECK STREET

St Mary's Well flowed on the south side of this street until urban development in the mid-nineteenth century. There is no record that it was ever a holy well, but the name is suggestive.

Above left: St Cuthbert holding the severed head of St Oswald in St John's Church. *(Geoff Holder)*

Above right: The mysterious mural on the chancel arch in St John's, apparently painted well before it 'could' have been. *(Ségolène Dupuy)*

DEE STREET

The building occupied by the China Town restaurant is decorated with six Classical-style heads within roundels, all painted.

LANGSTANE PLACE

Lurking in an alcove on the corner with Dee Street is the 'Lang Stane', an irregular stone 5ft 11ins (1.8m) tall. Its history is unclear; it is probably a prehistoric standing stone, and seems to have originally stood on the north side of Windmill Brae, the steep descent opposite Langstane Place. Some time in the 1860s the name 'LANGS-TANE' was carved on it. However, it is also sometimes claimed to be the 'Crabstone' or 'Craibstone' mentioned in several early accounts. On 20 November 1571 another episode in the internecine warfare between the Gordon and Forbes clans became known as the Battle of Craibstone (the score was sixty men dead on each side, but the Gordons won on penalties by capturing Forbes of Brux). John Spalding, in *The history of the Troubles and Memorable Transactions in Scotland*, recorded that William Forbes murdered Alexander Irvine of Kingcausie at the Craibstone on 17 August 1644 (Spalding was very keen on the justice of Providence; he gleefully reported that a year later Forbes accidentally shot his own hand off, 'a token that the Lord thought not this innocent blood good service!').

   In both these and other accounts it is clear the Craibstone was further south-west than Windmill Brae, near Hardgate, probably at the top of the hill (now the junction with Willowbank Road); it also seems likely it was a march stone for the lands of Rubislaw, which were once owned by the Crab family. So the Langstane may be the relocated Craibstone, or there may have been two stones, one prehistoric and one modern, and both may have been moved. It's very confusing, and no one really knows.

HARDGATE AND JUSTICE MILLS LANE

The Battle of Justice Mills of 11 September 1644 is one of the more notorious episodes in Aberdeen's bloody history. The Royalist Marquis of Montrose, incensed by the shooting dead of his drummer boy under a flag of truce, smashed through the forces of the Covenanters, killing 160, and unleashed his army of Irish merce-naries to plunder, rape and murder through the town. The fighting took place on the sloping ground between Justice Mill Lane, Bon Accord Crescent, Hardgate and Union Glen, with the dying and wounded taken to the 'Bloody Well' on Hardgate. A full account of the events can be found in Chris Brown's *The Battle for Aberdeen 1644*; like many before him, Brown cites the account of the battle by John Spalding, Aberdeen's first historian. Spalding notes that the night before Montrose's army arrived, many townspeople saw the moon rise 'as red as blood two hours before its time'. To a man of Spalding's disposition regarding omens and portents, the

Far left: The Langstane standing stone; or, at least, what may be the Langstane. *(Geoff Holder)*

Left: The curious Art Deco gas ventilator on the corner of Justice Mill Lane and Holburn Street. *(Geoff Holder)*

meaning was obvious; had he been in a movie he would undoubtedly have said 'Uh-oh'. Or possibly, 'I have a bad feeling about this.' In the best-known incident of the battle, a wounded Irish soldier cut his own leg off with his dirk and handed it to another man, saying, 'bury that lest some hungry Scot should eat it.'

At the junction of Justice Mill Lane and Holburn Street stands one of Aberdeen's quirkier sights, a brightly coloured Art Deco ventilator shaft that contrasts strikingly with its surroundings.

BON ACCORD SQUARE

The granite block in the centre of the raised garden is dedicated to Archibald Simpson (1790-1847), the architect who was largely responsible for making the Granite City what it is today. The stone was originally intended to become a lion on the George VI Bridge but wartime economies intervened; its three companions ended up as the Nascent Lions, the *faux* stone circle in HAZLEHEAD PARK.

UNION GLEN

This was the valley of the Ferryhill Burn, now culverted. Diane Morgan's *Lost Aberdeen: The Outskirts* describes how in 1904 the Bon Accord Distillery was destroyed by fire. In what must have been an unforgettable sight, the flaming whisky poured into the burn, creating a river of flowing liquid fire.

4

THE CITY CENTRE – NORTH-WEST OF UNION STREET

UNION BRIDGE – SKENE SQUARE – HUNTLY STREET

So easie a thing it is for fables to find good harbour,
wher verities would be beaten out with cudgelles.

Gilbert Blakhal, *A Breiffe Narration* (1666)

UNION BRIDGE

On 7 July 1801, accompanied by full Masonic honours, the face of Aberdeen was changed forever. On that date the foundation stone of a new bridge was laid. When the bridge was completed, it spanned the ravine of the Denburn, up until then the geographical western boundary of the old town. With the advent of Union Bridge and Union Street, Aberdeen finally left the Middle Ages behind. No longer did travellers from the south have to deal with inconvenient topography and struggle up the Hardgate, snake through the Green and into Castlegate via Shiprow. There was now a direct major thoroughfare that leapfrogged on great arches not only over the stream and valley, but across the tangle of narrow old streets that networked the sloping ground down to the harbour – and creating a subterranean, almost secret city of tunnels and vaults in the process. When author Robert Smith was exploring the former Commercial Union Insurance building on the north-west corner of the bridge, before it was converted into the restaurant and bar now called The Monkey House, he was shown a 'secret passage' behind one of the walls, which apparently led under Union Street. The episode is in his book *Grampian Curiosities*. The view over Union Terrace Gardens from the north side is a reminder of how much the modern street towers above the natural ground level. The Denburn itself is no longer visible, having long been culverted, the suppressed waters flowing invisibly in underground pipes to the harbour.

The bridge has a bronze panel with a group of allegorical figures representing various virtues, but the bridge's most famous feature is Kelly's Cats, the leopards that decorate the north parapet. The south side used to be leopardine as well, but the beasts, removed in 1961, are now in the Winter Gardens in DUTHIE PARK. (The 1961 works also created a line of shops on the south side of the bridge itself, thus eclipsing any sense from that direction that Union Bridge is actually a bridge.) The standard story is that the creatures were designed by the architect and antiquarian Dr William Kelly. However, in her book *Lost Aberdeen*, Diane Morgan scotches this, stating the designer was Sidney Boyes of Gray's School of Art. Kelly's name became attached to the statues because he lambasted students who had tied ribbons around the leopards' neck during 'Rag Week'.

The granite statue of the well-padded King Edward VII opposite the Monkey House sports an elaborate bronze frieze, with St Andrew holding the X-shaped cross on which he was crucified; Britannia, overseen by an angel, breaking a sword (a symbol of peace); and a group representing the imperial possessions of the British Empire.

The Victorian Baronial-style structure on the south side, now part of the Trinity Shopping Centre, hides one of the city's nineteenth-century treasures. This was the location of Trinity Hall, the former home of the Seven Incorporated Trades, originally guilds of craftsmen from medieval times, who evolved into one of Aberdeen's most significant social and cultural organisations. The Trades sold the building during the redevelopment of the 1960s and moved out to their new headquarters on HOLBURN STREET. But they left behind their magnificent meeting hall built in 1848, with its high mock-medieval hammerbeam roof, chandeliers and vibrant Victorian wallpaper. The hall, on the top floor of the building above the busy shopping floors of Primark, was once used as a restaurant but now remains echoingly empty and is not open to the public.

In 2007 Graeme Milne, author of *The Haunted North*, felt the icy presence of an invisible spirit in the hall, and was told by a member of staff of rumours that the basement area was haunted. On my visit the store manager elaborated on these stories, stating that the area – known as the sub-sub-basement, the lowest of the multiple storeys within the building that rises from the Green through the split-level city to 'street level' on Union Bridge – was supposedly haunted either by a piper or by the spirits of children kidnapped to be sold as slaves in the eighteenth century. The area is now unused and inaccessible, but by its description is a windowless, cold, stone-built vault, the perfect place for the imagination to create terrors. Stories of the phantom piper have been circulating for decades but the 'kidnapped children' theme seems to originate only with Milne, who found that the original building was close to the 'kidnappers' house' on The Green, and shared this information with his contact in the store in 2007.

The 'kidnapped children' saga of the 1740s is, along with the witchcraft persecutions, one of the most infamous blots on Aberdeen's history. It was a classic case of supply and demand: the British colonies in America were short of labour, while the cities of the mother country were swarming with 'surplus' people. To some the solution was obvious, as is made clear in the subtitle to Peter Wilson Coldham's magisterial study *Emigrants in Chains*: 'A Social History of Forced Emigration to the Americas of Felons, Destitute Children, Political and Religious Non-Conformists, Vagabonds, Beggars and Other Undesirables'. The British authorities emptied their jails and workhouses to populate America. In Aberdeen, the great and the good of the city conspired in a variation on the theme. Up to 600 children were kidnapped, imprisoned in various locations such as the Tolbooth or the house on the Green and, when sufficient numbers were made up, bought by ships' captains who then sold the children at a profit to colonists in the New World. Technically the unwilling transportees were sold as 'indentured labour' for a set amount of years, although in some cases 'slavery' was a more apt term.

The entire process was legal and above-board, and was a nice little earner for Aberdeen's elite. But then it all went pear-shaped. In 1758 Peter Williamson of Aboyne, who had been kidnapped as a ten-year-old while staying with his aunt in Aberdeen, beat the system and unexpectedly re-appeared in the city. Not only that, he had written a book which detailed how the authorities had mistreated him. Unsurprisingly, the Aberdeen magistrates, not being big supporters of free speech – especially when it revealed their own crimes – took the huff and prosecuted him for 'an infamous libel'. Williamson was imprisoned, fined, and banished from the town, while the 'obnoxious' parts of his book were torn out and burnt at the Mercat Cross by the public hangman. So Aberdeen high society breathed a sigh of relief – until Williamson, an energetic type, raised an action in the court at Edinburgh, and won £100 in damages, plus costs, all of which had to be personally met by the Provost, the four bailies, and the Dean of Guild.

Later Williamson published an extended autobiography, *French and Indian cruelty exemplified, in the life, and various vicissitudes of fortune, of Peter Williamson: who was carried off from Aberdeen in his infancy, and sold for a slave in Pennsylvania*. It detailed his adventures in America – his lucky purchase by a kind Scotsman who had himself been kidnapped from Perth as a child many years previously, and his involvement in the wars with the French and Indians. The chapter headings give a hint of the contents:

- His house burnt by the Indians and himself carried off by them
- The cruel treatment he suffered while among the savages
- The shocking massacre of Jacob Snyder and his family
- The author meditates his escape and accomplishes it at the risk of his life
- His arrival at the house of John Bell, who takes him for an Indian, and threatens to shoot him
- A full account of the Indians, their manner of living, fighting etc
- The French discovered coming to attack Oswego
- An Irishman scalped when drunk, yet recovers

Torture, rape and murder on the frontier are the keynotes of the narrative. Williamson took to publicising his book dressed in 'authentic' Native American costume.

By and large the story told by 'Indian Peter' has been accepted as a true account, and certainly the kidnapping from Aberdeen did take place – interestingly enough, Williamson claims he was held on board a ship in the harbour, not in any building. But recently academics having been casting doubt on the American adventures. A typical case is the 2004 piece entitled 'Peter Williamson: faker' by B. Bruce-Biggs in the journal *Northern Scotland*, published by the University of Aberdeen Centre for Scottish Studies. Williamson is shown to have plagiarized some of his accounts from contemporary magazines and newspapers; many of the battles he said he took part in did not actually take place; and it seems Williamson may have gathered up stories from other frontiersmen and claimed them for his own. He may not ever have fought with the Indians. Throughout his later career as a successful Edinburgh businessman Williamson never once hinted that anything in his book was fraudulent, and, maintaining the story of 'Indian Peter' to the end, he was buried with his war-bonnet.

SKENE TERRACE

In December 1865 the first ever photograph of the moon was taken from the garden in front of No. 48. Altogether photographer George Washington Wilson and astronomer Sir David Gill made six images; Gill later achieved more lunar fame when a crater on the Moon was named after him. On a related space note, Aberdeen is one of several Scottish places that claims it will be the birthplace of Chief Engineer Montgomery Scott in the year AD 2222. After a brilliant education 'Scottie' will join Starfleet and serve on the Starship *Enterprise* under Captain James T. Kirk. The race to claim the future birthplace of the iconic engineer was prompted by the death in 2005 of actor James Doohan, who played Scottie in original *Star Trek* television series and films. All together now: 'The engines canna take it, Captain!'

SPA STREET

Just in front of the unlovely car park on the corner of Spa Street and Skene Street stands an attractive sandstone monument, now mostly ignored but once a healing well of great repute. The Well of Spa was first mentioned in 1580, and in 1615 was in ruins, the remains bearing carvings of six of the Apostles; this suggests it had been a holy well in the days before the Reformation. Perhaps people came here hoping for miraculous cures. Under Protestantism miracles were eschewed but the 'healing virtues' of the waters continued to attract rich and poor alike. In 1700 James Brome, author of *Travels over England, Scotland, and Wales* observed that the well was 'very efficacious to dissolve the stone, to expel sand from the reins [kidneys] and bladder, being good for the collick and drunk in July and August'. According to Andrew Jervise, reporting to the Society of Antiquaries of Scotland in 1862, in the seventeenth century the well bore the legend:

PETER WILLIAMSON
In the Dress of a Delaware Indian
1 *Tomehauk.*   6 *Powderhorn.*
2 *Scalping Knife.*   6 *Indian Canoe.*
3 *Shot Bag.*   7 *Bush Fighting.*
4 *Purse & Belt of Wampum*   8 *War Dance.*

Above left: 'Peter Williamson in the dress of a Delaware Indian', from his autobiographical book *French and Indian cruelty exemplified*. A war-dance is going on behind him.

Above right: The seventeenth-century wellhead of the Well of Spa, with a thistle, rose, fleur-de-lis and sunburst. *(Geoff Holder)*

> The Stomack, Reins, the Liver, Spleen, yea sure
> A thousand evils this wholesome Spring doth cure.

The structure was rebuilt in 1635 by the artist George Jamesone (who drank from it daily for his health), though this succumbed to the Denburn in flood fifteen years later. A replacement appeared in 1670, but a century later the medicinal chalybeate or iron-bearing water supply dried up, probably due to building operations in the area. In the Victorian period the stone wellhead was restored and moved to the east side of the valley. In 1977 the structure was repaired again and relocated to its present position, a short distance from its original location. The crisply restored carvings include the Scottish Thistle, the Rose of England, and the Fleur-de-lis of France, plus a superb sunburst. There are also three inscriptions: 'As Heaven gives me / So give I thee'; *spada rediviva 1670* (*rediviva* can mean 'reconstructed' but I am unable to make sense of *spada*, which relates to 'sword' – could it be a reference to 'spa'?); and *Hoc fonte derivata Salus / In patriam populumque fluat*. The latter is a clever reworking of a quote from the Roman poet Horace. The original, *Hoc fonte derivata clades in patriam populumque fluxit*, can be translated along the lines of 'from this fountain of evil the stream of disaster has poured in full flood upon our dear native land'. By changing two words the new inscription means something like 'from this fountain of health, benefits pour in full flood upon our dear native land'.

WOOLMANHILL HOSPITAL

The hill on which the hospital is built was just outside the medieval burgh, which meant it could be pressed into use in a crisis. In 1647, with plague ravaging the town, the sick were placed in temporary huts here (along with the Links at the Beach). The settlement was guarded to prevent the spread of infection; those who died here were buried on the hill. That same year the election of magistrates was removed to neighbouring Gilcomston, while the Universities held their classes in Fraserburgh and Peterhead.

SKENE SQUARE

This was the area of a settlement known as Gilcomston, whose history stretches back to at least the twelfth century. Its location was a strategic one, on high ground between the Gilcomston Burn and Denburn. The name is usually thought to come from Gilcolm's-town, Gilcolm presumably being the local landowner. An alternative derivation is that it was from Gilcolm's (or Gilcon's) Stone, as two prehistoric standing stones could be found here until at least 1871, although they had disappeared a decade later. One was around 8ft (2.4m) tall, its companion about 6ft (1.8m) in height, and they were located near where Hill Street blends into Skene Square. It is possible they were part of a stone circle, although like everything else in the vicinity whether this was so is unknown. 'Gilcolm' himself, a man with a Celtic name, does not appear in any records and nothing is known of him. And why Skene Square is so named is also a mystery, as there was never a square here. The Gilcomston Bar, on the corner of Skene Square and Baker Street, sports a pub sign painted with the name Gillecoaim's Toun, showing a medieval motte topped by a wooden castle, a settlement encompassed by a moat – and, nearby, a stone circle.

SOUTH MOUNT STREET

The arches of the oval of flats at Rosemount Square are graced with two wonderful Art Deco sculptures of the Elements, represented by streamlined naked maidens pouring out water or flying upon the wind on an imperious horse. The development was the first major post-war build of municipal housing, and the sculptures were by T.B. Huxley-Jones. A plaque states the flats were 'Commended for Good Design by the Saltire Society' in 1948.

The pub sign of the Gilcomston Bar, Skene Square. Note the castle motte and stone circle. *(Geoff Holder)*

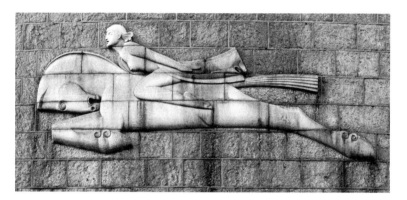

Sculptures of the Elements – Wind, Rosemount Square. *(Geoff Holder)*

Sculptures of the Elements – Water, Rosemount Square. *(Geoff Holder)*

MACKIE PLACE

Along with the grounds of Aberdeen Grammar School, Mackie Place is one of the few locations where the Denburn can be seen flowing in the open. Here on this cul-de-sac off Skene Street once stood a classic 'haunted house' whose story has something of the quality of *Scooby Doo* about it. The building was known as the White House or The Castle, a forbidding early nineteenth-century structure five storeys high, far larger than anything in the area at the time. As Diane Morgan told the story in *Lost Aberdeen: The Outskirts*, the house grew to this size because the builder, a Mr Taylor, was in a construction war with George Dickie, his neighbour in the now-demolished adjacent building called Cherry Vale. Dickie erected a wall to prevent his property being overlooked, so Taylor added another storey. Dickie responded by raising the height of his wall to 30ft (9.1m) but the White House kept growing upwards, eventually reaching its formidable size. In the 1860s tea planter Alexander D. Forbes retired here with his family. Soon a reputation for ghostly activities spread, although the origin of the spooks was explained in the first issue of the *Castle Spectre*, an informal journal produced by the Forbes family and printed at the house in October 1876:

> We are the dwellers in that house in the neighbourhood of Skene Street known to the oldest inhabitants as the Haunted House, to younger inhabitants as the Castle, and to the Post Office as No. 6 Mackie Place. In former days we were 'desp'rate wicked'. We dressed ourselves in white sheets and popped out upon passers-by, frightening them into fits. We used to scoop out the largest turnips (which we always stole) and, having cut out slices to represent eyes, nose and mouth, light candles in them and stick them on poles in hedges, just where they would suddenly glimmer out upon the greatest possible number of women and children. We used to lie behind low walls and growl like bears, or howl like dogs, or caterwaul like cats whenever any weakly-looking person was passing. We were very careful not to play our tricks upon strong-looking men – or women either for that matter – for fear of being found out and getting a thrashing.

If it wasn't for those pesky kids … !

The story of the *Castle Spectre*, which came out every month for twelve years until 1888, is told in Robert Smith's splendid book *Aberdeen Curiosities*. In later years the magazine was virtually entirely written by Alexander Forbes. When his wife died he withdrew into himself, swearing he would never go outside his door. He grew his hair to his waist and wandered the vast building in his dressing gown. His eccentric behaviour combined with the earlier pranks of the Forbes children to produce a rumour that the house was genuinely haunted. After Forbes' death the building decayed and although it survived into the early twentieth century, it is now long gone.

HUNTLY STREET

The Roman Catholic Cathedral of St Mary, with its immense spire, sports a fine collection of Victorian sculpture: a roaring lion, a crowned woman and the head

Right: A strange winged demon, moulded in metal on a drainpipe of St Mary's Cathedral. *(Geoff Holder)*

Far right: A roaring lion below a symbol of the Trinity, St Mary's Cathedral. *(Geoff Holder)*

of a bishop, as well as a statue of St Peter holding the key to the heavenly gates, and the Virgin Mary within a Gothic niche. There are also abstract demonic heads, and a truly strange winged gargoyle-like head poking out of the black-painted metal drainpipes. Gargoyles traditionally protect places which contain secrets and mysteries; this seems appropriate, as within the cathedral is a replica of the statue of the Virgin Mary known as Our Lady of Bon Accord or Our Lady of Aberdeen (there is another copy in St Peter's Church on CASTLEGATE). The original statue is held in Notre Dame de Finistere in Brussels, and the story of how it got there, and why it is held in such high esteem, takes us to the heart of medieval religious belief, with its miracles, visions and messages from the Divine.

Because the statue was lost (and found) during the chaos of the Reformation, and then became an icon of Catholic propaganda, much of its history is dubious. The more supernatural elements are collected in William Walsh's *The Apparitions and Shrines of Heaven's Bright Queen* of 1904, which maintains a pro-miracle and anti-Protestant tone throughout ('Heaven's Bright Queen' is of course the Blessed Virgin Mary). The basic story is that the original wooden statue was in ST MACHAR'S CATHEDRAL, where Bishop Gavin Dunbar prayed to it every day. In 1520 the statue of the Virgin audibly spoke to Dunbar, telling him where to build a bridge over the Dee. (On another occasion the image warned Dunbar, who died in 1532, of the Reformation that would come several decades later.) When the BRIDGE OF DEE was completed in 1527, Dunbar built a shrine to the Virgin Mary at its north end and installed within it the statue, which now started to dispense miracles and caused a healing spring to well up at the spot.

In December 1559 a rabble of Protestant fanatics swept into the town, bent on the destruction of 'idolatrous images'. The Lady Chapel at the bridge fell victim to their rage, although what actually happened to the statue is unclear. In one version it was thrown into the river, picked up by a Flemish ship and taken to the Continent. Another variant says it was deliberately hidden within the riverbank before being recovered by Catholic sympathisers and transported to Brussels.

Walsh gives a much more elaborate version. According to him, the statue's hiding-place was discovered by the Protestants. Strangely enough, those charged with its destruction could not bring themselves to actually complete the task, dropping the hammer at the last moment. One Protestant who took it into his house witnessed so many miracles there that he and his family re-converted to Catholicism. Iconoclasts forced themselves into the house but failed to carry out their destruction of the statue because, as Walsh puts it, 'although it had been put in one of the most conspicuous places in the house, they could not see it'.

If Walsh is to be believed, the statue remained hidden until 1623 or 1625, when renewed Protestant investigations prompted Catholics to take it out of the country. It was thus placed on a Spanish vessel lying in Aberdeen harbour and despatched with orders to be delivered to the Infanta, Archduchess Isabella, the Spanish ruler of the Low Countries and a key figure in the Catholic Counter-Reformation that was attempting to head off Protestant rumblings in the Netherlands. Satan sent a storm to sink the ship, which survived despite losing its sails and masts. Then a Dutch pirate vessel attacked the stricken ship, to be miraculously driven off with the help of Our Lady of Aberdeen. The ship limped into Dunkirk, whose Governor attempted to seize the statue, only to be struck down with a deadly illness. By a remarkable coincidence Archduchess Isabella happened to visit Dunkirk shortly afterwards, and when the Governor handed over the statue to her he was – of course – instantly cured of his disease, 'to the wonder and admiration of all the people', as Walsh says.

Isabella had the image taken to Brussels, where it continued to dispense miracles. The Abbot of Cundenberg was healed of an incurable disease. Catherine Raes, bed-ridden with a badly-damaged knee, rose up and walked as normal. In 1633 Louis Clarisse, a magistrate from Amiens, was cured of a fatal illness. In 1695, while much of Brussels was destroyed by an artillery siege, the church of the Augustinian Fathers containing the statue remained completely untouched. A century later the iconoclasts of the French Revolution failed to locate the statue, despite having ransacked churches and shrines. In 1814 Our Lady of Aberdeen was installed in Notre Dame de Finistere, where it remains to this day, although the miracle-count has gone down.

More variations on this story are recounted in Gilbert Blakhal's *A Breiffe Narration of the Services Done to Three Noble Ladyes*, written in 1666 or 1667. Father Blakhal was a Scottish Catholic priest operating in post-Reformation difficulties and his book recounts his experiences in Catholic France and Protestant Aberdeenshire between 1631 and 1649. At one point Blakhal was in Brussels and in a brief aside mentions Our Lady of Aberdeen. He claims the statue travelled on a merchant's ship from Aberdeen to Ostend (not Dunkirk), and its arrival prompted a miraculous Catholic victory over the Protestant Dutch rebels. He also noted that 'the vulgar people' believed the image had been thrown into the sea at Aberdeen and carried by the waves (and the hand of the Virgin) to Ostend. He concludes his comments with an appropriate observation: 'So easie a thing it is for fables to find good harbour, wher verities would be beaten out with cudgelles.' Quite.

5

EAST AND NORTH-EAST OF THE CENTRE

FOOTDEE – THE LINKS – MOUNTHOOLY – PITTODRIE

One, two, three,
What a lot of fishwives I do see.

Alex McAldowie, *Personal Experiences in Witchcraft* (1896)

FOOTDEE

Pronounced 'Fittie', this delightful former fishing village has two petite squares of eighteenth-century cottages and houses, accompanied by the huts that were formerly used for fishing nets but are now converted to a variety of uses, many decorated with various variations of folk art. One house has an amusing sculpture of a seagull, and the old metal well-heads bear grotesque faces.

As with the inhabitants of TORRY, the fishers of Footdee were culturally different from all those around them, maintaining an inward-looking, clannish society in which superstition thrived. Despite living only a few streets away from the city centre, they may as well have been occupying a remote coastal outpost. *The Goodwife at Home: Footdee in the 18th century*, written by Ann Allardyce in 1918, gives something of the flavour of how supernatural belief saturated daily life in the cramped, sea-swept houses:

> They had considerable personal courage, but great timidity toward everything which they supposed to be under supernatural influence, and stout men who would have faced any danger by day would not have passed the churchyard alone at night. They believed firmly in ghosts, wraiths, witches, fairies, mermaids, and water kelpies.

A fisherman named Andrew Brand was found unconscious one day on the Hill of Torry. When roused he was incoherent, and spent the next few weeks in a fever. Finally he was able to give an account of what had befallen him. He had been employed as a look-out and had seen 'a creature like a woman with a white sheet about her sitting on a stone, sometimes combing out her long hair and sometimes tossing up her arms in a fearsome way.' This individual then rushed into the sea and vanished. Immediately Brand became paralysed, blind, and slipped into unconsciousness. He clearly believed he had seen a mermaid or some other cursed thing, but it was more likely his already fevered brain had misinterpreted the ordinary sight of a woman out bathing.

Women gathered soon after midnight on New Year's Day to obtain the precious 'cream of the well', the well water that brought good fortune if gathered at dawn on the first day of the year – 'a scuffle generally ensued as to which of the numerous pans and buckets should be permitted to carry off the precious 'first draught.'' Grandparents were often thought to be healers, and their advice sought in preference to doctors; but some also had dark powers and were also dreaded as being an 'unlucky foot'. Anyone regarded as an 'unlucky foot' was not allowed to cast off the moorings, and had to be avoided at all costs before a voyage – if a fisherman met one of these people on his way to his boat, he simply abandoned the day's work and remained in his house all day. Unlucky people were therefore not merely a danger to life and limb – meeting them might cause a storm to get up or a boat to sink – but also to livelihoods. Pointing at a boat with a forefinger was sure to bring the evil eye down on it. Various apotropaic precautions were therefore taken to ward off evil influences – wives sprinkled husbands with salt as they crossed their threshold at the start of the working day, and at sea many words were taboo, including clergymen, rabbits, rats, salmon, and pigs ('pig' and 'salmon' were still words that were never spoken by trawlermen well into the twentieth century).

Writing in the journal *Folklore* in 1896, Alex McAldowie contributed his own memories of living alongside the fisher-folk as a child:

> Their superstitions were the butt of every Aberdeen schoolboy. They had a dread of having their boats counted when at sea. On several occasions we have been chased off the pier for counting the boats in the bay in a loud voice. It was also commonly supposed that they dreaded being counted individually, an idea which gave rise to the popular couplet shouted by all urchins: 'One, two, three, What a lot of fishwives I do see.' They believed that a hare's foot brought bad luck. I, like other boys, have been pursued many a time for throwing a clod of earth or some other missile into their creels and shouting, 'There is a baud's fit [hare's foot] in your creel!

A piece in *Scottish Notes and Queries* in 1910, reprinted from the *Penny Magazine* of 1840, explained that the hare's foot was feared because one day many fishermen lost their lives at sea, and a hare had been seen running through Footdee the previous evening.

McAldowie continued:

> A third popular idea was that they would not cross a line drawn across the road in front of their path, but would make a detour or climb the wall to avoid stepping

over it. I never saw the experiment made, so I cannot vouch for its truth. I know
I firmly believed it, but it had to be done right in front of an advancing column
of fishwives, and all my experimental researches into their superstitions were conducted in a safer strategical position at the rear.

In 1938 another report in *Folklore*, this time by Dr David Rorie, noted that when a
few months previously an Aberdeen trawler was lost at sea and its crew drowned, a
newly-widowed fishwife of Footdee had told a reporter that she knew disaster was
brewing because she had dreamed of being followed about by a black and white dog.

POCRA QUAY

The Footdee fishers jealously guarded their marginal, unpredictable livelihood. In
1600 they cut the mooring ropes of visiting fishing boats tied up at Pocra Quay
and set them adrift in the harbour. The Council warned one and all that anyone
caught in the act would be tied to a stake at the water's edge – just far enough out
so that the incoming tide would only reach up to their necks – and then whipped
through the streets and banished from both Footdee and Aberdeen. In a later
century the Footdee folk were still out to get the competition, throwing stones at
steam trawlers as the new-fangled vessels left Torry.

More stone-throwing took place in 1630, only this time it was seven witches
casting a spell by chucking pebbles off the quay to sink a fishing boat. There was
once a military blockhouse here, for defence of the harbour. The notorious witch
Janet Wishart was accused of meeting her master the Devil by the blockhouse
one night in 1591. (*see* INTERLUDE: WITCHCRAFT IN ABERDEEN)

Pocra Quay was where the whaling ships tied up – the boiling of their blubbery
cargoes creating an intolerable stink, as shown in a letter of complaint to the
Aberdeen Journal in 1784. In 1836 the whaler *Dee* became trapped in the Arctic
floes. After months of continual darkness and deprivation nine of the original
crew of forty-six finally reached Orkney in April 1837, their captain dead and the
first officer having lost his mind. To complete the Gothic tale, one man had his
frozen-off toe bones in his vest pocket.

The tall obelisk-like brick structure on North Pier is Scarty's Monument, named
after a harbour pilot of Victorian times. It is, however, neither a monument to him
(or anyone else) nor indeed anything to do with Scarty (other than both it and
he were fixtures in this part of the harbour for many years). The strange item is in
fact an air-vent for a now-disused sewer. The pier also hosts a sculpture consisting
of a tilted white half-sphere atop a grey sloping disc, a reference to the way ships
roll in the sea. It is inevitably known as 'the egg on a plate'.

Somewhere nearby a special gallows was erected in 1596 to hang Andrew
Brown, Robert Laird, John Jackson and Robert Breuklie or Brewster for piracy
(they had stolen a ship at Burntisland). The Accounts of the Burgh of Aberdeen

1596-97 record the expenses of the case: building the gallows cost £1 18s 4d, the hangman was paid £1 6s 8d, and the 'Council officers' supper' came in at £4. Eat, drink and be merry, for tomorrow someone else dies.

YORK STREET

In the sixteenth and seventeenth centuries Aberdeen was afflicted by many outbreaks of what was called the 'plague', although only one – the epidemic of 1539 – may have actually been the Black Death. Other outbreaks may have been typhus, paratyphoid or other virulent and deadly diseases. During the outbreaks the town was sealed off, the town gates locked, and the harbour and bridges patrolled by armed guards. In 1585 a gibbet was erected at the harbour mouth – anyone bringing in infected people by ship, or sheltering them, suffered swift execution at the end of a rope. In 1647, in the worst outbreak, over 1,700 Aberdonians died of 'plague', almost a quarter of the population. The sick were sent to live in the Lodges, encampments of temporary huts on the Links and at GALLOWHILL. Soldiers ensured the infected did not leave, while would-be escapees were hanged. Those who died of the disease were buried in mass graves on the sites. When sewer pipes were being laid in the late nineteenth century, the largest plague pit was uncovered just east of York Street.

In a bizarre echo of these earlier events, when typhoid broke out in Aberdeen in May 1964 the sufferers were sent to the City Hospital, which happened to have been built on the site of one of the 1647-era Lodges on the Links. During the scare there were 500 cases of typhoid although only one person died, and that from a condition not directly related to the outbreak. This sensibly-controlled, relatively minor epidemic was not juicy enough for some of the more frothy-mouthed areas of the European press, which hyped up the horrors to an incredible level, conjuring up a state of affairs bordering on a medieval apocalypse. Aberdeen was said to be a no-go area, all exits barred and controlled, with the dead piling up in the streets to such an extent that the bodies had to be thrown into the sea.

THE AMUSEMENT PARK

Skulls! Volcanoes! Pirates! How can you resist? The Codonas funfair between Links Road and The Esplanade has two splendid attractions side-by-side – a Haunted House ride with well-executed ghoulish signs on the exterior, and, best of all, a giant skull in the crazy golf area called Pirate Island. The course, which is disabled-accessible, also features an erupting volcano and a pirate galleon.

LINKS ROAD

Norman Adams' book *Haunted Scotland* relates the episode of George Millar, who on a summer's day in 1932 saw a phantom army on the Links. George and his

The giant skull on Pirate Island, Codonas Amusements. That's what I call crazy golf. *(Ségolène Dupuy)*

brother had been playing with their grandfather's dog and were lying on the grass when they spotted a body of armed men, some of them on horseback. The bayonets and bandoliers were clearly visible. The two boys went up to the spot – the ridge of Broad Hill, which also overlooks TRINITY CEMETERY – and searched the area, but found nothing. An old man told them he had been there for hours and would certainly have seen an army if there had been one. Phantom armies were a relatively common paranormal phenomenon in the eighteenth and nineteenth centuries, but the reports tail off after about the 1860s – for some reason, ghost armies were no longer in fashion after that date. (For examples see LANG STRACHT and KINGSWELLS.) George Millar's experience is an unusual modern example of the genre. As to what George actually did see, it is now impossible to reconstruct the exact events. Does the fact that both boys saw the same thing suggest there was some kind of visible phenomenon actually present?

THE ESPLANADE

Further north, beyond the golf course, the Esplanade passes a group of three hollowed-out stones. Sculpted by Lourdes Cue in 1984, this artwork, entitled *Windows to the Sea*, has become an impromptu shrine to commemorate loved ones. On my visit there were seven bouquets or flower-arrangements of varying vintages. Perhaps the nature of the sculpture – which combines the memorial-like permanence of stone with views out to or 'windows' on the elemental waters, and is easy to access – has encouraged this practice. It is a fascinating example of how a modern work of art can re-use or re-think in an unanticipated manner, a folkloric efflorescence of remembrance and loss in a secular age.

The Windows to the Sea sculpture on the Esplanade, which has become an impromptu shrine. *(Geoff Holder)*

CONSTITUTION STREET

One of the most famous cases of spontaneous human combustion took place here on the night of 18 February 1888. SHC, as the phenomenon is usually known, is one of the more controversial areas of what might be termed medical Forteana: a human body is consumed by fire, without the flames affecting items around it such as furniture. What makes this particular episode so intriguing is that the burned body was examined by a trained and diligent medical observer, Dr J. Mackenzie Booth, Physician to the Aberdeen General Dispensary and Lecturer on Diseases of the Ear and Larynx at the University of Aberdeen, who later wrote a detailed account of the case in the 21 April 1888 edition of the *British Medical Journal* (all emphases are my own):

> I ascended to the loft, and found the charred remains of a man reclining against the stone wall, and kept only by one of the joists and the burnt remnant of the flooring under him from falling through into the stable beneath. What struck me especially at first sight was the fact that, *not-withstanding the presence of abundant combustible material around, such as hay and wood, the main effects of combustion were limited to the corpse,* and only a small piece of the adjacent flooring and the woodwork immediately above the man's head had suffered. Several of the slates had fallen in over the corpse, making a small hole in the roof above it, and a small piece of the flooring had fallen through immediately round him into the stable below, leaving the hole through which he had been first seen. *The body was almost a cinder, yet retaining the form of the face and figure so well, that those who had known him in life could readily recognise him.*

The extent of the burning, and the fierceness of the fire, was obvious:

Both hands and the right foot had been burnt off and had fallen through the floor among the ashes into the stables below, and the charred and calcined ends of the right radius and ulna, the left humerus, and the right tibia and fibula were exposed to view. The hair and scalp were burnt off the forehead, exposing the bare and calcined skull. The tissues of the face were represented by a greasy cinder retaining the cast of the features, and the incinerated moustache still gave the wonted military expression to the old soldier. The soft tissues were almost entirely consumed, more especially on the posterior surface of the body where the clothes were destroyed, and the posterior surfaces of the femora, innominate bones, and ribs exposed to view. This was doubtless in a measure caused by the falling of the slates on the body, and a more perfect cinder would have been found had we arrived earlier on the scene. Part of the trousers on the anterior aspect of the legs that had escaped the impact of the slates was still represented in cinder.

Dr Booth arranged to have the photograph (shown below) taken of the victim, who was a sixty-five-year-old pensioner named as 'A. Al.', an ex-soldier noted for his excessive drinking. He had been seen drunk at 9 p.m., and smoke had first been noticed around twelve hours later. When the body was removed it collapsed, and so the internal organs could not be inspected. The report's conclusions are fascinating:

From the comfortably recumbent attitude of the body it was evident that there had been no death struggle, and that, obfuscated by the whisky within and the smoke without, the man had expired without suffering, the body burning away quietly all the time. So much for the condition of the corpse. *The strange fact remains that while round about in close proximity were dry woodwork and hay, loose and in bundles, these had escaped, and the body of the man was thoroughly incinerated.*

One of the few pictures in the world of a case of spontaneous human combustion. The features and legs are still recognisable. Slates have fallen onto the chest from the burned roof above. (*Fortean Picture Library.*)

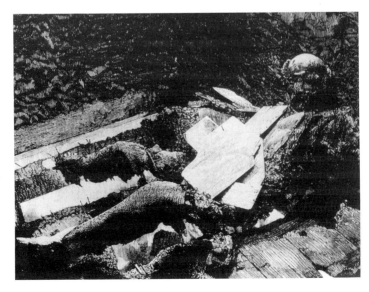

This case and others like it continue to attract controversy to this day, partly because some researchers deny SHC is possible. Intense heat is needed to consume a human body, and yet here we have a clear case where the combustible surroundings had been barely touched.

In an entirely separate case, Eileen Clark told Graeme Milne that in the early 1900s her grandmother saw the apparition of Priest Gordon – and smelled the tobacco from the pipe she could see him smoking. The figure was partly-solid, dressed in a Catholic priest's robes, and bore every resemblance to the much-beloved Gordon, who had died in 1855. The sighting was in Gordon's former home in Constitution Street, next to the school he founded.

TRINITY CEMETERY

This extensive graveyard stretches up from both sides of Park Road, and, in the western section in particular, offers several fine examples of late Victorian and Edwardian sculpture, including angels, weeping women and cherubs. One truly astonishing slab features a lady in a diaphanous garment who appears to be crawling over – or escaping from – the tombstone. Elsewhere there are several graves marked with the set-square and 'G' of the Freemasons, while atop the slope of the later twentieth-century extension to the east is the angular 1970s modernistic memorial 'In Memory of Those Who Gave Their Bodies for the Advancement of Science and Medical Knowledge.' It's hard to avoid the conclusion that the erection of this unique monument to those who have donated their bodies to science since the 1920s was in some way an atonement for the crimes of the bodysnatching era.

Above left: Trinity Cemetery. This young woman appears to be trying to escape from her tombstone. (*Ségolène Dupuy*)

Above right: A monument to those who donated their bodies to science, Trinity Cemetery. (*Geoff Holder*)

GALLOWS HILL/ERROL STREET

Aberdeen has had several official execution sites over the centuries. After the location at the north of Gallowgate was abandoned, the second Gallows Hill was established further east. Although the name appears on no modern maps, the site was on what is now the small patch of grass immediately west of Trinity Cemetery, next to the splendid baronial-Gothic gatehouse on Errol Street. Some years after the executions moved to Castle Street, Gallows Hill was used as the town's gunpowder magazine. When the building was extended, the works uncovered many skeletons, showing that the criminals had been buried where they died.

Some of the executions on this spot attracted more than the usual notoriety. On 24 November 1752 Christian Phren and William Wast were hanged on the same day for two separate crimes. Phren, a farm servant, had killed her illegitimate new-born infant and tried to hide the evidence by (unsuccessfully) burning the body. On the journey to the gallows she was forced to carry the half-charred corpse as a mark of her particular crime. At this period, women sentenced to death were usually drowned, so Phren's death by hanging was novel. But times had changed as a result of the Murder Act of 1751, which stipulated that 'some further terror and peculiar mark of infamy be added to the punishment' and forbade the simple burial of murderers – they had to be either hung in chains or given to the surgeons for dissection. 'Hanging in chains' involved taking the body down from the gibbet, coating it in tar and fitting it with a made-to-measure set of chains (and sometimes a metal cage as well). The cadaver was then displayed on the execution site until the bones finally fell apart some years later. Phren appears to have been hung in chains but this may have been merely a token display, as her body was soon taken down and put to use on the anatomists' table.

William Wast, a wife-murderer from Seaton, was also hung in chains, and the sailor's decaying corpse creaked eerily in the wind for another nine years. Norman Adams' *Scotland's Chronicles of Blood* relates a tradition among youths from Old Aberdeen, who would dare each other to visit the gibbet at night and offer a bowl of hot soup to the be-chained bones. One night a prankster hid behind the post and when his nervous friend arrived and held up the soup, called out in the sepulchrous voice of the corpse, 'It's too hot!' 'Well blow, ye bugger!' came the panicked reply, and the youth promptly ran back to the safety of a howff on the High Street, where he was no doubt ragged by his mates.

Wast's corpse became a fixture, a curiosity, and eventually ceased to scare the citizens – or at least some of them. Robert Wilson's *An Historical Account and Delineation of Aberdeen* describes how in 1763 – by which time the body was a wasted collection of bones – some 'impious wags' removed the corpse and placed it at the door of the Methodist meeting house near LODGE WALK, with a message pinned to the front: 'I, William Wast, at the point of damnation, Request the prayers of this congregation.' As part of the ongoing Aberdeen tradition of religious intolerance, the Methodists had been badly treated in earlier years; by 1763 the violence had died down, so having a murderer's bones dumped at their door was probably a relatively minor affair. Wilson notes that the young man who took the skeleton down from the gibbet hung up his father's cart in its place.

On 16 November 1753 James Miller was hanged for housebreaking, and buried at the gallows foot pending dissection. The delivering of corpses up for dissection was a source of horror among many people, as shown by the fate of Miller's body, given in James Bruce's *The Black Kalendar of Aberdeen*: 'some friendly sailors saved it from the dissecting knife, by soon after taking it up, and carrying it out with them in a yawl, and sinking it in the sea.' John Hutcheon was less lucky, being taken for dissection after being hanged for theft on 28 June 1765. The *London Magazine, or, Gentleman's Monthly Intelligencer* reported that on 17 October and 14 November 1766 respectively, Helen Watt and her son William Keith, both from Gamrie, Banffshire, were hanged for the murder of Alexander Keith, husband and father. Helen's cadaver was dissected, while William's was hung in chains. The murder had taken place some years earlier, and only came to light when mother and son fell out and each accused each the other of the crime. The last person to be executed on Gallows Hill was wife-murderer Alexander Morrison. He was also the last malefactor to be hung in chains after his death, on 6 November 1776. From this date the site of execution moved to CASTLE STREET. In 1810 Andrew Hossack was hanged outside the TOLBOOTH for theft, although he was widely believed to have also committed a double murder. His body was taken for burial to Gallows Hill, where that night it was dug up and stolen by medical students.

MOUNTHOOLY

The area bounded by Nelson Street, King Street, Mounthooly roundabout and Mounthooly Way was once the Lepers' Croft, where those unfortunates suffering from the disfiguring disease of leprosy were forced to live. Although known for millennia, leprosy became a major disease within Europe in the eleventh century. Lepers' colonies were set up outside towns, partly based on the Biblical injunction in the Book of Leviticus (13:45-46): 'Unclean, unclean … without the camp shall his habitation be.' For this reason lepers also had to cry 'Unclean! Unclean!' as they moved about, begging for alms. Giving charity to lepers was popular because it was a part of the medieval insurance policy for saving your soul. It was thought that lepers were undergoing the punishments of Purgatory here on earth, and therefore, unlike all other sinners, they would by-pass Purgatory after death and get to Heaven earlier than anyone else. So if you were benevolent to lepers in this life, they would intervene on your soul's behalf when they reached Heaven long before you did. This explains why wealthy citizens donated the land and built a chapel and infirmary on the site. Of course generosity was to an extent circumscribed: Aberdeen lepers were forbidden from washing at the commonplace wells or streams, and had to use the filthy Lepers' Myre on the Croft, and they could not leave their reservation after sundown.

The Mounthooly colony was known as the Lazar House (the name is another reference to an episode in the Bible). In the Gospel of St Luke, the parable of Lazarus and Dives tells how Lazarus was a deformed beggar sitting outside a rich man's gate. St John's Gospel then relates the more famous episode of Jesus raising a different Lazarus from dead. Although the two Lazaruses (Lazari?) are clearly separate individuals, medieval readers mixed them up, and as the deformed beggar was assumed to be suffering from leprosy, lepers became known as Lazars.

For some unknown reason the incidence of leprosy declined Europe-wide in later centuries, and by 1574 the chapel dedicated to St Anna was no longer needed and was sold off. The last leper living on the Croft died about thirty years later, the ruins of the Sickhouse remaining until the 1750s. The bodies of the lepers were probably buried on or near what is now Nelson Street. Nearby is the former John Knox Free Church (now apartments); the tiny burial ground behind it is chiefly notable for having a gravestone that is completely ordinary in every respect – except that it is made out of wood (so it should presumably be called a memorial rather than a grave*stone*).

ST PETER'S CEMETERY

This extensive and atmospheric graveyard on King Street is lined with mature trees and is home to a wide range of high quality Victorian and Edwardian funerary sculpture, including numerous angels, anchors, lamenting ladies, and two women holding up the lamp of Truth or Resurrection. Some damaged stones in the south-east section still bear the effects of shrapnel from bomb blasts in the Second World War. Two prehistoric burials were uncovered in 1855 and 1865, but the urns dug up at the time have been lost. The older part of the cemetery to the east has the outline of St Peter's Church and several eighteenth-century stones decorated with skulls, crossed bones, and other symbols of mortality. The church appears to have been founded in the twelfth century and abandoned after the Reformation. Its adjacent medieval hospital has vanished entirely, leaving only the name 'Spital' for the adjoining street and for part of the cemetery.

Right: St Peter's Cemetery. The family crest of the Moirs of Scotstown, with the mysterious severed heads of three black men. The symbol may go back to the wars against the Moors. Or it may not. *(Ségolène Dupuy)*

Far right: An angel peeking through the branches, St Peter's Cemetery. *(Ségolène Dupuy)*

Skulls, bones, and the Angel of the Resurrection on a gravestone in St Peter's Cemetery. *(Geoff Holder)*

The great wrought iron gates on King Street feature a skull and crossbones symbol with the inscription *Non Sibi Sed Cunctis*, Latin for 'not for self but for all'. The symbol is repeated on a memorial within the large mausoleum that occupies part of the site of the old church, and also sculpted in bronze above the entrance from St Peter's Gate off Spital (this entrance is often locked). This latter symbol features a shield showing the busts of three black men. Initially I thought this might have been some reference to the Slavery Abolition Act, the Act that sounded the death-knell for slavery within the British Empire, as it coincided with the year that this part of the graveyard was walled (1833). However further digging found a far different story.

In 1913 Alexander Moir of Lowell, Massachusetts traced his family history in a book entitled *Moir Genealogy and Collateral Lines*. The death's head symbol and the Latin motto are part of the coat of arms of the Moirs of Scotstown. In the late seventeenth century several Aberdeenshire families by the name of Moir had registered their coats of arms; the details varied but they all had one feature in common – three severed African heads with splashes of blood dripping out. Why were these heads on the arms? Alexander Moir was unable to discover a definitive answer. One suggestion was that it was a play on words of the kind often found in heraldry – Moir/Moor, Moors being the name of the North African Muslim armies who occupied Spain in the medieval period before being expelled by Christian forces. An alternative explanation has all the air of a legend, as set out by

Dr Nathaniel Holmes Morrison, Provost of the Peabody Institute in Baltimore, who provided the foreword to Moir's book:

> It is asserted that Kenneth Moir was one of the brave soldiers who accompanied Lord James Douglas, or 'The Good Sir James' into Spain with the heart of King Robert the Bruce, about the year 1330, and when they landed, they engaged with Alonzo XI of Spain, to fight on the Christian side against the pagan Moors. Lord Douglas was killed in attempting to rescue Sir William St. Clair of Roslyn; but in the charge, and before this happened, Kenneth Moir slew three Moors and cut off their heads, when one of the Scottish host exclaimed 'One Scottish Christian Moir can kill three pagan Moors.'

Were medieval soldiers, like movie action heroes, fond of coming out with punning quips in the heat of battle?

As with most other Aberdeen graveyards, St Peter's/Spital attracted the attentions of those who needed fresh corpses to dissect. In October 1801 Charles Jameson, the student secretary of the Aberdeen Medical Society, was convicted of stealing the body of miller James Marr from Spital. He was bound over to keep the peace, on payment of a surety of £50 provided by his father. On 23 February 1806 a body was discovered on the Society's Hall, leading to a hasty after-dark reburial at Spital. An indication of how Aberdeen professional society winked at the activities of the bodysnatchers can be found in the consequences of the discovery. The society was fined the token penalty of one guinea, which the procurator fiscal was happy to defer, but the widow of the disinterred man made such a fuss that the sum was passed to her. To keep up appearances and preserve his reputation, Dr William Livingstone, the society's first honorary president, had to evict the society from their premises, although he continued to support the resurrectionist policy in private.

SUNNYSIDE ROAD

Beside the Sunnybank bowling green stands the Firhill Well or Gibberie Wallie, whose intriguing history was summarised in the September 2009 issue of the *Auld Toon News*, the news-sheet of the Old Aberdeen Community Council. The well used to be west of College Bounds, some 40yds (37m) east of its current location. Although there is no pre-Reformation record of it being regarded as a healing well, in 1721 it cured a man called John Forbes of his gallstones, at least temporarily. Local farmers claimed it also worked for asthma, conjunctivitis and stomach pains. In 1798 a stone fountainhead was built by public subscription, and the popularity of the well in healing various ailments increased to the point that the water had to be rationed. Between 1815 and 1830 a locally notorious character named Baubie Courage sold gingerbread or 'gibberie' at the well, thus giving the alternative name Gibberie Wallie. In 1937 the structure fell victim to urban development and was relocated to its current neglected location; its healing virtues vanished.

6

SOUTH OF THE DEE

TORRY – KINCORTH – GIRDLENESS – COVE BAY

Names on a mossgrown tablet; underneath,
Death and the final mould.

From 'St. Fittick's Churchyard' by 'W.G.S.', quoted in *The Book of Saint Fittick*

TORRY

Once Torry was a tiny fishing hamlet at the mouth of the River Dee, roughly where Sinclair Road and Abbey Road are now. Part of it was lost when the Dee was re-routed as part of the harbour improvements. In the nineteenth century the centre of gravity shifted up the hill to the tenements and industries around Victoria Road. Post-war housing accelerated the transformation and in 1974 the last remnants of Old Torry were swept away, to be replaced with oil industry hardware. Only the two tall lighthouse-like Leading Lights, designed to guide ships into the harbour, indicate where the village once stood.

Like other fisher communities in the North-East, the Torry folk were noted as being insular and prone to superstition. The local minister, Revd Cruden, writing in the *Old Statistical Account* of 1793, commented:

> On the sudden deaths of their relations, or when in fear of such catastrophe from the sea becoming stormy, the fisher people, especially the females, expressed their sorrow by exclamations of voice and gestures of body like the eastern nations, and those in an early state of civilization.

Thomas White Ogilvie's *The Book of Saint Fittick* (1901) plausibly ascribes the belief systems of Torry fisherfolk to the high-risk nature of their occupation:

The sea, winter by winter, brings them face to face with danger and death, and, winter by winter, some father, or son, or brother comes back from the sea no more. So the idea of the world beyond, where there is no sea and no storm, is ever present with the fisher folks.

About 1892 a Dr Crombie learned of a case where a Torry man, on his way to his boat one morning, was greeted by another fisherman. This violated the taboo that no human contact should be engaged in before setting off, and so the man immediately abandoned the day's work. Further, he believed his boat was now bewitched, and could only be made safe if 'rechristened' with the blood of the man who had unknowingly bewitched it. Consequently the mischief-worker who had greeted him was casually invited to the house, where an 'accident' occurred and a needle pricked his thumb. The drop of blood so gathered was then taken and smeared on the boat, which removed the curse. Dr Crombie was told the story by an old Torry resident who found the whole thing hilarious, not to mention ludicrous, so presumably this was an archaic superstition for most fishers by the 1890s. Crombie's notes were published by M.M. Banks in the journal *Folklore* in 1934.

In a scholarly review of the seventeenth-century author Sir Thomas Browne in *The Aberdeen University Review*, J. Russell Lowell mentioned that in 1921 an advertisement had appeared in the *Aberdeen Journal*: 'Birth Caul for Sale. What offer? No. 1411 Journal Office.' The caul, the membrane sometimes found covering a child's head at birth, was long thought to grant good fortune to whoever owned it. Lowell quoted Browne's report that lawyers believed a caul would make them perform better in court, and speculated that a sharp Aberdeen advocate may have snapped up the charm, although it was more likely that a Torry skipper was the buyer, as cauls guarded against death by drowning. On 8 May 1848 *The Times* described a caul that had been 'afloat with its late owner thirty years in all the perils of a seaman's life, and the owner died at last at the place of his birth.' Such a boon was of course expensive, and in Victorian times a caul cost between six and sixteen guineas (very roughly £450-£1,200 at contemporary prices).

Another Torry curiosity was reported in the *Aberdeen Journal* in 1797. On 28 November twenty-year-old James Shepherd, a barber and field preacher, married Nelly Auld, aged seventy-seven. As the report noted:

The bride was three feet high, and deformed to the last degree of distortion. Though the day was very stormy and rough, so great was the public curiosity that not only the ferry-boats, but the whale-boats were employed a great part of the day carrying people across the river, to witness nuptials so extraordinary.

The reference to boats is a reminder that Torry was a world apart, reachable only by a ferry across the harbour and river from Pocra Quay at Footdee. On 5 April 1876 the overcrowded boat overturned, drowning thirty-two out of seventy-three passengers. The tragedy prompted the construction of the Victoria Bridge, which now links Market Street with the south shore of the Dee. A plaque commemorates the victims.

Craiginches Prison on Grampian Place was the site of the last execution in
Aberdeen (Henry John Burnett, hanged for murder on 15 August 1963), while
Victoria Road School has a vague story of some kind of alleged supernatural
manifestation. Between Baxter Place and North Balnagask Road stands Balnagask
motte, a tree-grown mound which may have once supported a wooden castle in
the Middle Ages but that definitely had a summerhouse in the early twentieth
century. The only Torry name to appear in medieval documents is a thirteenth-
century landowner named Cormac de Nugg (who gave his name to Nigg), but
there is no evidence to definitely link him with the site, which has never been
excavated.

Torry is the site of Aberdeen's most enduring murder mystery. On 12 December
1945 beachcomber Alexander King found a severed woman's arm on the fore-
shore. Fingerprints identified it as belonging to seventeen-year-old Betty Hadden,
a 'good-time girl' who was often seen on the town with sailors. Richard Wilson,
in *Scotland's Unsolved Mysteries of the Twentieth Century*, detailed the lengths the
police went to in an attempt to find the rest of the body and the killer. It was
thought the arm may have been thrown from a ship so weather scientists from
Aberdeen University conducted forensic tests, placing the foreleg of a pig into
the water to establish how the tides had moved the arm. In fact this showed
that the arm had not been in the water long and had been placed on the shore
from the land. Thus Torry had been the site of the disposal of the body, if not the
murder itself. More tests showed that the limb had been expertly removed with
a saw and knife. The notion was advanced that the murderer had tried to fit the
body into a trunk, and had to saw the arm off to make it fit. Twine attached to the
wrist may have been attached to a weight intended to sink the arm – the weight
slipped off and thus the arm came to light.

As to the culprit, there were two notions. The first was that Betty had been
picked up by some sailors, was injured or died during sex or rape, and the remains
disposed of. The second, and the generally more favoured idea was that the killer
was a local man. He may even still be alive, possibly continuing to live in Torry.
The preserved forearm was kept in the university's anatomy department, devel-
oping an occasional but minor notoriety, but at a later date was unceremoniously
disposed of during a clear-out. So the only item of investigative value in the case
was lost, denying any possibility of being of use in future advances in forensic science. And Betty Hadden's murder remains unsolved.

ST FITTICK'S CHURCH

By far the most interesting location in Torry is the much-abused ruin of St
Fittick's Church on St Fittick's Road. The roofless eighteenth-century husk
stands on a site that has been Christian since at least the twelfth century, although
it may go back to the Dark Ages. The church was abandoned in 1829 when the
population shifted away from this area. Unsympathetically smothered in modern

Above left: The roofless Kirk of St Fittick, with the tower blocks of Torry in the background. *(Geoff Holder)*

Above right: An eighteenth-century graveslab in St Fittick's Kirk, with skull, crossed-bones and hourglass. The second panel, presumably intended for the man's wife, is blank. *(Geoff Holder)*

harling and subject to vandalism, it is probably best visited in the morning, before the alcohol and narcotics brigade arrive. If the lock to the graveyard gate has not been smashed off, the key can be obtained from the starting box of Balnagask golf course, at the top of the road. Despite these problems, treasures lie within.

There are numerous stones carved with symbols of mortality such as skulls, hourglasses and crossed bones, as well as heraldic panels and other carvings such as a splendid sailing ship. When the whaler *Oscar* struck rocks in Greyhope Bay during April 1813 only two out of the crew of forty-four survived. Many families could not afford to take the bodies of their loved ones home so the corpses were buried in a communal grave in the churchyard. A tablestone has a now-eroded Latin inscription which translates as:

> William Milne tenant of Kincorth, slain by his enemies on 10th July, 1645, for the cause of Christ, here rests in peace from his labours, whom piety, probity, and God's Holy Covenant made happy, fell by the sword of a savage Irishman — I am turned to ashes.

A space in the north wall of the church was long thought to be a leper's squint – a gap which allowed lepers to view the Mass without entering the church – but this idea has now been dismissed, as the current building is too late for the period when it is known leprosy was common in Aberdeen. To the right of the main door is a metal link that may be the base of a chain for jougs or another punishment item such as a scold's bridle.

Above left: A carving of an eight-man fishing vessel at St Fittick's, with fish leaping to escape. *(Geoff Holder)*

Above right: An almost abstract skull-and-bones, St Fittick's. *(Geoff Holder)*

In the north-east corner of the kirkyard stands the roofless watcher's house, erected to see off the bodysnatchers for whom the proximity to Aberdeen and the dissecting tables of Marischal College made St Fittick's a tempting target. The only problem for the resurrectionists was that any stolen corpse had to be transported back via the ferry. On 22 December 1808 the funeral party accompanying the coffin of ninety-year-old Janet Spark, née Young, took the ferry from Aberdeen to Torry for the burial at St Fittick's. Unbeknownst to them, also on the ferry were two medical students, their bags filled with tools for graverobbing. The following morning the violation was discovered, as described in John Henderson's *History of the parish of Banchory-Devenick*: 'The grave was left in a most gruesome fashion – broken pieces of the lid of the coffin, tatters of grave linen, and marks of blood, being left scattered about the grave.' The night-time visitors, however, had been disturbed by the minister's dog, and, fearing pursuit at the ferry, had buried the body in the sands on the north side of Nigg Bay. Presumably they had hoped to return to reclaim their prize when the heat had died down, but a storm washed the body onto another part of the bay where it was found by the relatives. One of the careless students also left behind a spade with the name Rae carved on the handle. Mr Rae senior, whose spade it was, was obliged to pay compensation money to the family, while his feckless son wisely left the country for a few months.

It seems there was at least one other unsuccessful attempt to steal bodies from St Fittick's, although who did it and who the victims were are unknown. In 1874, decades after the bodysnatchers had ceased their depredations, harbour works near Jessie Petrie's Inn uncovered two skeletons. The inn was at the site of the ferry, north of Sinclair Road. Presumably the resurrectionists had hidden the corpses there for fear of being discovered on the ferry, and for one reason or another, they never returned. This, at least, was the tradition in the village, and no one suggested the bones might have been from an older grave on the spot. The graverobbers must have found their style cramped when in 1816 a huge mort-stone was installed in St Fittick's, courtesy of Superintendant Gibb of Aberdeen Harbour Works. The granite block, too heavy to move by hand, was placed on top of any new grave for several weeks, until the body was too decayed to be of use to the anatomists.

One of the key texts for the history of the church is Thomas White Ogilvie's *The Book of Saint Fittick*, published in 1901. Ogilvie recorded two unlikely traditions associated with the old graveyard. The first was that when the left foot of William Wallace's dismembered corpse was displayed on the Justice Port by CASTLE STREET, patriotic Aberdonians removed it from its nail at night and brought it across the river to be secretly buried in the south-east corner of St Fittick's. The second is that the cemetery was founded with soil carried from Ireland after St Patrick had banished worms and snakes from the Emerald Isle, 'since when no worm has ever been found in the holy precincts of St. Fittick.' If only the supernatural injunction equally applied to broken bottles and drug paraphernalia.

Like many saints with a single dedication, Fittick is utterly obscure. In fact he seems not to have had an independent existence, and to be a potpourri of other saints, including the little-known second-century St Fotin and the more cele-brated St Fiacre, an Irish missionary active in France in the seventh century AD. An entry in the Aberdeen kirk session records for 1630 refers to 'San Fiacker'. Fiacre is distinguished by being the patron saint of gardeners, sufferers from vene-real disease, and – through an accident of language derived from the fact that the place for carriage-hire in Paris was called the Hotel de Saint Fiacre – of French taxi-drivers. North of the church along St Fittick's Road is the abandoned South Kirkhill Farm, the garden wall of which contains an Iron Age saddle-quern found in the area during ploughing. Querns were used to grind cereal grains, but here it has become mythologised as 'St Fittick's Virtue Seat', graced by the saintly posterior. It seems to have been (incorrectly) regarded as some kind of repentance stool, while sitting in it also cured piles and, appropriately, sexually transmitted diseases. I suggest it would be unwise to depend on this alleged function.

Looking at the area today it is a little difficult to imagine that this was once a landscape of sanctity, filled with shrines and other religious sites – the *genius loci* has definitely undergone a transformation. Like all good saints, Fittick had a holy well named after him. Ogilvie relates the legend that the (fictional) saint, *en route* to converting the Picts in 650 AD, was shipwrecked off Girdleness. At the spot where the holy man's hand first touched dry land, the spring bubbled into exist-ence to quench his thirst. The well was 500yds (457m) south of the church, but was lost to sea erosion in the early 1900s.

There is no record of the veneration of the well during the Middle Ages, but it must have been special because following the Reformation and the official ban on visiting holy wells, the local people continued to defy both Church and Council and make pilgrimages to the well for magical cures. Not surprisingly this defi-ance produced a reaction by the authorities, who, judging by the records, seem to have taken about thirty years to fully suppress visits to the holy well. In 1603 the Aberdeen Kirk Session authorised three of its members to wait at the ferry-boat, taking the names of those making the journey on a Sunday so they could be punished at the next session. On 1 June 1606 four men were fined 4*d* each for visiting the well on Sunday. These were relatively minor fines, and presumably had little impact, because in 1616 we find the Town Council setting out a more draconian decree, establishing fines of 40*s* for people of substance and 20*s* for servants. In addition, heads of households were to be answerable for their wives, children and servants, which meant they would have to pay any fines incurred by these dependents. Interestingly the decree expressly forbids visiting the well in the night-time. This may mean that people travelled or camped through the night so that at dawn they could drink 'the cream of the well,' believed to be the most potent and health-giving draught.

Perhaps the threat of substantial fines quietened things down, because we hear of no more punishments until 1630, when Margaret Davidson was fined a hefty £5 for sending a nurse to the well to wash her sick child. An unspecified offering was left at the well. After Margaret and her nurse repented in front of the Session, St Fittick's Well vanishes from the records, so presumably there were no more transgressions.

The sanctity of the well continued to hold strong in popular belief, however, and up to the early 1800s people were still leaving rags, nails and pins at the well, all as offerings in exchange for health. The supernatural power providing the cure, how-ever, was no longer St Fittick – now it was the fairies. Around 1900 Ogilvie spoke to a woman in her late nineties who remembered a mother called Jessie taking her sick child to be washed in the well on a moonlit night. She left two loaves of bread for the fairies, and the child got better and, at the time of the story, was a mother in Torry herself. The old lady also claimed to be the last woman in Torry to have cured a child using 'unspoken water'. The infant was wasting away and the mother was convinced it was a fairy changeling or had been otherwise cursed by the fairies. Ogilvie's informant said she had collected water from the Struak burn in Torry and placed a shilling in the pail – if the coin turned heads up the problem was 'in the bairn's head', whereas if it showed tails it was the body that was sick. She then washed the child and it got better – but only because whilst going to and from the burn the woman had not said a word, despite meeting several people she knew. It was this 'unspoken' aspect of the water that had provided the cure.

This episode with the unspoken water may have been in the 1830s or '40s. The old woman then told Ogilvie of 'three times roon the crook,' a practice that probably dated from two or three decades earlier. If someone was sick the women of the house would take three round stones from the Bay of Nigg and heat them in a fire. One represented the head, the second the heart and the third the body. Whichever one cracked first indicated the source of the problem. The invalid was then carried three times round the 'crook' or angle of the chimney with the sick part – as diagnosed by the fire-cracked stone – held next to the crook. Perhaps sensing Ogilvie's scepticism, the old woman finished with an appropriate com-ment on the efficacy of the procedure: 'Sometimes they got better an' sometimes they didna, jist the same as wi' the doctors noo-a-days.'

A couple of hundred paces south from where St Fittick's Road joins the coastal road is a small, little-noticed stream, Tullos Burn. The tiny Bridge of Nigg once stood where the road crosses the burn. Funeral parties bringing coffins on their shoulders from Cove Bay to St Fittick's would pause here and doff their hats at nothing in particular, simply because it was the custom. The origin of the action was that once upon a time a statue of the Virgin Mary stood here. The shrine was removed along with the Catholic religion, but Presbyterian mourners continued the tradition of removing their hats at the bridge even though the original meaning of the act was lost to memory. Doubtless many Protestant participants in the custom would have been offended to learn it was the echo of a mark of respect to what they would have seen as 'Popish superstition'. Leading from the bridge to the church the path passed the vaulted cover and worn stone steps of the Lady Well, but this too has vanished.

GIRDLENESS

Greyhope Road leaves the north-east of Torry to circle the peninsula, providing views of Footdee and the harbour and passing several pieces of maritime architecture, from jetties and capstans to breakwaters and Girdleness lighthouse. Somewhere near here the very first meetings of the Aberdeen Freemasons were held, probably in the sixteenth century; at the time the society was forbidden from meeting in houses 'where there is people living', hence the choice of this isolated spot (although secrecy may have had something to do with it as well).

Next to the car park is Torry Point Battery, a large gun emplacement built in 1861 to protect Aberdeen harbour. Over the decades the scale of the armaments here expanded or shrank depending on the war footing of the country (and the economy). The site's most expansive phase was in the Second World War. Rather bizarrely the bunkers and blockhouses became temporary accommodation for families during the housing crises of the inter-war years and the later 1940s. Like many ex-military sites this large structure, with its massive walls surrounding an extensive courtyard and numerous abandoned gun platforms, has a particular atmosphere. The exterior is bounded by several rectangular stones marked 'WD' (for War Department).

Opposite the lighthouse a pair of large access-blocking boulders have been painted with cheerful faces. Below the foghorn is the penstock and valve house, part of the Girdleness Outfall sewage scheme. A bronze plaque above the door has two Tritons (Neptune's marine assistants) holding up a sign marked 'City of Aberdeen, Main Drainage Works'.

One of the boundary markers of Torry Battery. 'WD' stands for War Department. *(Geoff Holder)*

The stony gaze: a pair of smiling faces at Girdleness foghorn. *(Geoff Holder)*

TULLOS HILL

Here lies a major Bronze Age cemetery, with three large cairns prominently situated on the crest of the hill, possibly sited here for reasons of territory and display as much to commemorate the dead – 'these are our ancestors, and they guard over our land as far as the eye can see'. Much of the hill has been used for landfill; a recent scheme has improved the interpretation and access to the monuments (a new path leads up from the car park next to Doonies Model Farm). The first (most north-eastern) pile of stones is Crab's Cairn (NJ96320376), damaged by the concrete base of a Second World War installation. Thomas White Ogilvie, writing in *The Book of Saint Fittick* in 1901, states the mound was used for a fire beacon to warn of the approach of enemy ships, and the foundations of the watchman's house could be seen nearby. A cist grave and a beaker were found here in the late eighteenth century. About 600 paces west, on the summit of the hill, is the massive Baron's Cairn (NJ95760369), surmounted by an Ordnance Survey triangulation pillar. Another 800 paces or so west along the ridge beings you to Cat Cairn (NJ95190317); these three mounds are intervisible from each other, while a fourth structure, Tullos Cairn (NJ95900410), is out of sight down the slope north-east from Baron's Cairn.

The hill also holds more recent archaeology, from nineteenth-century consumption dykes used to 'consume' the huge number of stones taken out of the land during agricultural improvements, to a Second World War prisoner of war camp and anti-aircraft battery. Ogilvie mentions a 'curious mound known as the Elf Hillock' and a small bridge to the west called The Fairies' Briggie, but I have been unable to identify these features; they may well have disappeared beneath the landfill. Ogilvie also dug up some of the local folklore: the River Dee, so the tradition went, once flowed through the Vale of Tullos; it will again in the future; and, rather strangely, long, long ago, a Dutchman offered to lead the Dee down this way. Why, we are not told.

KINCORTH

Abbotswell Drive in the housing estate is a remembrance of the farm of Abbotswalls, itself apparently named after a chapel and burial ground that existed until the seventeenth century. The name referred to the ownership of the chapel by an abbey elsewhere: there was no monastery here, although there may have been a 'hospital' (a lodging-house for travellers). This vague monastic connection may have influenced the description of a monk-like figure reported near a Kincorth bus stop in 1970. However, given that the apparition was seen at 5.45 a.m. on New Year's Day, and was said to be cloaked, hooded *and masked*, this perhaps suggests it was a reveller returning from a Hogmanay costume party.

Kincorth Hill Nature Reserve to the south of the estate has a small number of archaeological remains, including a large (possibly modern) cairn topped by a disused Ordnance Survey triangulation pillar (NJ94010261), a smaller cairn and prehistoric hut-circle to the south-west (NJ93420219) and a large eighteenth- or nineteenth-century consumption dyke further east (NJ936022).

COVE BAY

The Cove Bay, Altens and Kincorth area seems to be a hot-bed of UFO sightings, possibly because, in contrast to the sometimes cramped skyscapes within the city streets, here there are open spaces and extensive sea views. Ron Halliday's *UFO Scotland* records a sighting from December 1957 when Mrs J. Esslemont and her husband saw from their car a 'streak of light moving slowly across the sky with a very bright light at the centre'. The trajectory was from the sea, crossing the coast and heading inland, and the light was clearly seen in the darkening sky of 3.30 in the afternoon. Several other witnesses spotted something, including Jim Thomson, the owner of the Cove village shop, who described it as 'something like fire,' while Howard Smith's remembrance was that it was an orange pyramidal object with fire at the point and 'a ball shape at the end.' Three days later a pair of Stonehaven police officers driving into Aberdeen after dark saw a large light above and just in front of them. It appeared not to be an aircraft. More lights were seen in December 2002 and January 2003, while in 2006 the website www.ufocasebook.com reported an experience related by Neil Prosser. At 20.45 on 17 November he saw a flare fired out to sea from Girdleness, followed by some kind of flashing light. He thought it might be a ship in distress so phoned the coastguard who told him they had received several similar reports. Then looking to the south-west both Neil and his partner saw a stationary 'copper coloured star' which then changed colour to white. He drove south keeping it in view but lost it before reaching Cove.

7

THE SOUTHERN SUBURBS
AND DEESIDE

FERRYHILL – BRIDGE OF DEE –
GARTHDEE – PETERCULTER

Study their monuments, their gravestones, their epitaphs, on the spots where they
lie: study, if possible, the scenes of the events, their aspect, their architecture, their
geography; the tradition which has survived the history; the legend which has
survived the tradition; the mountain, the stream, the shapeless stone, which has survived even history and tradition and legend.

Dean Stanley, *History of the Eastern Church* (1861)

FERRYHILL ROAD

There's nothing like a big, strange hole to attract attention – and strange tales. The
Round O was indeed a big, strange hole, and attracted attention as far back as
1611, with eighteenth-century mentions describing it as 'A Circular Quagmire'. It
may have been a glacial kettlehole, although a Mr P.J. Anderson, writing in *Scottish
Notes and Queries* in September 1905, made the assertion that it was a gravel-pit.
Anderson wrote that in 1830 it was firmly believed that the hole opened up to
swallow a house with two men who had been playing cards on a Sunday. The
'Sunday gambling' motif is a common one in moralising Scottish folk-tales – usu-
ally one of the card-players is revealed to be the Devil himself, although in the
Ferryhill it is not His Satanic Majesty who conducts the wicked poker players to
Hell, but the Earth itself. The Round O was filled in and built over in 1990.

FONTHILL ROAD

This street name commemorates Fonthill Abbey in Somerset, the most grandiose, ridiculous and insane architectural conceit in British history. In 1822 John
Farquhar, a retired Aberdeenshire brewer and gunpowder merchant, had bought

Fonthill Abbey (which was never a religious building) from its builder, the mightily eccentric William Beckford. (For more on Beckford, see the author's *The Guide to Mysterious Arran*.)

WELLINGTON SUSPENSION BRIDGE

One of the parapet stones on the north-east entrance to the 1886 pedestrian bridge is incised with a cross. I have no idea why.

DUTHIE PARK

This is a happy hunting ground for anyone seeking curios, sculptures and general oddities. The park itself sports a fountain supported by some rather sinister-looking swans; a statue of Hygeia, the Greek goddess of health, on a column guarded by four lions; and a totem pole carved with seagulls, fish, modern technology and flowers, topped by a majestic big cat (presumably a leopard); the feline backside is decorated with a burning oil or gas vent. Outside the Winter Gardens the Alexander Taylor Fountain has a lioness' head as a spout and a pair of wonderfully expressive male and female heads.

The Winter Gardens themselves are the main attraction, with all sorts of architectural bric-a-brac scattered round the glasshouses of tropical and desert plants. Here you can find:

Above left: The Wellington Suspension Bridge. On the far right is the mysterious carved cross. *(Geoff Holder)*

Above right: One of the expressive heads on the Alexander Taylor Fountain, Duthie Park. *(Geoff Holder)*

Above left: McPuddock the Frog rises from the depths at Duthie Park Winter Gardens. *(Geoff Holder)*

Above right: The water monster that stalks the dank tropical swamps of the Winter Gardens. *(Geoff Holder)*

- A gaily-coloured Aberdeen coat of arms with a pair of wonderfully agile leopards
- A water-spouting gargoyle brought from VICTORIA PARK
- Two sections of extraordinary semi-circular stained glass rescued from a building at the beach. One shows a barrel-chested trident-bearing Neptune with seahorse legs and a fish-tail encompassing all sorts of sealife, while the other has Venus water-skiing in her scallop shell, drawn by two fish
- Wooden sculptures of two drunken revellers, and a mournful lion with a bandaged paw
- The railing of Kelly's Cats brought from the south side of UNION BRIDGE, along with the accompanying bronze panel showing Commerce surrounded by allegorical figures representing Agriculture, the Sea, Shipbuilding, Engineering, Navigation and Railways
- A square-pillar multi-face sundial from 1707 carved with an apothecary's mortar and pestle
- 'Peace', a female figure holding a lamp, superbly sculpted from granite
- A nineteenth-century cheese-press

The best sight, however – and worth coming a long way to see – is McPuddock the Frog. This giant green-and-yellow amphibian lurks in the carp-pond, where, at the behest of a hydraulic system, he submerges and emerges at regular intervals. Watching McPuddock bubble up from the bottom is a delightfully daft experience. McPuddock has two companions, although these are static: one is another frog, while the other resembles a combination of a conger eel and the Loch Ness

Monster, painted green with yellow-and-black spots. Given its setting amidst tropical vegetation, I surmise this creature is meant to be the *mkole-mbembe*, the legendary (and possibly real?) dinosaur-like beast rumoured to live in the swamps of West Africa. Finding a tribute in Aberdeen to one of the key cryptozoological mysteries, and an African one at that, is a real treat.

ALLENVALE CEMETERY

This vast cemetery is the best place in Aberdeen to study the late Victorian and Edwardian way of death and commemoration. Bounded by the Great Southern Road, Riverside Drive and Allenvale Road, and with superb views over the Dee, this is a wonderful place to just potter around and marvel at the monuments put up by the more affluent members of society. There are entire squadrons of angels in various poses; lamenting ladies so lifelike that in poor light they can be mistaken for living mourners; doves, eagles, anchors, sheaves of wheat, winged souls, crowns and musical instruments; eternal flames and the Greek letters Alpha and Omega, the Beginning and the End; a three-masted sailing ship; bronze portraits of the deceased; and Masonic symbols (lots of these). One slab bears a quote from John Donne: 'one short sleep past, we wake eternally and death shall be no more'. Another is carved with the Magi adoring the Holy Child in the stable at Bethlehem, a highly unusual subject for a gravestone; not surprisingly it commemorates, in part, a very young child. Two modern stones strike the eye: one is inscribed 'resting in God's waiting room' while a second bears a *Braveheart*-type sword and the word 'Freedom'.

A corner of Allanvale Cemetery which includes carvings of an angel and a lamenting lady. *(Geoff Holder)*

One of the many magnificent sculptures of angels in Allanvale Cemetery. *(Geoff Holder)*

Above left: A gravestone symbol in Allanvale Cemetery. The shape in the square is the 47th Problem of Euclid, a mathematical proposition of great significance to Freemasons. *(Geoff Holder)*

Above right: The Magi adoring the Holy Child at Bethlehem, a very unusual subject for a gravestone. One of those commemorated on the stone is a very young child. Allanvale Cemetery. *(Geoff Holder)*

RUTHRIESTON AND BRIDGE OF DEE

If the River Dee gave Aberdeen its harbour and communications by sea, the bridge over the Dee connected the town with the rest of Scotland (although people stuck in the bridge's notorious traffic jams may not appreciate this bounty). There may have been a wooden bridge as early as 1384 but it certainly did not last long and the seven-arched stone-built structure, one of the wonders of the age, finally spanned the Dee in 1527. Apart from some widening, the traffic-clogged bridge of today is essentially the same as that built nearly 600 years ago. Let's hear it for the skills of medieval engineers.

The medieval, pre-Reformation origin of the Bridge of Dee – and its funding by a bishop of the Catholic Church – explains its association with two alleged miracles. In May 1636, almost a century after the Reformation, an Aberdonian monk in Brussels, Brother Alexander Kennedy, penned a document in which he swore to 'bear witness and take my oath that I heard from my ancestors the following facts'. According to Kennedy, Bishop Gavin Dunbar of ST MACHAR'S CATHEDRAL was in the habit of praying daily to the Virgin Mary. Then, one day:

> The statue of the Blessed Mary the Virgin, called Of Good Success … gave *audible indications* to the Most Reverend Father … whilst he was praying concerning the spot where he should lay the foundations of the bridge over the rapid river Dee, and pointed out to him on both sides the points between which he afterwards built the magnificent bridge of seven arches that to this day is to be seen.

The manuscript was quoted in the *Aberdeen Journal* for 18 August 1887, although I have taken it from *A History of the Parish of Banchory-Devenick*, written by John Henderson in 1890. Kennedy's tale that the statue of the Virgin spoke to Bishop Dunbar, acting as a engineering consultant on a major construction project, was dismissed by most authorities as Catholic propaganda, designed to boost the status of the statue of Our Lady of Good Success, which was by then working miracles from its new home in Brussels, Kennedy's base.

Dunbar certainly did build a chapel dedicated to Mary at the western end of the bridge for the benefit of travellers, and he did install within it a statue of the Virgin. This statue may or may not have been the one from the cathedral that allegedly spoke to him, the image variously known as Our Lady of Aberdeen, Good Success or Bon Accord. In 1904 a Catholic writer named William Walsh published *The Apparitions and Shrines of Heaven's Bright Queen, in Legend, Poetry and History*, a catalogue of visions and miracles associated with the Blessed Virgin Mary. In it he made the following claim:

> Not far from this chapel, near the end of the bridge, sprang up a little fountain of limpid water, and many miracles are recorded to have been wrought by its use through the intercession of Our Lady. One day a heretic, to show his hatred for the Mother of God, threw a quantity of filth into the well. But God's vengeance soon overtook him. On the spot he was seized with a terrible malady; a hunger

which nothing could satiate seemed to consume his bowels, and he cried out: 'I am stricken by God for what I have done!' And he warned all who saw and heard him never to speak against, or in any way dishonour, the Holy Virgin, lest a similar evil should overtake them. The heretics themselves [i.e. the Protestants], who were witnesses of the crime and of the awful punishment which followed, were forced to acknowledge that it came from the hand of God.

The chapel was ransacked at the Reformation, and now even its exact former location is uncertain. The confused story – or legend, or propaganda – of how the statue eventually made it to Brussels is told in the section on the ST MARY'S CATHEDRAL on Huntly Street in Chapter 4; the cathedral holds a replica of the statue.

The bridge was a boon to trade and communication; it also meant access to the city was now much easier for less welcome visitors, such as those infected with plague. The bridge was guarded during the 'visitations' of pestilence in 1529, 1538 and 1545. In 1566 drowsy watchmen who let their attention slip were fined 40s; failure to pay meant being nailed up by the ear and forced to wear the branks. Further epidemics prompted greater deterrents, such as the construction of a temporary wooden port or locked gate and the erection of a gibbet at the Ruthrieston crossroads in 1585. Anyone entering who was infected, or those who gave them hospitality, were strung up or, if they were women, drowned. (The gallows were still there in 1748, when they were used to despatch housebreaker James Davidson.) Despite these precautions, in 1647 a woman from Brechin somehow sneaked past the guards and settled somewhere around Broomhill Road. She died three days later and the subsequent 'visitation' of the plague killed some 1,760 people out of a population of 8,000.

In June 1639 a Covenanting army commanded by the Marquis of Montrose attacked Aberdeen from the south. The Royalist forces barricaded the bridge at the eastern end and held out for two days before being overrun, the action involving some fierce exchanges of artillery. Five defenders were killed, Montrose losing two men. Five years later Montrose was back for another victory at the BATTLE OF JUSTICE MILLS, although by that time he had switched sides and was now fighting for the Royalists against the Covenanters.

The bridge bottleneck also caused some problems for a party of bodysnatchers in the early 1800s. 'Long Ned' and his fellow medical students had lifted a body from Banchory-Devenick church on the south bank of the Dee but the frozen soil had slowed them down so much they had attracted unwelcome attention. Pursued by local people the party fled towards the city, only to be stopped at the bridge by the townsfolk. Long Ned tried to drop the sack into an ice hole in the river but failed and the body was recovered.

The green space down by the river on the west bank contains a minor curiosity, the seventeenth-century Ruthrieston Pack Bridge that once spanned the Pot Burn but now has little purpose, having been relocated 35yds (32m) to the east in 1923. Its heraldic panels are heavily eroded, and in its stranded location it seems a tad forlorn.

KAIMHILL

The city's first crematorium was built off Broomhill Road in the 1930s, but has long been superseded. In 1944 James Dewar, the managing director of the crematorium, was found guilty of stealing coffins lids and coffins. Effectively, he and his co-accused, an undertaker from Woodside, were not burning the coffins but collecting and re-selling the wood. Typically a body was either burned without a coffin or tipped into a second coffin so two bodies were burned together. It wasn't quite bodysnatching but the case provoked such strong reactions locally that it was tried in Edinburgh, while numerous sick jokes and songs made the rounds in Aberdeen.

GARTHDEE

'Granite City in a spin over "flying saucers"' claimed the *Press & Journal* on 2 August 2006. A couple in Gaitside Drive had reported six orange lights hovering in the sky before 'disintegrating'. The lights were 'said to resemble balloons more than saucers.' From the description it is obvious what they had seen were what are called Chinese or Thai fire lanterns. The fragile paper lanterns are given lift from the temporary burning of their limited fuel, which also creates the characteristic orange glow. Fire lanterns are very popular at parties, weddings and festivals. And on UFO websites.

The Baron of Pitfodels, an alleged wizard, had a cat as a familiar. One night he beat the animal, which promptly left. Some months later the Laird was riding home at night along the old highway that ran through the marsh called the Clash. He never made it home. The following morning his mangled body was found floating in a peat-hag on the Clash. And in subsequent years the bloody-mouthed apparition of the 'Clash Cat' was seen in what is now Auchinyell Road.

That, at least, is the story told by Fenton Wyness in *Royal Valley: The story of the Aberdeenshire Dee.* John Henderson's *History of the Parish of Banchory-Devenick* has a slightly different version of the tradition, in which the laird, who is not a wizard, is simply surprised to see his favourite cat scampering through the bogs of the Clash. Back at home in Pitfodels the cat jumped up his table, and, as cat-owners often do, the Laird spoke to it, asking it why it had been in the marsh. Somewhat unexpectedly the cat answered in a human voice: 'Whare ye saw me ance ye sail see me na mair' – and promptly clawed its master to death.

PITFODELS

On 29 September 1983 taxi driver George Murdoch was murdered in Pitfodels Station Road. Despite descriptions from eye-witnesses and an intense police investigation, the killer was never caught. In 2000 Dr Peter McCue, a consultant clinical psychologist in Glasgow and member of the Scottish Society for Psychical Research, received a letter from an Aberdeen man in his sixties who claimed he had had precognitive knowledge of the murder before it took place. McCue described what then happened in the September 2001 issue of *The PSI Report*, the SSPR's newsletter, and Norman Adams wrote up the case in *Blood and Granite: True Crime from Aberdeen.*

Brian Parry (not his real name) said he had switched on his car radio one morning in 1983 and heard the details of the murder on the news. He mentioned it to two work colleagues but they hadn't heard the story, and, even more strangely, there was nothing in the newspapers. Five weeks from the day Parry woke up when the radio was on, to hear the real report of the murder. McCue wrote to the former colleagues to check on the story. Only one replied but he couldn't recall if Parry had discussed the murder before or after 29 September. Parry's wife however stated he had definitely told her about the murder before it actually happened. Six months after sending the letter to McCue, Parry was visited by two detectives who handed him Murdoch's cloth cap and pen, in the hope that he would be able to psychometrise the items (psychometry is the technique used by some 'sensitives' to obtain impressions from an object). Parry picked nothing up, but he did tell the police they would not get the killer.

John Henderson's 1890 book *History of the Parish of Banchory-Devenick* mentions an isolated grave beside Daveny's Meels, somewhere not far from the old Castle of Pitfodels, which is now the Norwood Hall Hotel. The tradition is that a local man 'used to endeavour to make a lie pass current by praying that he might be buried out of sight of kirk or kirkyard if his tale was untrue'. Somewhat inevitably, when the funeral party were carrying his coffin through the countryside to the churchyard, it suddenly became so heavy the mourners found they could take it no further. They were forced to bury it at the remote spot where it had been dropped, and so the man's oft-repeated prayer was fulfilled.

CULTS

Henderson also mentions three large stone cairns north of Cults Avenue; two contained stone-lined cists with skeletal remains. The legend was that they marked the graves of the dead slain in a battle between the Scots and Picts. It is much more likely that they were prehistoric burials, but Henderson says that when one was removed for building stones, arrowheads and a sword were found, the latter being of 'quite modern manufacture'. Perhaps the prehistoric cairns were re-used for a secondary burial in the Dark Ages? Sadly we will never know, as the sword, skeletons and stones are all long lost, and the exact site of the cairns is now unknown. Also vanished is a stone circle at NJ89470351. *The Ordnance Survey Name Book* for 1865 simply noted: 'The stones of this circle have been removed and nothing remains.'

BIELDSIDE

More prehistoric heritage has been lost here. The site of a cairn where bones were found within a stone-lined cist in 1815 is now occupied by the primary school, while a second cairn further east has also gone. One survivor can be found in the residential area north of Cairn Road, a mound of loose boulders around 13ft (4m) in height.

During the days of the bodysnatchers, a minister found an abandoned body in a sack in the outhouse of the manse, while a second body came to light in a flour sack in the bakery. The culprit was probably the medical student son of the baker; the discovery ruined his father's business.

MILLTIMBER

A skull, some bones and a prehistoric beaker were dug up in 1899 south of what is now the Old Deeside Line Walk. The beaker is now in Marischal Museum. The Binghill stone circle to the east of Contlaw Road is badly damaged, but its setting in beech woodland is so attractive it is worth a visit (NJ85520237). Eight stones remain, three of them upright, including the recumbent stone. This was the focus of the circle, a large horizontal block flanked by two upright pillars, all oriented to the south-west. Recumbent stone circles are a speciality of the north-east of Scotland: for descriptions of the dozens scattered throughout the area, see the author's *The Guide to Mysterious Aberdeenshire*. A ring cairn can just be made out within

The recumbent stone circle at Binghill in Milltimber. *(Geoff Holder)*

the circle. The wood contains three further cairns, two of them barely noticeable unless you are really looking for them. The most obvious, a substantial pile of boulders south-east of the stone circle, may be the one described in John Henderson's *Annals of Lower Deeside* as the traditional burial place of the Irvine family in medieval times. On the other hand, the descriptions of the three cairns have been so confused over the years that the Irvine sepulchre may be one of the almost eradicated cairns. And on the other other hand, the tradition of relatively recent burial may be entirely spurious, and the trio of cairns are entirely prehistoric.

Binghill may be the 'Binhill' where Andro Man said the Queen of Elfland and a host of other supernatural spirits held regular conventions – see INTERLUDE: WITCHCRAFT IN ABERDEEN for the full details.

PETERCULTER

With its delightful riverside location, collection of carved eighteenth-century gravestones, and anti-bodysnatching watchhouse, the former St Peter's Church on Station Road South makes for a fine visit. There was a church here from the twelfth century, although the current building dates from 1779 and was substantially reno-vated by the Victorians. Wandering around the gravestones turns up fine examples of *memento mori* – carved skulls, hourglasses, crossed bones, gravedigger's tools and winged souls – as well as heraldic panels. St Peter's Well, possibly a holy well, used to flow to the east but it was destroyed by the construction of a sewer in 1962. The small watchhouse is a reminder that the graveyard was vulnerable to attack by bodysnatchers, who would arrive by road or river. A large unshaped stone south of the church may have been a mortstone, placed over graves to hinder access. Norman Adams' *Scottish Bodysnatchers* book states that, fifty years after the passing of the Anatomy Act of 1832, a group of medical students decided to emulate their forebears and, for a dare, rowed from Aberdeen and stole a body from St Peter's.

The church, along with the adjacent corrugated-iron hall, is now St Peter's Heritage Centre (typically open early March to early December, Wednesday, Saturday and Sunday, 2-4 p.m., modest admission charge). Within are mementos of the Culter Paper Mill, a fairground organ, a 1904 motorcycle – and Rob Roy MacGregor. This gaily painted figure stood above the Culter Burn from 1926 to 1991, the third statue to do so. Its contemporary replacement can be seen in its floodlit glory from the A93 bridge over the burn, at the west end of the village.

The first 'Rob Roy' was a ship's figurehead in the form of a Highlander, set up around 1850. Being a figurehead it obviously lacked legs, so it was supported on two upright logs, aided by impromptu boots and a kilt. There is no direct evidence that Rob Roy – outlaw, cattle thief, Jacobite rebel, and, thanks to Sir Walter Scott, famous folk hero – was ever in the area. The tradition however is that he came to Aberdeen on a Jacobite recruitment drive amongst his kinsfolk, and, finding the burn in spate, leapt it with ease (folk heroes have a tendency to perform mighty leaps across ravines). Once the wooden figure was erected it was linked with Rob's leap, and the 'Highlander' became 'Rob Roy'. Soon the figure became a tourist attraction and when it decayed in 1865 a better quality replace-ment was commissioned. This lasted until 1926, even weathering military target practice before the First World War. The next model (the one in the Heritage Centre) served until 1991, to be replaced by the current incarnation.

The *Statistical Account* of 1791-1799 mentions a rampart called the guard-dike further west along the Culter Burn near its junction with the Gormack Burn by the weir at Newmill, where it overlooked the main road to and from north Deeside. The tradition was that this was where armed guards were stationed during the time of plague, preventing the passage of anyone who might be infected. Another local legend was recorded by John Henderson in *Annals of Lower Deeside*. North along the Culter Burn was a deep hole known as the Linn Pot, wherein a great treasure was hidden. The tenant of North Linn Farm dammed the river above the Pot so the hole would empty, but was interrupted by a cry that his farm was in flames. He rushed back home to discover there was no fire, and on returning to the river discovered the dam had been mysteriously removed. He therefore wisely abandoned his search for the

A figure of Rob Roy stands ready to leap over Culter Burn, Peterculter. *(Geoff Holder)*

Culter Treasure. This motif – the search for hidden treasure, the warning of a fictitious fire, and the discovery that the treasure-seekers' workings have been covertly destroyed by the fairies, or some other supernatural force – is one of the most widespread in Scottish folk literature; there is probably not a single county that does not have some version of it.

Opposite Rob Roy, on the south side of the A93, a path leads uphill to the square castellated war memorial, designed in imitation of Belskavie Tower to the south-west. This lonely structure (NJ822002) is reputed to be a watch-tower for Drum Castle further west. On the other hand, it could just be a nineteenth-century folly. To the south, west of Oldtown, are the scant remains of a temporary Roman marching camp (NO830994). The most obvious structure is the rampart and ditch running along the north edge of the wood. Some time in the nineteenth century a hoard of silver Roman coins was found nearby. At one point the camp was clearly believed to be a medieval work, as it is called Normandykes, the adjacent fields are the Norman Faughs, and the well at Oldtown is Norman's Well. John Henderson adds that a hollow close by was still called the Bloody Stripe in the 1890s, and was thought to be the site of a deadly battle.

8

THE WEST END

HOLBURN STREET – QUEEN'S ROAD –
RUBISLAW – HAZLEHEAD

UFO crash lands in Aberdeen!

Headline in the *Evening Express*, 14 August 2009

HOLBURN STREET

From the outside the dull slab of 1960s concrete on the corner with Great
Western Road appears singularly uninviting, although passing it at dark when the
lights are on reveals an intriguing set of very out-of-place stained-glass windows.
Within, however, it is a different story. For this is Trinity Hall, the headquarters
of the Seven Incorporated Trades of Aberdeen, a crafts guild organisation with
roots stretching back to early medieval Aberdeen. The first Trinity Hall of 1633
occupied the shell of the former Trinitarian Monastery between Guild Street
and THE GREEN. The second was on UNION BRIDGE, where the Victorian hall still
survives, empty and unused; the Trades moved out to Holburn Street in the 1960s.
And with each move they brought their treasures with them: magnificent six-
teenth- and seventeenth-century carved chairs, paintings, plaques, mementos
and banners, all of which – along with much wonderful Victorian stained glass
– adorns the ornate interior.

Trinity Hall is not normally open to the public except on special occasions
such as Doors Open Day. The history of the Seven Trades has been extensively
covered in works such as *Inscriptions from the Shields or Panels of the Incorporated
Trades in The Trinity Hall, Aberdeen* (Andrew Jervise, 1863) and *Merchant and Craft
Guilds: A History of the Aberdeen Incorporated Trades* (Ebenezer Bain, 1887), while
a more portable digest can be found in a booklet published by the Aberdeen
Town & County History Society, *A Brief History of The Seven Incorporated Trades of
Aberdeen* (Lys Wyness, 2009). For our purposes, there are several items of particular
interest.

Above left: The elaborately-carved chair belonging to the Weavers' Incorporation, Trinity Hall. Note the crowned angel, the pair of mermaids, and lions (or bears) with shuttles in their jaws. *(Ségolène Dupuy)*

Above right: Another amazing chair at Trinity Hall. *(Ségolène Dupuy)*

Each of the Seven Trades (Hammermen, Bakers, Wrights and Coopers, Tailors, Shoemakers, Weavers, and Fleshers) has its own insignia, and these appear frequently on the woodwork, paintings and stained glass. The Weavers' emblems include three lions (or bears) with shuttles in their fanged jaws, plus a winged angel-like being and a pair of topless mermaids. Elsewhere can be found grotesque human and animal faces, Wildmen, Green Men, smiling Suns, Adam and Eve, the heads of birds and monstrous creatures, and, on the corners of a frame, burnished rams' heads. A contemporary reference links to the Fleshers' painting of their crest. The painting contains a long poem giving the mythological history of the craft of the Fleshers (i.e. the butchers), placing its origins in Old Testament times:

> From ancient times, our origin we draw,
> When priests were cons'crate to keep God's law,
> When sacredotal sacrifice and feasts,
> Made altars smoak with blood of slaughter'd beasts.

In *Flesh House,* Aberdeen author Stuart MacBride's 2008 crime novel, a cannibalistic serial killer is dubbed the Flesher by the press, because of the way the victims are butchered for meat. In a clever plot device, the only person to survive an attack writes a book about the murderer, *Smoak with Blood: The Hunt for the Flesher.* This quotes the verse from the painting, leading the police to visit Trinity

Hall to see if there is any connection with the killer (there isn't). *Flesh House* is just one in MacBride's superb series of bloody *policiers* set in Aberdeen; they are not for the faint of heart.

Amongst the sober portraits of former members, one painting stands out – a truly odd work that, from its inscription, purports to be a portrait of William the Lion, King of Scotland 1165–1214. It depicts a fulsomely-bearded man wrapped in chains and wearing a helmet decorated with a grotesque animal face. The individual is graced with a saintly halo. Revd David Roberts, writing in the Catholic journal *The Innes Review* in 1960, describes the painting as 'exceedingly bizarre … like some respected citizen who has taken leave of his senses and turned up, in fancy dress, at a Kirk Session meeting'. Great antiquity has been claimed for this work, with the standard tradition (as given in, for instance, Bain's book) being that it belonged to the Trinitarian Friary in The Green. When the post-Reformation ruins became the first Trinity Hall, the medieval painting, so the story goes, found its way into the possession of the Seven Trades. The connection between King William and the Trinitarians is that he invited the order to set up bases in Scotland and gifted some land or buildings to them on The Green. The chains symbolise the origins of the Trinitarian Friars, who would sell themselves into captivity as ransom paid to release Christian knights imprisoned by the Saracens during the Crusades. The halo in the painting is a flattering indication of William's piety and love for the Church; he was never considered for sainthood.

Above left: A hairy Wildman peeks out from a painting of the Shoemakers' Incorporation, Trinity Hall. *(Ségolène Dupuy)*

Above right: The perplexing and peculiar portrait of William the Lion at Trinity Hall. *(Ségolène Dupuy)*

The anonymous painting has never been thoroughly studied by an expert, but even a cursory examination clearly shows its style is not that of the medieval period, and the long inscription is couched in handwriting that has the hall-mark of the eighteenth century. Attempts to trace the definitive history of the painting have foundered on the reefs of poor records and possible propaganda, made worse by the credulity of earlier writers (a recent attempt, *From Hungary to Holburn Street* by Albert Thomson, assesses the key documentation and comes up with nothing substantive – no one knows when the work was painted, by whom, or how exactly it came into the possession of the Trades). The painting awaits a definitive study, but my guess is that it is an eighteenth-century or late seventeenth-century work, and that the purpose of whoever painted it was to create a bogus link between the Trades and a fictionalised 'glorious past', with all the status that antiquity and royalty can bring.

Other possibly invented traditions hang about the three great swords on display. They are claimed to be spoils of war, brought back from the invading Highland army defeated by the Aberdeen men at the bloody Battle of Harlaw in 1411. They may be the genuine article, or they may have been acquired at a later date and, Harlaw being so infamous it lived long in tale and ballad, the story of heroic deeds at the battle became attached to the swords.

The first Trinity Hall owed its establishment to the munificence of Dr William Guild, Minister of the Kirk of St Nicholas and Principal of King's College University. Guild died in 1657, and 200 years later coal merchant Alexander Fidler put up a commemorative well at the junction of Market Street and Guild Street. In 1957 'Fidler's Well' was moved to Duthie Park, to be re-sited in 2003 in a more appropriate location outside the current Trinity Hall. This really is a curious structure – the metal wellhead is inscribed:

> Fountain Hall 1st August 1857
> Water springs for man and beast
> At your service I am here
> Altho' six thousand years of age
> I am caller, clean and clear.
> Erected for the inhabitants of the world by Alexander Fidler.

I have not read any interpretation of the truly strange verse, and do not know what it means. My only guess is that 'six thousand years of age' may refer to Bishop Usher's notion, based on study of the genealogies of the Old Testament, that the world was created in 4004 BC (on Sunday 23 October, no less); or perhaps it is a wave to the *Anno Lucis*, the Masonic year of Creation (4000 BC). But what is the meaning of 'caller' in 'I am caller, clean and clear'? Another oddity is the writing on the stone trough: 'Dedicated to Dr William Guild died 1657 Lammas AF'. 'AF' is obviously Alexander Fidler, and Lammas ('loaf-mass day') is 1 August, the date on which the fountain was dedicated. In medieval times Lammas was the

festival of the first wheat harvest of the year, and in Gaelic-speaking areas cor-
responded to the harvest festival of Lughnasadh. It is a curious thing to put on a
public monument in Victorian times – did Lammas have some special or cryptic
meaning for Fidler?

NELLFIELD CEMETERY

This walled cemetery on Great Western Road is mostly Victorian and Edwardian,
with grave furniture such as lamenting ladies, anchors, sheaves of wheat, and
portraits in stone and bronze of the deceased. One slab is inscribed 'ALEXR
FRASER who died 21 Octr 1834 Aged 26 Years and was the first Interred in this
CEMETERY'. In 1899 Nellfield was at the centre of a scandal brought about
by lack of space. Graves were unceremoniously emptied and the human remains
dumped willy-nilly or thrown into holes beneath the paths; the plots were then
resold. Coffins were smashed up and burned, sometimes with their bodily contents (the caretaker's furnace was specially enlarged for the purpose). One grave
had been used for eighteen funerals in just three months, the bodies being dug up
and disposed of as soon as the mourners left. Another gravecut had seen twenty-
nine interments in a year. The total number of sepulchres violated was unknown,
but was at least 200, and the newspapers were filled with endless stories of gruesome finds as the crime scene was investigated. Cemetary Superintendent Coutts
was arrested and sentenced to six months' imprisonment.

Across Nellfield Place from the cemetery is the Short Mile pub, named because it
is flanked by two of Aberdeen's march-stones – #3 is beside the cemetery wall at
the corner of Nellfield Place, and #4 is immediately west of the pub, a distance of
some 30yds (27.4m). March-stones marked the one-time boundaries of Aberdeen;
these two were mistakenly taken for milestones, hence the name of the pub.

GRAY STREET

Ian Taylor spotted an 'extremely vibrant, almost neon-like' orange-red light
moving above the roof-line in April 2009. At one point the light stopped still,
before heading east out of sight. There was no sound. The sighting, which hints
at a helicopter, lasted for some two-and-a-half minutes and was reported in the
Evening Express on 14 April.

ALBYN PLACE

St John's Well stands outside Albyn Hospital at No. 24. It used to be located on
St John's Croft at the junction of Skene Row and Hardweird, Upper Denburn,
where it had a reputation for health-giving waters in the seventeenth century

and was known to some as 'the Knight Templar's wallie'. In 1885 the construction of Rosemount Viaduct displaced the well and it virtually vanished, only to be rescued and rebuilt on Albyn Place in the 1950s, when the hospital was owned by the Venerable Order of the Hospital of St John of Jerusalem. The tap is in the shape of the Hospitallers' star. The current structure incorporates a datestone of 1852, when the well was given a roof. Further west, a peculiar fountain in Queen's Terrace Gardens features a curving stone pipe snaking its way between two leaning granite boulders.

QUEEN'S ROAD

Bring me the head of ~~Alfredo Garcia~~ Queen Victoria! When Robert Smith wrote *25 Walks In and Around Aberdeen* in 1995 there was a sculptured head of Queen Victoria, of unknown provenance, at the foot of the steps of No. 10 Queen's Road. In the intervening years it has migrated elsewhere. There is a modern stone circle in the front garden of the investment company 3i (No. 70) and a fierce bearded bronze head on the keystone of No. 94. But the sight *par excellence* on this street of grand houses is No. 50, John Morgan's House.

Sphinxes and other details on John Morgan's House. *(Geoff Holder)*

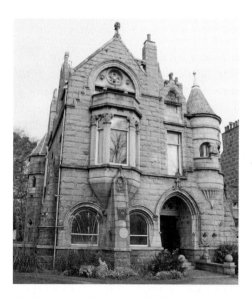

Aberdeen's only Franco-Gothic Hammer Horror Art Nouveau Scots Baronial building: John Morgan's House, Queen's Road. *(Geoff Holder)*

It is hard to pin down what exactly makes this extraordinary Victorian building so unique and so appealing – it is not one feature, but the combination of the whole that works. The house was designed in a distinctive asymmetric style by architect John Bridgeford Pirie for John Morgan, the master mason who constructed the equally striking Queen's Cross Kirk to the east. Morgan was a well-travelled bibliophile open to new ideas in art and architecture. In an article entitled 'The architecture of Pirie and Clyne', Mark Chalmers described the house as having 'elements of both fairytale castle and Hammer Horror mansion' combined with Scots Baronial, Franco-Gothic and Greek architectural motifs. Design elements include a pair of human-headed sphinxes at the entrance, a bronze sundial, and curvilinear, almost Art Nouveau decorative touches. An inscribed stone set subtly into the entrance paving is inscribed 'Built This House 1887' around a monogram, presumably John Morgan's.

ST SWITHIN'S STREET

In September 1952 Mrs Robert Smart was in her back garden at 4.25 p.m. when she saw a flying saucer travelling fast at great height in a north-north-east direction. The white object resembled 'a saucer with a chip out of it.' The sighting is mentioned in Ron Halliday's *UFO Scotland*.

HILL OF RUBISLAW

Something like six million tonnes of granite were extracted from Rubislaw Quarry, making the Granite City what it is (and creating the largest man-made hole in Europe in the process). In December 1931 daredevil Charles Ludwig crossed the quarry hand-over-hand on the Blondin wire that stretched across the crater-sized space. The wire was used to raise the granite blocks from the rocky surface hundreds of feet below. Ludwig was the same chap who later scaled the Mitchell Tower of MARISCHAL COLLEGE and planted a skeleton on the top. Someone needs to make a film about him. The quarry is now closed, inaccessible, filled with rainwater, and a conundrum for anyone trying to work out exactly what to do with it.

HAZLEHEAD PARK

As with many of Aberdeen's parks, Hazlehead is a bit of a treasure trove of curios and street furniture bric-a-brac. The oddest sight is the Nascent Lion stones, three large granite blocks originally intended to be sculpted into lions for the George VI Bridge. War economies scuppered that plan, and in 1970 the blocks were deposited here in the form of a stone circle, inevitably nicknamed Hazlehenge. The accompanying interpretation makes things even stranger by informing the visitor that the blocks are not 'Druidical stones'. The many stone circles of Aberdeenshire and elsewhere were built in the Neolithic period and the Bronze Age, long before the Druids of the Iron Age were active; antiquarians used to regard stone circles as 'Druidical' back in the nineteenth century, but it's been many decades since that view was scotched. But the non-Druidical not-a-stone-circle Nascent Lions stone circle is still marvelous.

Close by is another wonder, a privet hedge-maze of considerable extent, laid out in 1935 and, although not up to Hampton Court standards, is still a challenge to navigate. One of the attendants used to stand on the raised viewing platform and guide panic-stricken people out with a megaphone. The maze is closed in winter. The park also abounds in abstract works of art and Victorian fountains, including one with four splendid leonine heads. On the southern edge of the park is a substantial stone wellhead inscribed 'He sendeth the spring Psalm CIV 10' and 'The Well Spring of Nethertown'; the bronze waterspout is in the form of a Green Man. The most moving sculpture is the memorial to the 167 victims in the Piper Alpha disaster of July 1988. The powerful work shows three men vigorously active in their offshore workgear, and the legend 'Lest We Forget'.

The Nascent Lions stone circle, Hazlehead Park. Definitely not Druidical stones. *(Ségolène Dupuy)*

Robert the Bruce splits open the skull of Henry de Bohun at the Battle of Bannockburn. One of the Bruce cairns at Hazlehead. (*Ségolène Dupuy*)

Next to the restaurant is a pod of modern cairns, each sculpted with a scene from the life of Robert the Bruce. The 1970s carvings, some of which have not aged well, show Bruce and the spider, Bruce's coronation at Scone, the Herschip of Buchan (where Bruce slaughtered his fellow Scots so he could take on the English without having to worry about rivals for the Scottish throne) and Bruce triumphing at Bannockburn. One of the sculptures has Bruce presenting the 'Freedom Lands' to the citizens of Aberdeen, so this is as good a place as any to tackle one of the most persistent of Aberdonian myths.

The standard story, repeated *ad infinitum*, is that Bruce gifted the hunting ground of the Stocket Forest to Aberdeen in 1319 as a thank-you for the town's help during the Wars of Independence. The Stocket Forest then became the lion's share of the Freedom Lands, from which the town derived the Common Good Fund. The key problem is the word 'grant' – it was not a gift, free gratis and for nothing; it was a business transaction. Bruce granted Aberdeen rights over the Stocket in exchange for a fee, an annual payment or feu, of £213 6s 8d Sterling. In modern terms that is around £91,000. So Bruce made over £90,000 out of Aberdeen *every year* – a nice little earner for the Royal Exchequer.

UFO crash lands in Aberdeen! That was the come-on headline in the *Evening Express* on 14 August 2009. But before visions of a McRoswell Theme Park could materialise, the small print revealed that what had actually happened was that two brothers out walking their dog on Hazlehead football pitches found something that may have been a meteorite. Perhaps. Possibly. You never know. No follow-up appeared in the press so I suspect the rock turned out to have a more earthly origin. And using the description 'UFO' for a possible meteorite is, I suggest, pushing the tabloid abuse of language just a little far.

9

THE NORTHERN AND WESTERN SUBURBS

HILTON – ASHGROVE – LANG STRACHT – KINGSWELLS

Thou scarest me with dreams, and terrifiest me through visions.

Job vii: 14-15

HILTON

A massive standing stone dominates the manicured landscape of the Hilton Heights housing development off Hilton Drive. Known as the Hilton Stone or Lang Stane, it formerly served as a feature within the playground of the school that stood here until recently. In 1886 Revd J.A. Wylie claimed in *History of the Scottish Nation* that the monolith was once flanked by two stone circles, each 30yds (27.4m) in diameter, with eighteen stones between them. The eastern circle was broken up for building materials in 1830, its companion lasting just a few more decades. Wylie was of that breed of antiquarian for whom stone circles were Druidical, a point of view long superseded. His imaginatively over-the-top reconstruction of what went on at the Hilton Stone is a classic of the genre of Victorian Druidical nonsense:

> Victim after victim is led forward and slain — mayhap in the number is babe of some poor mother in the crowd, who seeks by this cruel and horrid deed to expiate her sin — and now the altar streams with blood, besmeared are hands and robe of officiating priest, and gory prints speckle the grassy plot which the granite mono-liths enclose. The sound of the rude instruments waxes yet louder, till at last their noise drowns the cries of the victim, and the smoke of the sacrifices rises into the sky and hangs its murky wreaths like a black canopy above the landscape.

There's nothing bookish intellectual antiquarians like better than a bracing bit of human sacrifice.

Above left: The Hilton Stone, Hilton Drive. Entirely imaginary Druidical blood sacrifices not shown. *(Geoff Holder)*

Above right: From the Arctic to Aberdeen. The Stewart Park whalebones, installed 1903. *(Geoff Holder)*

ROSEHILL

A mysterious pair of large whale rib-bones form an arch close to the Rosehill Drive entrance of Stewart Park. Following some puzzled newspaper queries, an article in the *Evening Express* of 11 July 1973 stated the bones were presented by the Captain of the Arctic whaler *Benbow* in 1903. There was once a blue enamel interpretive plaque, but this has vanished. When I was in the park a middle-aged woman asked me what I was taking photographs of, so I pointed out the whale-bones. She looked at them for a moment, then said, 'I've lived in this area for thirty years and never noticed them before!'

ASHGROVE

The bulk of the information in this section is drawn from Diane Morgan's won-derfully-researched book *Lost Aberdeen: The Outskirts*. In the Middle Ages the area near what is now Berryden Road was a bleak and remote spot called Barkmill Moor. Here in 1351 Provost William Leith of Ruthrieston slew Baillie Catanach and buried the body in a shallow grave on the moorland. Leith was later found out – or he suffered an attack of conscience – and in penance he gifted two bells to ST NICHOLAS KIRK. Centuries later the area became the pleasure ground of wealthy druggist Alexander Leslie, who, like other late eighteenth-century gentlemen, delighted in adorning his property with follies. On the top of the hill was a pictur-esque copy of the crown of King's College, constructed in brick. To the west was a grotto, a temple of science and religion, with a model of the solar system outlined by a silvery-white mineral, walls adorned with shells and quotations, and a small cell with a cross, which inevitably (and erroneously) was believed by the local people to have been a chapel. Sadly the grotto and the pleasure gardens are long gone, their place taken by a somewhat less romantic retail park.

The longest-lasting of Leslie's eccentricities was a rough brick obelisk which somehow become attached to the floating legend of Downie's Slaughter. Downie supposedly accidentally died of fright during a student prank (*see* TILLYDRONE ROAD for the full story). In 1926 the Ordnance Survey map showed the obelisk standing opposite Chestnut Row, clearly labelled as Downie's Cairn. When the 9ft (2.7m) obelisk was relocated to Old Aberdeen in 1926, the legend migrated with it.

ABERDEEN ROYAL INFIRMARY

The Pathology and Forensic Medicine Collection at the University of Aberdeen's School of Medical Sciences holds numerous specimens of human tissue showing pathological conditions, and items relating to forensic investigation of crimes in Aberdeen. Two skulls in particular are of interest – one was used in the 1991 film *Hamlet* starring Mel Gibson, and partly filmed at Dunnottar Castle, while the other displays an exit wound caused by a bullet. Sadly the collection is not open to the public.

VICTORIA PARK

There was once a small knoll here, surmounted by a miniature castle known as 'Tom's Castle' because the local children believed Tom Thumb resided there. The castle has been dismantled but a gurning gargoyle head that adorned the well at its base is now in the Winter Gardens of DUTHIE PARK.

LANG STRACHT

One of the best Pictish stones in the country can be seen in the foyer of Woodhill House, the headquarters of Aberdeenshire Council sited between Ashgrove Road, North Anderson Drive and Lang Stracht. Rhynie Man, as the figure is known, was found in 1978 in the Aberdeenshire village of Rhynie, an area that has produced numerous carved stones and must have been a cultural and religious centre in the Dark Ages. The carving shows a fierce bearded man carrying an axe. Only six of the hundreds of known carved Pictish stones depict single figures; their rarity suggests they were something special. Perhaps Rhynie Man is a Pictish god? Could his axe be an emblem of his role as a spirit of the woods? Or as the deity of the arts of civilisation? He can be viewed – and worshipped, if you are so inclined – during normal office hours, Monday to Friday.

A phantom army appeared twice on White Myres moor in 1719. On 29 January a force of 7,000 men were seen forming up in battle array on the moor. It was 8 a.m., and a clear sunny day. Drums could distinctly be seen strapped to the drummers' backs. In one curious aside, the long line of soldiers was 'seen to fall down

Rhynie Man, the Pictish stone in Westhill House. He may be a Celtic god, so show respect. (*Ségolène Dupuy*)

to the ground, and start up all at once'. After about two hours a commander rode along the line on a white horse, and the army set off in the direction of Aberdeen, visible until it passed behind the Stocket Hill. Around thirty people saw the host, but the only reference to a specific witness was to 'a very judicious man, who had been long a soldier in Flanders, and is now a farmer at this place'.

What was apparently the same force reappeared on the afternoon of 21 October, visible in the clear sunlight for three hours until it became too dark to see. This time the numbers were estimated at 2,000. The soldiers had blue and white coats, shining white insignias, and carried weapons. As before, they were seen to fall down *en masse*. This time a smoke appeared as if they had fired their muskets; but there was no noise. An officer on a white charger rode along the line, and the force marched off in the direction of the Bridge of Dee – but not before the most extraordinary aspect of the apparition. That day the great annual fair had taken place in Aberdeen. Hundreds of people returning home passed through the army without noticing them. Only when they met the crowd looking east at the spectacle did they turn around – and were astonished to see, on the ground they had just crossed, the phantom army.

Researching three famous English phantom army sightings of 1735, 1737 and 1745 for *The Guide to the Mysterious Lake District*, I came across accounts of phantom armies seen in Leicestershire (1707), Ujest, Silesia (1785), Vienne, France (1848), Lough Foyle and Bannmouth (both Ireland, 1848 and 1850 respectively) and Buderich and Paderborn in Germany (1854 and 1860). Clearly phantom armies were a feature of eighteenth- and nineteenth-century paranormal experiences, and for some reason they have been seen less frequently since. For another Aberdeen example, see BRIMMOND HILL below.

The two White Myres episodes were recounted in a letter sent in November 1719 by Alexander Jaffray, the Laird of Kingswells, to Sir Archibald Grant of Monymusk. The document was reproduced in *The Miscellany of the Spalding Club* (1841) and again in the *Edinburgh Topographical, Traditional, and Antiquarian Magazine* (1849). Ultimately, the credibility of the visions depends on the quality of this initial report, because there is no other documentary evidence. Jaffray had not seen the phantoms, but was an intrigued investigator: 'Both these visions I enquired about immediately after, and examined many of the spectators with the utmost care, who all agree with the greatest confidence imaginable, so that there is no room left of doubting the truth.' We do not have any of these witness statements, and none of the hundreds of spectators were identified. So the 'reality' or otherwise of the phantom army depends on whether we believe Jaffray. His account is plausible, but is it true? From this distance, it is impossible to say. The laird concluded his letter by telling his friend, 'This will puzzle thy philosophy but thou needst not doubt of the certainty of either.' In the end, the Phantom Army of White Myres certainly puzzles our philosophy, and remains a genuine mystery.

KINGSWELLS

For his book *The Hidden City* the indefatigable Robert Smith visited Gillahill, a farm east of Kingswells. There he was told a patch of woodland marked an unofficial graveyard where the resurrectionists reburied the dismembered remnants of their dissection experiments. No bodyparts or graves had ever been seen in the soil, and, in the absence of any other evidence, Smith concluded the story was unlikely. The farmer mentioned he had also been told the spot was where Quakers were buried. This is an understandable confusion, as there is a Friends' burial ground in the area, but it is on the west side of Kingswells, in a clump of trees on the hill north of East Kingsford Cottage at NJ85670665. In keeping with the Quaker desire for simplicity, the tiny enclosure has no gravemarkers. To the north-east, reached by a lane off the Kingswells by-pass, are some spectacularly large consumption dykes, massive field walls built solely to 'consume' the field stones removed during agricultural improvements (NJ85870688). The dykes, built in the 1850s, are fitted out with steps, a paved central path and even a watertank.

The minor road that passes East Kingsford Cottage towards Clinterty navigates a largely rural landscape rife with archaeological interest. A heavily-robbed but still substantial Neolithic long cairn can be seen from the road in a field at NJ85120705. It is 170ft (51.9m) long, although this may have been augmented by field clearance stones in recent years. Sometime before the First World War the slabs lining the burial cist were removed and used to construct a roadside water-trough, which sadly has also disappeared. The quarry at Borrowstone Farm (NJ851081) yielded six prehistoric burials, the most recent being discovered in 1984. As well as human remains, the rich grave-goods included flakes, knives and scrapers of flint, beakers, a quartz pebble, and arrowheads, while three very unusual items – a greenstone wristguard, a bone pulley ring and what might be animal sinew used to string a bow – suggest the deceased was a high status individual similar to the 'Amesbury Archer' found near Stonehenge. The finds from these six cists are in the (currently closed) Marischal Museum.

Some readers of a certain age may remember being on the receiving end of 'birthday bumps', in which one's compatriots repeatedly lifted and dropped the unlucky birthday boy or girl on the floor, generating considerable discomfort. Something similar took place at the Douping Stone, a large granite boulder in

The Douping Stone and its adjacent boundary marker near Kingswells, site of a painful initiation involving burgess' backsides. *(Geoff Holder)*

a field west of the road to the north of Wynford Farm (NJ83980938). The occasion was the annual Riding of the Marches, when the burgesses of Aberdeen patrolled the march-stones to ensure the lands belonging to the city had not been encroached upon. As the decades passed the Riding became less serious and more drunken, with the last hurrah of the old order taking place on 4 September 1889. Whenever a new burgess took part in the Riding, it was the custom for him to be 'douped'. The eighteenth-century writer Francis Douglas left a description of the process in *A General Description of the East Coast of Scotland*:

> After dinner, the ceremony was very solemnly gone about, in presence of all the company … Two of the company took the novice by the shoulders, and two others lay hold of his legs, lifting him breast-high, above the point of the rock, to which they returned his posteriors, with a velocity proportioned to their respect for his character. The elevation and depression being thrice repeated, the person was inrolled a free brother-burgess.

Ouch. Next to the Douping Stone, marked No. 31, is one of the march-stones marking the old boundary of Aberdeen, erected sometime after 1790. Stone No. 30 is about 200 paces to the south-west, in the corner of the field beside the burn.

Around 8 a.m. on 12 February 1643 William Anderson, the tenant of Crabeston farm, saw a phantom army upon Brimmond Hill. Both cavalry and infantry were visible to him, but when the sun cleared the mist away the host vanished into a moss, accompanied by some undescribed noise. The episode was recorded in John Spalding's *The History of the Troubles and Memorable Transactions in Scotland*; as with pretty much everything he reported, the credulous Spalding regarded the vision as a bad omen of grim events to come. Given that he was living in the plague-, famine- and warfare-ridden seventeenth century, he was almost always right.

NEWHILLS

The largely-ignored roofless kirk and small graveyard at the bend in the road from Kingswells to Stoneywood (NJ87170947) is actually rather special, for within lurk tales of witchcraft, bodysnatching and madness. The first hint is the anti-bodysnatching watchhouse at the entrance. In the early nineteenth century the gravedigger's nickname was 'Resurrectionist Marr', which gives a clue about the way he earned some extra cash on the side. For years the sexton happily plundered graves in the company of farmer Peter Brownie from Fintray, a notorious bodysnatcher who operated throughout the Garioch but was never caught. One day, however, Brownie repented his evil ways and converted to Quakerism. In a classic case of poacher-turned-gamekeeper, he designed a graverobber-proof mortsafe, a very heavy metal lattice-work that encased the whole coffin and needed to be lowered into and raised from the grave by a workgang using a lifting apparatus. The mortsafe was in use in Inverurie and is currently in storage. Peter Brownie died at Kinmuck in 1886, a happy Quaker. It is not recorded what Resurrectionist Marr thought about his former comrade's apotheosis.

The parish church of the newly established parish of Newhills was established in 1666. In 1702 it gained a new minister, Revd Robert Burnett. Two years later the General Assembly of the Church of Scotland agreed to address his grievances about his stipend – or lack of it. Sometime between 20 May and 22 June 1715 the sixty-year-old hanged himself in his own church with the bell rope, having apparently lost his mind through the continuing financial disputes over his stipend. Popular belief, however, had it that he was a victim of witchcraft. The tradition went that the pulpit Bible was found open beside his hanging body, with the passage from Job vii: 14-15, marked by his own hand: 'Thou scarest me with dreams, and terrifiest me through visions; so that my soul chooseth strangling, and death rather than my life.' So entrenched was this belief that it was mentioned in the *Fasti Ecclesiæ Scoticanæ*, the soberly definitive 1920s 'database' of Church of Scotland ministers from the Reformation.

KINGSWELLS (SLIGHT RETURN)

A UFO flap was sparked in 2006 when a wedding party in Kingswells let loose some fire lanterns into the night sky. UFO websites and the local press logged dozens of sightings of bright orange lights, and there was talk of an alien invasion. The bride, Sharon Forrest, told the *Sunday Mirror* on 13 August, 'I couldn't believe all the fuss. The lanterns are bright, but I'd never think about them being UFOs. We thought they were a bit of harmless fun, but obviously not everyone agreed.' So here's a hint: if it's bright, orange and floats in the sky in the way that a fragile paper fire lantern would, it is *not* the advance fleet from Zeta Reticuli.

The ruined Newhills church, site of bodysnatching, witchcraft, and a monkey-puzzle tree. *(Ségolène Dupuy)*

10

NORTH BY NORTH-WEST

BRIG O'BALGONIE – DANESTONE – DYCE – KIRKHILL

By turns my blood ran cauld an' warm,
My brain began to crack,
When out it stretched a fleshless arm,
And thus the spectre spak.

William Anderson, *Rhymes, Reveries, and Reminiscences* (1851)

THE DON

John Spalding's *The History of the Troubles and Memorable Transactions in Scotland* has a 1635 sighting of a water monster that sounds suspiciously like a walrus:

> In the month of June, there was seen in the river of Don a monster having a head like to a great mastiff dog, and hand, arms, and paps [breast] like a man, and the paps seemed to be white; it had hair on the head, and its hinder parts was seen sometimes above the water, whilk seemed clubbish, short legged and short footed, with a tail. This monster was seen body-like swimming above the water about ten hours in the morning, and continued all day visible, swimming above and beneath the bridge, without any fear. The town's people of both Aberdeens came out in great multitudes to see this monster; some threw stones, some shot guns and pistols, and the salmon fishers rowed cobles with nets to catch it, but all in vain. It never sinked nor feared, but would duck under water, snorting and bullering, terrible to the hearers. It remained two days, and was seen no more.

Spalding then signed off with one of his customary musings on bad omens: 'It appears this monster came for no good token to noble Aberdeen, for sore was the same oppressed with great troubles that fell in the land.' To Spalding, everything was a bad omen.

BRIG O' BALGOWNIE

This single-span medieval bridge was built around 1320, making it one of the earliest stone bridges in the country. It was largely superseded by the larger and downstream Bridge of Don in 1830, and is now closed to motor traffic. The steep brae up from the south side passes through the attractively-renovated seventeenth- and eighteenth-century houses of Cottown of Balgownie. The house nearest the Brig was once called the Black Nook alehouse, its name coming from a dark pool to the west of the bridge. The 33ft (10m) deep Black Nook Pot was thought to be the habitation of evil spirits whose joy in life was to drag travellers to a watery doom. Quoting the traditional couplet 'Bloodthirsty Dee she needs three; Hungry Don he needs one!' in his book *City by the Grey North Sea*, Fenton Wyness mused on the folklore of the appetites and behaviour of water-spirits. He considered that in the old days the quota of human sacrifices required to placate the river-gods was met by drowning accidents; when people started building substantial bridges like the Brig o'Balgownie, the evil ones relocated to the deepest pools in the hope of snaring the occasional passer-by. Perhaps a Jacobite spy named Daniel Campbell provided the appropriate sacrifice. In 1746, when the Duke of Cumberland was in Aberdeen before the Battle of Culloden, Campbell was hanged from a tree at the Brig, with a paper pinned to his chest proclaiming his treason.

Thomas the Rhymer is attributed with pronouncing a curse on the bridge:

> Brig o' Balgownie, wicht [white]'s thy wa' [wall].
> Wi' a wife's ae [only] son an a mare's ae foal
> Doon shalt thou fa' [fall].

The poet Byron knew the rhyme when he lived in the area as a child, and in *Don Juan* recalled the frisson it gave him to cross the bridge and peer over the edge, knowing he was an only son. In *Popular Rhymes of Scotland* Robert Chambers cited the case of a recent Earl of Aberdeen, another only son. Careful not to test the prophecy to destruction, he would dismount at the Brig, walk over, and only when he had crossed would he signal a servant to bring his horse over. Most of what is told of 'True Thomas' is lies, or at least folkloric speculation. If, as is some-times thought, he died in the late thirteenth century, he could not have crossed the bridge, was which completed in 1320.

William Anderson's *Rhymes, Reveries, and Reminiscences* of 1851 has a long, jokey poem about a drunkard taunted by a ghost at the Brig. 'Jamie Cockmalone's Vision in 1847, Travelling from Aberdeen to the Printfield' has the titular char-acter crossing the bridge on a dark and stormy night and being accosted by a tall figure in white: 'By turns my blood ran cauld an' warm, My brain began to crack, When out it stretched a fleshless arm, And thus the spectre spak.' The loquacious spirit then takes several dozen lines to condemn the evils of alcohol and extol the virtues of teetotalism, before vanishing at cock-crow. Jamie's response? 'I wish I had a drappie more.'

DENMORE

A single pointed standing stone, probably a flanker (and sole survivor) of a recumbent stone circle stands in a field west of the B999 at NJ94001309. Access to the 6ft 1in (1.85m) tall stone is not possible if the field is in crop.

DANESTONE

The former Grandholm woollen mills long dominated part of the north riverbank. *Druidism Exhumed*, an enthusiastically eccentric antiquarian work by Revd James Rust, tells how the construction of the factory destroyed one or more stone circles, plus a number of prehistoric graves. The disturbance of the dead caused some local people to predict some kind of supernatural retributive justice. 'And every misadventure for a long period, every accident within the works to limb or life, every bad commercial speculation, every seizure by the enemy, or loss by war, every vexatious lawsuit in which the company required to engage, to sue or be sued, was attributed to that cause.' The mill flourished for many a decade but has now been developed for housing.

There is a place called Fairy Hillock on the east bank of the Don north of Grandhome estate at NJ898131; there must be a story about it, but I do not know it.

DYCE

At the end of the sixteenth century the citizens of Dyce were badly troubled by spirits. On 19 January 1599 Thomas Lorne of Overtoun of Dyce was accused of communication with bad spirits. Sometimes he stayed away from home for seven weeks conversing with the spirits, to the despair of his wife and children. Lorne agreed that from now on he would pay no attention to the spirits, and that he would always inform a friend or family member if he went away anywhere. If he failed to obey these injunctions, he laid himself open to a trial for 'dealing with spirits', for which the penalty was death. The initial hearing took place in the presence of Alexander Rutherford, the Provost of Aberdeen, and occurred just over a year after the witch-burning mania of 1597; Lorne got off lightly. Of course, there are reasons why a man might want to absent himself from his domestic arrangements for a time, and invoke persuasive spirits as an excuse; but the records are silent as to the exact details of Lorne's behaviour.

On 20 November 1601 Walter Ronaldson of Kirktown of Dyce was up on a charge before the presbytery of Aberdeen. Ronaldson was regarded as a pious man, but he confessed to 'familiarity with a spirit'. Twenty-seven years previously the spirit had come to his door and called out his name, 'Wattie, Wattie!' The spirit then returned twice every year, but in invisible form. At Michaelmas [29 September]

1601 Ronaldson woke to a voice calling 'Wattie! Wattie!' and he saw a small figure or manikin sitting on a chest near his bed. It had a trimmed beard and was wearing a white linen sark or shirt. The spirit – or hobgoblin or fairy, because that is surely what is being described – told Ronaldson that he could solve his financial woes if he went to the Weachman's house in Stanivoid, where he would find silver, gold and valuable vessels (I have been unable to identify where 'Stanivoid' might be). Ronaldson directed three friends to dig at the spot, as he was unable to do anything physical himself (the inference is that he had no strength after the encounter with the spirit). Nothing was found, although Ronaldson was convinced a thorough examination would unearth the treasure. Like Lorne, Ronaldson was lightly treated: the presbytery simply ordered his parish minister to give him a good talking to.

The cases are in two monumental works edited by John Stuart for the Spalding Club: Lorne's can be found in *Extracts from the Council Register of the Burgh of Aberdeen* (1843) while Ronaldson's is in *Selections from the Records of the Kirk Session, Presbytery, and Synod of Aberdeen* (1846).

Dyce Old Parish Church, by Kirkton off Dyce Drive at NJ87531541, has a superb location overlooking a bend in the Don. The roofless pre-Reformation kirk holds a number of treasures: a Pictish stone incised with a double-disc and Z-rod symbol and the 'Pictish beast' which some interpret as a dolphin, or an elephant, or a sea mon-ster; a magnificently-carved cross-slab with other Pictish symbols (crescent and V-rod, mirror case, double disc and Z-rod, and a triple ring) and, running down the edge, an inscription in the primitive Celtic writing called Ogham; and four cross-marked stones, each cross carved to a differ-ent and unusual design. All the stones were found on the site, which indicates there was an early Christian settle-ment here. A roughly-incised medieval stone is cemented

One of the Pictish stones in the ruined Dyce church, showing the Z-rod and double-disc symbols, and the enigmatic 'Pictish beast'. *(Ségolène Dupuy)*

into the exterior south wall, the broken medieval font sits outside the west door, and an anti-bodysnatching watch-house stands in the south-east corner of the churchyard. Those interested in the Second World War will gravitate to the war memorial: next to the graves of RAF personnel can be found those of ten members of the Luftwaffe. A well-preserved Second World War brick pillbox still guards the bridge over the railway line, on the access road to the church.

To the west is Liddell's Monument, erected in 1614 to commemorate Dr Duncan Liddell, Laird of Pittmedden House and Professor of Mathematics and Medicine at the University of Helmstadt. His portrait in bronze is on his graveslab in ST NICHOLAS KIRK. South of the railway and Pitmedden House is a second monument, this one raised in 1898 to mark the fiftieth anniversary of Queen Victoria's first visit to Aberdeen (NJ86321430). Decorations include a sailing ship and the Latin motto *Per Perigulum Vivo* (I think this is meant to be *Per Periculum Vivo*, 'We Pass Through Dangers to Life'). A private walled cemetery can be seen on the west bank of the Don at Mains of Dyce (NJ89221359); it belonged to the Skene family, who had a mansion on the estate. The mansion is long gone, and the nineteenth-century graveyard is disused, with only a few stones remaining.

The Times for 7 April 2006 reported that Loretta Walker claimed to have seen a panther-like animal in the Dyce area of in 2003. The big cat was black and larger than an Alsatian.

ABERDEEN (DYCE) AIRPORT

Ron Halliday's *UFO Scotland* has two episodes from 1991. On 26 March a helicopter pilot *en route* to the airport at 11.20 a.m. picked up a major radar trace. Air Traffic Control could not identify it so RAF fighters were scrambled, the standard response when Soviet aerial incursions were suspected. No contact was made but around the same time, a suspiciously loud bang was heard over Aberdeen, as if something fast had broken the sound barrier. On 9 November an employee from an operation at the airport saw a cube-shaped object in the sky at 12.15 p.m. He reported it to Air Traffic Control, who could not locate it visually or by radar.

The standing stones on the airport roundabout are a piece of modern landscaping; the boulders were dug up during the construction of the aircraft parking apron in front of the terminal building, and erected here as a contemporary reference to Aberdeenshire's extensive heritage of stone circles.

CHAPEL OF STONEYWOOD

Tucked away in a corner just south of the A96, the chapel of St Mary's of Stoneywood is now little more than foundations and a small graveyard of nineteenth-century stones (NJ86631118), most notable for an episode in 1827 when medical student Alexander C. Matthews was fined £20 and jailed for a month for stealing a body. But in the corner of the burial ground is a holy well that was still being visited in the nineteenth century, when visitors would drop pins in the water to obtain the grant of a wish. The first documentary mention of the well is in MacFarlane's *Geographical Collections*, written around 1749. St Mary's Well was 'reck'ned medicinall and good for the stomach and for cleansing and curing any ulcerous tumours on any part of the body when bathed within it.' Crowds flocked to it about the beginning of May. The well must have been in use in medieval times, although there is no record of this. The chapel was completed in 1367, and two of the adjacent plots were of old called Waterton and Wellton, suggesting the well had been a feature for centuries. After 1930 the well dried up and became neglected; in recent years it has been cleaned out, and good interpretation installed.

CLINTERTY

A prehistoric burial was uncovered in a sand pit in 1897. As well as a skeleton, the rich grave goods included an axehead, a topaz crystal, arrowheads, a bone pulley ring, a bone needle, flint flakes, and a beaker. Most of the items are in Marischal Museum. A second beaker was found in a cist near Elrick Hill sometime before 1850. There is a standing stone at Little Clinterty (NJ83121207) but the one marked on the OS map near Clinterty Home Farm (NJ84381052) has been

Fancy a cuppa? Folk-art or tea-break practicality? A 'mug-tree' near Meikle Clinterty. *(Geoff Holder)*

removed; it was probably not prehistoric, but a relatively modern cattle rubbing stone. The excitingly-named Robber's Cave in Clinterty Woods (NJ85131079) is in a gulley north of the southernmost track, but has been blocked off with logs. It was probably originally an early iron mine; whether or not it was ever a base for brigands is not recorded; possibly the presence of a cave close to the road prompted a romantic speculation. The woods are home to modern sculptures of varying quality.

KIRKHILL FOREST

Walking boots are required to explore this extensive Forestry Commission plantation. Following the signage north-west from the car park off the A93 brings you to the Tappie, a nineteenth-century lookout built by Dr William Henderson of Caskieben to define the summit of his property: a folly with a view (NJ84431268). The external stairs take you up to the platform. Down the southern slope from the Tappie, and now difficult to find because of tree clearance, is the boundary marker called the Bishop's Stone (NJ84311212). This was one of several markers that delimited the Bishop's Lands, properties belonging to the Bishop of Aberdeen on Tyrebagger Hill. Look for a large moss-covered glacial erratic at the angle of the wall of Gueval Croft. Below the moss on the sloping surface two small cup-shaped stones and the letter 'M' can just be made out.

The stone is mentioned in a 1926 paper read to the Society of Antiquaries of Scotland by James Cruickshank. Cruickshank also described two other markers, the Great Stone (which had recently been destroyed by quarrying), and a 'large flat cross of stone and turf' with shafts 48ft and 64ft long (14.6m and 19.5m). The arms of the cross were 3ft 6in (1m) broad and 2ft (61cm) high, although much overgrown. Cruickshanks' illustrations, carefully drawn by Douglas Simpson, show the cross on the 600ft (183m) contour on the south-eastern slope of the hill. You don't find giant crosses every day. Sadly this extraordinary feature of the medieval landscape, something almost unique in Scotland, is hidden somewhere in the heavily wooded part of the forestry plantation, and no one knows where it is; it may even have been entirely obliterated.

East from the Tappie is Pitdouries Well (NJ85101247), once a noted wishing well much visited on May Day, while the piece of detached woodland known as the Slacks, to the north-west, holds an impressively large Bronze Age cairn some 75ft (23m) in diameter (NJ84171442). In the surrounding trees are several prehistoric hut-circles — one can be found immediately south-east of the cairn — and a number of smaller cairns. Further north-east, approached from Kinaldie, is the Gouk Stone (NJ83451516) a towering 9ft 10in (3m) tall monolith standing in a broken-down field wall. There are several Gouk Stones in Scotland, the name meaning a cuckoo. However, no cuckoo legend is attached to this one, the only piece of folklore being an eighteenth-century reference to the stone marking the grave of some forgotten general. Before the true antiquity of prehistoric standing stones was understood, it was common practice to assume they commemorated some prominent individual. In the nineteenth century several cist burials containing bones and beakers were uncovered some distance north of Gouk Stone

The greatest sight in this corner of Aberdeen, however, is Tyrebagger Stone Circle, also known as the Standing Stones of Dyce (NJ 85951322). This spectacular circle commands an extensive view and looks down onto the airport. It is best reached along the very rough track that leads north-west from where the road north from Chapel of Stoneywood turns abruptly east towards Dyce Drive. There is also a route uphill from Cairn Industrial Park, which is often used by lunchtime joggers. Whichever route you take, a longish walk is on the cards. The circle is unsignposted; when the track first enters the wood, turn immediately left (south) along a track/path alongside the treeline to a wooden field-gate. The stones are prominent on the horizon.

Tyrebagger is a recumbent stone circle, a form peculiar to Aberdeenshire. For some unknown reason the peoples here built many of their stone circles with a massive horizontal stone – the 'recumbent' – flanked by two great teeth-like uprights, the entire arrangement creating a 'frame' of the south-west horizon. Why this did this, no-one knows. The other stones in the circle are graded in height away from the recumbent. Despite its previous use as a cattle-fold, and its popularity with Victorian picnickers, the circle is still in good condition, with ten stones still upright, including the recumbent and flankers. A smaller inner circle can just be made out. Sitting in this beautiful Bronze Age site, watching the jets and helicopters take off below, is one of life's enduring pleasures.

Tyrebagger recumbent stone circle, overlooking Aberdeen airport. *(Ségolène Dupuy)*

11

OLD ABERDEEN

KING'S COLLEGE – ZOOLOGY MUSEUM –
ST MACHAR'S CATHEDRAL – TILLYDRONE

Ye're a' airt an' pairt in Downie's slauchter.

Street chant directed against students, nineteenth century

Old Aberdeen may be one of the most enchanting and olde-worlde areas described in this book, but it is no older than 'New Aberdeen' (the city centre); indeed the settlement by the Dee may actually predate its companion on the Don. Old Aberdeen was an independent town from 1489 until 1891 when it was finally incorporated into the City of Aberdeen. The street plan and some of the buildings are medieval, but the current appearance is largely eighteenth and nineteenth-century.

COLLEGE BOUNDS

The minarets of Powis Lodge gates were erected in 1834 by John Leslie, the young laird of the grand estate of Powis. Their Near Eastern appearance may have been a fan-boy tribute to Lord Byron, the nearest the early nineteenth century had to a rock star. The turrets are topped with gold-leafed orbs and crescent finials; the crescent is the emblem of the Fraser family, the previous owners of the estate. The towers now form the entrance to some of the University's halls of residence.

Hidden behind the buildings at Nos 21-31 and accessed through the car park is the miniscule site of St Mary Ad Nives (of the Snows), usually known as the Snow Kirk. The sixteenth-century gateway of the churchyard can be seen in the garden wall of No. 19. The kirk was founded in 1497 and, despite lacking a priest or formal congregation, survived the Reformation as a continuing focus of Catholic faith. In 1640 the authorities had had enough of this, and the church was demolished. This still did not stop the faithful, and on 4 March 1649 the Kirk Session admonished people who were going to the churchyard 'to say ther prayers upon ther husbands or friends graves which is playne superstitione' (Alexander

Macdonald Munro, *Records of Old Aberdeen*). Roman Catholic families continued to use the now-crowded site as a place of interment up until the early twentieth century. The *Press & Journal* for 11 November 1963 reported on a number of bones found in the back garden of No. 53 during extensions to Crombie Hall; the conclusion was that they were from the overflow of the burial ground. In 1921 Rachel Blanche Harrower wrote an article for *The Aberdeen University Review* in which she mentioned the children of Professor Hugh Macpherson's extended family playing in the churchyard; the MacPherson boys eagerly consumed the raspberries that grew in profusion among the graves, but the girls refused to do so because they believed the berries were dyed with the blood of the dead.

KING'S COLLEGE

Founded in 1495, this was Aberdeen's first university and the third oldest in Scotland. The quadrangle is classically collegiate, and is complemented by New King's, built in a sympathetic style in 1913. Now part of the University of Aberdeen, the College is a delight to explore, its precincts bursting with heraldic plaques, statues of lions and unicorns, and ornate memorials decorated with skulls and bones. An astonishingly detailed twentieth-century monument to Bishop William Elphinstone sits outside the west door of the chapel. Elphinstone founded King's College and was a leading intellectual and political figure of his time; an effigy of him lies on the marble sarcophagus, surrounded by bronze angels and Classical gods, the latter sitting on bound prisoners (presumably representing the various evils of mankind) and a rather fetching dragon.

Above left: The minaret-like towers of Powis Gates, on College Bounds. *(Geoff Holder)*

Above centre: Bishop Elphinstone's monument outside King's College. Note the cuddly dragon. *(Geoff Holder)*

Above right: A statue of a student lounging outside New King's; he holds the apple of knowledge. *(Geoff Holder)*

Among Elphinstone's many achievements was the compilation of the *Aberdeen Martyrology and Breviary* in 1510, usually just called the *Aberdeen Breviary*. He employed various clerics to travel the length and breadth of Scotland, visiting shrines and collecting what was known – or believed – of the lives of the saints. The *Breviary* forms the basis of most later writings on Scottish saints, including their legends and miracles. *Especially* their legends and miracles. Elphinstone also had an ulterior motive for its creation, as for the first time it brought together the scattered traditions of a nation that sometimes felt itself on the fringe of Europe, and presented this deep Christian heritage in a single impressive corpus. The *Breviary* was in part aimed at a readership at the centre of Catholic Europe, the Papacy, and effectively said, 'Here in Scotland we have as many saints and as much piety and learning as any of our neighbours; take us seriously as a modern, sovereign state.' As a side effect, the *Breviary* revived interest in the cults of native Scottish saints, leading to an upsurge in pilgrimage to shrines and cult centres throughout the country.

A close companion of the Bishop was Hector Boece, the first principal of King's and author of *Scotorum Historiae* (1527), one of the very first histories of Scotland. Fact, fiction and fable were clearly indivisible in Hector's house, and the massively influential book has spawned innumerable legends and fantasies that are some-times still cited as reliable history, at least among the less critical websites and other arbiters of popular Scottish history. Boece also wrote a biography of his friend and patron, *The Life of Elphinstone* (reproduced in part in William Orem's *A description of the Chanonry, Cathedral, and King's College of Old Aberdeen*, 1791), in which we learn that when Elphinstone was a child the Virgin Mary appeared to him in a dream, urging him to take up a life in the Church, and promising that he would become a bishop. He was also instructed to take care of the Christian religion and repair the Virgin's shrines, and certainly Elphinstone had a deep personal bond with the cult of Mary. When he was four years old he strayed from his parents, to be eventually found lying prostrate before a statue of the Virgin in ST MACHAR'S CATHEDRAL; only with force, and many tears, could he be persuaded to leave the statue.

When Elphinstone died in 1514 Boece was keen to demonstrate that miracles and wonders accompanied the passing of such a holy man:

> At Foveran, a village ten miles from Aberdeen, a child was born with two heads and bodies, but only two legs, and otherwise not deformed. Another child born at Aberdeen could not be brought to suck its mother, nor look at her without horrid squalling, while it took the breast of their [servant] woman quietly. The vanes on the towers of Aberdeen church all fell down or were broken off …

At Elphinstone's funeral his silver pastoral staff was broken by accident, and when part fell into the grave, a voice 'from whence is not known' was heard to pro-nounce the words *Tecum Gulielme, mitra sepelienda* ('Thy mitre, William, should also be buried with thee'). Not surprisingly, the mourners complied. The bishop was laid to rest in front of the high altar of the Chapel; when Boece followed thirteen years later, he was buried beside his friend and patron.

King's College Chapel. Could it have been based on the proportions of King's Solomon's Temple? *(Geoff Holder)*

The highlight of King's is the medieval chapel with its staggeringly ornate crown atop the tower. The closed nature of the crown indicates the king (James IV) was the highest political authority in Scotland, and was not subject to rule from elsewhere; had the crown been open, it would be an admittance the king was subject to the Holy Roman Emperor. The little lead-panelled steeple adjacent is embossed with the letters C R (Charles Rex, Charles I) and the insignia of Bishop Elphinstone, three fishes and a pot of three lilies; the latter also symbolise the Virgin Mary, to whom, as we have seen, Elpinstone was particularly dedicated. When the Reformers came calling in 1560 the College Principal armed the staff and students, and the mob was driven off. Consequently the chapel was relatively untouched by the excesses of the Reformation, and its layout proved adaptable: part of the west end was turned into a library, while the east end became a meeting room for the Synod of the Protestant Church. Religious worship resumed in the church in 1824, and continues to this day (the chapel is open Monday-Friday, 10 a.m.-3.30p.m., admission free). A minor excavation during the installation of a new organ in 2004 uncovered a skeleton and some coffin nails; radiocarbon analysis gave a date of 1030-1220 AD, several centuries before the chapel was actually built. Perhaps there had been an earlier chapel or graveyard on the site.

The early sixteenth-century stalls, misericords and canopies are beautifully carved with vegetation and tracery, and many of the stalls have early graffiti. Behind the communion table can be found an altar slab that was re-used as a gravestone for Peter Udny, sub-principal from 1593-1601. The consecration crosses of the altar are visible in three of the corners. These crosses came to be identified with the Five Wounds of Christ, an important cult focus within the chapel during the early sixteenth century that may have continued after the Reformation – the inscription on the slab reads 'I have learnt and I have taught Thy wounds, O Christ'. All this suggests Catholicism died a lingering death at King's (MARISCHAL COLLEGE was founded as an expressly Protestant alternative).

But the chapel is not just a glorious medieval survival; it may also hide a deep esoteric secret. The revelation comes in a superb scholarly compendium edited by Jane Geddes in 2000, called *King's College Chapel, Aberdeen, 1500-2000*. On the west front of the chapel is a Latin inscription that translates as:

> Through the most serene, most illustrious and most victorious James IV King
> On the fourth day before the nones of April [2 April] in the one-thousand-and-
> five-hundredth year [1500]
> This eminent college the masons began to build.

In a contribution to the book, John Higgitt suggests 2 April was deliberately chosen as a direct allusion to the foundation date of the Biblical Temple of King Solomon, the first Temple of the Israelites, constructed in the tenth century BC to house the Ark of the Covenant. Solomon's Temple fascinated medieval minds, and spun off into all kinds of esoteric lore such as sacred geometry and architecture – for example, it had a profound effect on the mythology developed by the Freemasons (*see* CROWN STREET). The 2 April date is not in the Old Testament – it appeared in early medieval works of speculative Biblical exegesis such as Jerome's *Liber Quaestionum Hebraicarum in Genesim* and the *Postillae* by Nicholas of Lyra. Although the connection cannot be definitely proved, Higgit bolstered his argument by citing a 1985 article by G.P. Edwards in the *Aberdeen University Review*, which showed that Bishop Elphinstone could have been familiar with one or other of these works.

So the inscription *might* be a clue. Taking the Solomonic reference as a starting point, Jane Geddes examined the proportions of the chapel for her contribution to the book. They appeared to show that, yes, King's College Chapel deliberately echoed the Temple of Solomon. The ratio of external width to length of the Temple, as given in the Bible, 1 Kings 6:2-3, was 1:3 1/2. The chapel is almost the same. The Temple's innermost sacred space, the Holy of Holies, had a proportion of 1:3. At King's the measurements of the most sacred space, the sanctuary, from the altar steps east to the edge of the choir as indicated by the rood screen, are 1:3. Geddes concluded: 'Elphinstone's clue about Solomon's Temple in the inscription is manifest in his building.' With the secret encoded in the arithmetic of the architecture, the bishop built his chapel, the apex of his life's work, in the image of the Temple of Solomon.

Even more curiosities emerged in 2004. Workmen repointing the west exterior wall of the chapel found four pottery jugs placed in niches that had been deliberately created to hold them. The vessels were of local manufacture, and dated to the time when the chapel was built. They had been trimmed of their rims and handles and were set on their sides, their openings facing the exterior of the wall. Three were taken to Marischal Museum while the fourth remains *in situ*.

A small number of similar vessels have been discovered in the walls of other medieval buildings, especially churches. The practice was considered in an article by George Yates in *Antiquities and Curiosities of the Church*, edited by William Andrews in 1897. Yates thought the vessels were 'acoustic jars', used to improve the resonance of sound within the building. It was presumed that the early Christians had inherited the technique from the theatres and coliseums of Rome, where a similar form of sound enhancement had been described by ancient writers. This is fine as far as it goes, but some pots – as at Dundee, Abernethy and here in Aberdeen – were facing *outwards*, where the sound amplification could not work. Ralph Merrifield (*The Archaeology of Ritual and Magic*, 1987) thought the understanding of the practice simply degenerated over time, so that people knew the pots were important, but not why. Merrifield wondered whether the 'meaning' of the pots migrated from an architectural technique into the medieval folklore of demonology, so that the pots became to be regarded as 'spirit traps' for invisible evil beings. To an extent this is modern scholarly speculation, as no medieval writers recorded why these pots were installed; but the mystery, although minor, remains an intriguing one.

Susanna Clarke is a noted author of compelling works of dark fantasy, such as *Jonathan Strange and Mr Norrell* (2004), which retells British history as if magic was real. Her fiction is noted for its historically playful and scholarly quality; the short stories of *The Ladies of Grace Adieu* (2006) expand the mythos of the earlier work and claim to be edited by 'Professor James Sutherland, Director of Sidhe Studies, University of Aberdeen'. The Sidhe are the fairies, and the book is a collection of historical first-person accounts of interactions between humans and the realm of Faery. Sadly the professor is fictional and there is no Department of Sidhe Studies at the University of Aberdeen … if only there were.

TOWN HOUSE

This restored eighteenth-century building stands at the top of High Street, and now functions as a visitor centre (open Monday to Saturday 9 a.m. to 5 p.m., admission free; wheelchair access to ground floor only). A multi-use structure over the centuries, it retains its Victorian police cells, while the second floor, where the Masonic Lodge used to meet, has symbols of Freemasonry painted on the ceiling. A fragment of the old Mercat Cross sits on a modern pillar in front of the Town House. As with its equivalent in 'New' Aberdeen, this was the site of markets, proclamations, and the administration of justice. On 30 August 1699 convicted thief Patrick Falconer was bound to a stake, had his ear nailed to the wood, branded on the cheek and banished forever from the burgh.

In 1638 Revd Andrew Cant, whose two sons were attending King's College, had a prophetic vision. Looking out of his chamber window towards the Mercat Cross, he saw around 200 children, all dressed in white. The happy band were singing and playing musical instruments, and were led by his sons. A short time later the vision became true, as smallpox carried off many of the children of the town, his sons among them. The episode is quoted in Margo Todd's *The Culture of Protestantism in Early Modern Scotland*.

ZOOLOGY MUSEUM

Tillydrone Avenue. Open 9 a.m.–5 p.m. Monday-Friday, admission free. Wheelchair access to most of the displays, with some steps in one section. Although held in a brutalist concrete monstrosity, this wonderful collection of creatures great and small was founded as far back as 1775 and – if you are keen on fang and armour, tooth and tongue, bone and claw – is so full of marvels it takes hours to explore. There are skeletons of humans, gorillas, gibbon, orang-utan, chimpanzee, snakes, ostrich, lizards, bats, hippopotamus, rhinoceros, camel, giraffe, tapir and elephant. And more. There is a tiger that had been exhibited in George Wombwell's infamous Travelling Menagerie of the nineteenth century. There are whales and mightily-fanged sabre-toothed cats, giant spider crabs and a huge crocodile. There is a tuatara (the last living survivor of the Age of Dinosaurs) and the truly grotesque matamata turtle. There is a *faux* T.Rex made of drift-wood, a majestic Bengal tiger and a specimen of the passenger pigeon, the first creature to suffer a human-created mass extinction in modern times. There is the skeleton of a sei whale that allegedly drips oil on hot days. The overall experience is partly creepy, partly awe-inspiring, and entirely engrossing.

Two exhibits in particular have a cryptozoological interest. One is a full-size replica of the enormous fish called the coelacanth. Coelacanths were only known from the fossil record and were believed to have become extinct about 70 million years ago – until one was caught off South Africa in 1938. The discovery created a sensation and made the coelacanth the most famous fish in the world. Several other specimens of this relic of the Age of Dinosaurs have since come to light, and two breeding populations are known, at the Comoros Islands and in Sulawesi, Indonesia. For anyone interested in exploring the coelacanth story further, I recommend Samantha Weinberg's thrilling book *A Fish Caught in Time* (1999).

The second exhibit has a more local flavour – the Kellas Cat. The mounted specimen shows a large, black, grumpy-looking creature which has the appearance of a feral moggie that's been working out at the gym. Kellas cats are in fact a hybrid species of the domestic cat and the Scottish wildcat. They are named for the village of Kellas in Morayshire, where several of the cats have been caught.

Kellas cats have often been mistaken for much larger animals, and they may be behind some of the reported sightings of big exotic cats in the north-east of Scotland. The specimen on display was found in rural Aberdeenshire. The display interpretation makes the connection between Kellas cats and the uncanny black 'Wangie cat' or 'Cait sith' (fairy cat) of Scottish folklore. For more on this fierce feline, check out *My Highland Kellas Cats* by Di Francis (1993).

The Museum's website has a delightful story of an April Fool's joke in which an extinct species was brought back from the dead. The Great Auk, a once common flightless bird, was entirely killed off in 1844. The Museum has a Great Auk egg and on 1 April 1988 Dr Robert Ralph, a senior lecturer at the Zoology Department, announced on the local station Northsound Radio that he and his team had extracted DNA from the egg and successfully created a Great Auk chick. The bird, named Auky, had hatched a week previously and was enthusiastically consuming minced herring. Dr Ralph was now hoping to contact other museums with Great Auk eggs to see if the process could be repeated and a breeding population established. The hoax was brilliantly put together, with all sorts of details such as the scientists listening excitedly to the first faint scratchings from the fertilised egg. Dr Ralph signed off by looking forward to a time when the technique could be used to resurrect other extinct species: 'Who knows – it may be possible one day to visit an island full of dinosaurs!' This was two years before the publication of Michael Crichton's *Jurassic Park*.

THE CHANONRY

During 1837-8 an apparently supernatural assailant terrorised the streets of London. Nicknamed 'Spring-heeled Jack' for his ability to leap over high walls, he was reported to appear in a variety of guises, wearing armour, a cloak, a helmet or a white oilskin, had burning-red eyes, clawed hands, and the ability to breathe balls of fire. The demon, or monster, or superhuman – or whatever he was – made such an impression on Victorian culture that 'Spring-heeled Jack' became both a generic term for a prowler in the dark, and a folkloric 'meme' that appeared in dozens of British cities, and then travelled to Europe and America. Sightings of Spring-heeled Jack were still being reported well into the twentieth century.

Old Aberdeen was briefly visited with Spring-heeled Jack fever in the 1860s. Katherine Trail, who was born in that decade at No. 53 College Bounds, recalled her childhood impressions of Spring-heeled Jack in an article for the *Press & Journal* on 1 March 1933, entitled 'I Remember – when Old Aberdeen had only half a "bobby", and "Spring-heeled Jack" was the Terror of the Chanonry':

> I never saw him, nor was I acquainted with anybody who was supposed actually to have set eyes on him, but we children had not the slightest doubt as to his existence. We knew that he haunted the Chanonry at night, enveloped in a white sheet, and jumped over people's heads, and no maid would dream of walking along the Chanonry after darkness had fallen.

No. 16 has a sculptured finial from the cathedral in a window space, while No. 20 has a closed-up pend above which are the brightly-painted arms of Bishop Gavin Dunbar, who built the original building in 1519. In *Records of Old Aberdeen* Alexander Macdonald Munro recorded that in medieval times one of the manses of the college of canons in the Chanonry had a 'bad name' because for many years it was believed to be haunted by ghosts and evil spirits. The house was demolished in the seventeenth century.

ST MACHAR'S CATHEDRAL

The cathedral dedicated to St. Machar, tho' none knows who that Saint was.

Daniel Defoe, *A Tour Thro' the Whole Island of Great Britain* (1724)

Open 9 a.m.–5 p.m., admission free. Reasonable wheelchair access to most parts. This magnificent cathedral has full-colour guidebook available and a fulsome website, so here I will concentrate only on the stranger parts of the building's fabric, history and associations.

To start with the identity of St Machar, a shadowy saint of whom almost nothing reliable is known. He is supposed to have been one of the companions of St Columba on his voyage to Iona in 560. The same legend provides the founding miracle that was compulsory in all medieval wonder-tales associated with saints: in 580 Machar received instruction from Columba (or perhaps directly from God) to establish a church where a bend in the river resembled the shape of a bishop's crosier. The River Don meets this criterion. But this legend only stems from the fourteenth century, 200 years after the original cathedral was first established, and may have been part of an attempt to 'spin' the origin of Machar to provide a spurious antiquity and legitimacy to the dedication. The traditional story of the founding of the first church is illustrated in the 'St Machar' stained-glass window by Douglas Strachan. In *An Historical Account and Delineation of Aberdeen* (1822) Robert Wilson alternatively states that Machar was Macarius, a saint not of 580 but from the late 800s. To add to the confusion, on display within the cathedral is an incised Pictish or Celtic cross, which has been tentatively dated to the seventh or eighth century. It was found, reused, in a boundary wall in Don Street. So there may have been a Christian community on this spot in the Dark Ages, but whether it had anything to do with Machar, or whether he ever actually existed, is unknown.

The current building is only half a cathedral; in 1688 a storm brought down the central tower, annihilating the transepts, choir and altar, which were never rebuilt. A new wall closed off the nave, which then became the main church. Eroded carvings from what had been the columns of the internal crossing can be seen on the exterior east wall: they include a grotesque head and a mermaid and merman. The former transepts, now open to the sky, are filled with the gravestones of the great and good. Several slabs feature skulls and other symbols of mortality, while the crowded main graveyard also has many carved stones, with winged souls, hourglasses, skulls and heraldic panels all present and correct.

Of the two elaborate tomb recesses in the south transept, the one under the modern canopy is that of Bishop Gavin Dunbar, one of the 'building bishops', responsible for the BRIDGE OF DEE and much of the Cathedral. Dunbar died in 1532. The carvings on the tomb were mutilated by the intolerant Covenanters a little more a century later, possibly because they had heard of an episode later catalogued in Catholic writer William Walsh's 1904 compendium of Marian miracles and visions, *The Apparitions and Shrines of Heaven's Bright Queen*:

A Protestant gentleman having died, his relative chose for his interment the place where the remains of the saintly Bishop had been deposited. Their astonishment was great when, on digging the grave, the sexton came upon the coffin of the holy prelate. Opening it, they found the body robed in episcopal ornaments, without the slightest sign of corruption, as fresh and beautiful as the day on which it had been interred. Surprised at the news of this wonder, the minister of the cathedral went in person to witness it. On examination it was found that the body emitted no disagreeable odor, and was perfectly entire. The minister, through a sentiment of respect, commanded the grave to be closed at once, and forbade anyone to touch what had been so wonderfully preserved.

Above left: The twin towers of St Machar's Cathedral, with the anti-bodysnatching watchhouse in the foreground. *(Geoff Holder)*

Above right: The eroded carving of a bearded man on the eastern gable of St Machar's. *(Geoff Holder)*

As if an uncorrupted corpse was not enough, there was a second miracle of holy light:

> Seven years afterward the Regent, accompanied by thirteen schismatic bishops and a number of gentlemen of rank, went to the tomb of the holy man, and ordered it to be opened in their presence, that they might be personal witnesses of what had been recorded. When the grave was opened, the body was again found fresh and untouched by corruption, while from the countenance issued rays of light, which filled the beholders with astonishment, although their hearts still remained hardened, and they refused to accept the teachings of the true faith.

The collapse of the tower may have been accelerated by two factors. In 1568 (not at the Reformation of 1560, as is often claimed) the lead was stripped from the roof. Scotland was in economic crisis and its rulers were attempting to liquidate as many assets as possible. The ship carrying the valuable metal (along with the lead from Elgin Cathedral) sank on leaving Aberdeen harbour, an event many Catholics saw as God smiting the heretics for their sacrilegious act. Then in the 1650s Cromwell's troops built a bastion on CASTLEHILL using stone taken from the both the derelict bishop's palace to the east of St Machar's, and the choir, which had been largely unused since the Reformation. The fabric thus doubly weakened, the collapse may have been inevitable. The bishop's palace had a great stone-lined well in the middle of its court; when the Parliamentarians took the stones away, the sides of the well fell in and buried the men. More divine retribution.

There were two holy wells in the area, but we know little about them. St John's Well was at the bottom of the brae on the north side of the cathedral, while St Machar's Well was located in the neighbouring grounds of Seaton House (now Seaton Park). Their waters were used for baptisms and washing the holy vessels. In 1687 several church-goers caused a scandal by fighting at a baptism. The belief was that the first child baptised 'carried off the blessing of the water' and so the pushy parents traded blows in an attempt to gain precedence, a situation not unfamiliar to those seeking school places today. Ordinary water was sourced from the nearby Loch of Aberdon, which also supported a colony of Black-headed gulls, regarded at the time as domestic fowl. The young gulls were an important food source. John Milne's *Topographical, Antiquarian, and Historical Papers on the City of Aberdeen* describes how, 'just when the young birds were beginning to fly a string of men entered the water and drove all the young birds slowly before them. As they reached the side they were caught and killed as quietly as possible not to alarm the old birds, which were allowed to breed a second time without molestation to keep up the number of birds.' The superstitious Spalding (*History of the Troubles and Memorable Transactions in Scotland*) noted that in 1641 the gulls disappeared, this being God (or nature) expressing disapproval at the religious and military turmoil of the time. It was more likely the birds were seeking a better environment, as the loch was drying up (not to mention the harrying of their nests and slaughter of their young).

Above left: St Machar's Cathedral, showing the sixteenth-century heraldic ceiling. *(Geoff Holder)*

Above right: The Scourgal Monument: King Death brings down the final curtain. *(Ségolène Dupuy)*

Further strangitude can be found in a tradition that, when William Wallace was executed in 1305, his left arm ended up in Aberdeen and was buried at St Machar's. The usual spot pointed out is a five-pointed star on the south wall of the churchyard, beside the gateway leading into the south-east part of the Chanonry. The star, however, comes from one of the broken gravestones that were dispersed in the early eighteenth century. The legend of Wallace's arm probably prompted a ghostly experience claimed to have taken place when a party of schoolboys visited the cathedral in 1967. As reported in *Haunted Scotland* by Norman Adams, three of the boys said they had seen a severed hand emerge from a gap in the main door. There are more Wallace traditions, of equivalent believability, connected with JUSTICE STREET and ST FITTICK'S CHURCH in Torry.

The interior is a treasury of splendour. There is the unique flat rectangular heraldic ceiling decorated with the arms of the political and religious leaders of early sixteenth-century Europe – and arranged according to a very Scottish take on who owed allegiance to whom in that world. There are three effigies of medieval clerics, with superbly carved vestments. A twelfth-century cross-head on a modern shaft is a relic of the time the cathedral was surrounded by a sanctuary – if you could pass beyond the crosses, you were granted sanctuary and (theoretically) remained safe from your enemies for a year and a day. The 1950s font shows St Machar baptising converts. A modern carved wooden triptych commemorates archdeacon John Barbour, author of *The Brus*, a long poem glorifying the exploits of Robert the Bruce.

The most astonishing memorial is that to Patrick Scourgal, Bishop from 1664-1682. Winged souls, dour human figures and earnest angels fondling skulls form the basic décor, but the eye is drawn to the lower tableau. In a theatrical gesture, crowned King Death stretches his bat-like skeletal arms over two individuals struggling for their last breath. The final curtain is about to come down. Scourgal lived his later years in a first-floor apartment up the twisting stairs in one of the towers. Alexander Macdonald Munro, in *Records of Old Aberdeen*, notes that Scourgal was very fat when he died; the door and stairs proving too narrow, 'it was found necessary to remove the body through the window'.

In the seventeenth century the Kirk Session at St Machar's found themselves dealing with minor cases of folk magic and 'charming'. On 16 October 1642 David Craig of Clinterty confessed to using charms and was sentenced to make his repentance by appearing in the church in sackcloth. On 26 September 1649 Christane Simsone, the wife of Hendrie Adames, accused Isobel Kelman of taking a calf in her arms and so causing it to sicken and die. It seems both Isobel and Christane had wanted to buy the same animal, and Isobel, being bested in the deal, had cursed the creature. The case was not pursued further, but it was clear Isobel had a certain reputation. The following 21 November the Session reported they knew of no one in the parish suspected of witchcraft or charming, except Isobel Kelman 'against whom ther was no proofe'. Isobel had been due to be charged with crossing the River Don without a boat (that is, by witchery or with the aid of spirits); but the witness died before the Session could hear his evidence.

In 1673 Janet Watson took advantage of her neighbour's credulity and claimed she could discover who had stolen a pair of sheets and some money. She took up a sieve and shears – a classic form of Scottish divination – and asked the spirits who had the goods, making sure to use the protective incantation 'in the name of St Peter and St Paul'. Watson spoke several names, and the shears 'reacted' at one woman's name – the presumed guilty party. The Session considered the act had been done 'more through imprudence than any other way' and so only fined the women 40s.

On 5 June 1681 Jean Nimbrie confessed to healing Helen Collie in Sunnyside. She tied a thread around a hose (a garment) then placed the hose about Helen, saying 'The Lord Jesus Christ by the sea rode and the fevers on his side and buried them in a grave, in the name of the Father, Son and Holy Ghost.' This cured Helen of 'the fevers'. The following October the presbytery ordered Jean, 'being ane ordinarie charmer', to make repentance in church wearing sackcloth.

The final incident in the records is from 15 January 1727. Isabel Craffurd was accused of telling fortunes, locating stolen goods, and being able to tell if a person who had gone overseas was alive or dead. Isabel confessed only to fortune-telling, saying that she had learned how to do it from a book, and her practice was to 'read' palms. Isabel got a severe ticking off but otherwise she appears to have gone unpunished. All these cases can be found in Munro's *Records of Old Aberdeen*.

The invaluable Munro also has tales of graverobbing. When the tower collapsed in 1688 it smashed open a number of tombs. On 27 May William Gald, the sexton (gravedigger) confessed to 'sifting the ashes of the dead' in search of rings and other valuables. He lost his job (at least temporarily) and was ordered to make an apology in front of the entire congregation. Writing in 1725, William Orem noted that Gald 'never prospered one day after so unchristian an act'. During the time of the bodysnatchers a watchhouse was built at the western entrance of the graveyard (it is still there, now a tool shed). People were clearly on patrol at night with loaded firearms, and possibly some alcohol was occasionally imbibed – 'just to keep out the cold, like'. On 27 November 1809 complaints were lodged about stupid men with guns, and the forces of pulpit and Provost combined to suppress the foolhardy practice. It is not clear if they succeeded.

TILLYDRONE ROAD

This pedestrian thoroughfare departs The Chanonry opposite the cathedral and passes (to the north) Tillydrone Motte, an early medieval castle-mound, now overgrown. Inevitably it has an associated legend, and it can be found in Robert Smith's *The Granite City*. A group of nuns had committed some (unspecified) sin and in penance had to carry the soil to build the motte up from the low ground of Seaton – in their aprons.

Just before the junction with Tillydrone Avenue, the lane passes Benholm's Lodging, also known as the Wallace Tower. This Z-plan fortified house was built around 1588 on NETHERKIRKGATE; it was unceremoniously shunted here in 1964 to make way for Marks and Spencer. The tower has no connection with William Wallace, other than in that fervid part of the Scottish popular imagination that ascribes everything historical to Wallace, Robert the Bruce or Mary Queen of Scots. The tower is ornamented with the statue of a dog and a figure in armour (which these days gives him the comic effect of looking like the Michelin Man). By popular consent, any man in armour = William Wallace, hence the name. In fact the warrior is Sir Robert Keith of Benholm, the chap who built the original tower. At present the tower has no useful function and is forlorn and vandalised.

TILLYDRONE AVENUE

At the very point of the junction of Tillydrone Road and Avenue, well hidden behind the encroaching vegetation, is a roughly-made brick obelisk. The inscription, if you can see it, reads 'Downie's Cairn, formerly associated with the tale of Downie the Sacrist. I cannot tell how the truth may be; I say the tale as t'was said to me.' It may come as some surprise that this obscure, neglected and frankly dull spot is the focus of Aberdeen's most enduring urban legend: Downie's Slaughter.

The basic story is that Downie worked at the University as a sacristan, a kind of upmarket doorkeeper. He was diligent in making sure the students did not break any of the onerous rules about being outside of the College quadrangle at night, or drinking, or consorting with young ladies. And he maintained this discipline with a trusty cudgel. But this diligence in policing the student body was his undoing. One night the unpopular jobsworth was kidnapped and solemnly subjected to a mock trial, at the end of which he was formally sentenced to execution. He was bound and taken to a darkened room. He was blindfolded.

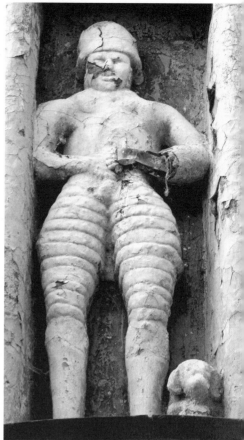

Above left: Downie's Cairn, Tillydrone Road, nothing to do with Downie and not a cairn. The hidden inscription reads, 'I cannot tell how the truth may be; I say the tale as t'was said to me.' *(Geoff Holder)*

Above right: The statue on Benholm's Lodging, Tillydrone Road. Often said to be William Wallace, it is actually the tower's builder, Sir Robert Keith of Benholm. The dog has not been identified. *(Geoff Holder)*

His head was placed on a block. A tub of sawdust was laid beneath his head. And when his neck was touched not with the axe but with the apex of the prank, the flick of a wet towel – he died.

This is the standard tale of 'the man who died of fright'; there is a particularly detailed account in Neil MacLean's *Life at a Northern University*, published in 1874, and I have several dozen references to its repetition in books, magazines and newspapers. It's so popular, so well attested, that it must be true. But. But…

But it's almost certain the whole thing is a farrago, a fable, a folkloric jest: a fib. In 1902-3 several former students of Aberdeen University attempted to get at the truth, their ongoing researches and polite disputes appearing in the multi-issue publication *Scottish Notes and Queries* (1903 edition). Nothing absolutely black-and-white yes-or-no was definitively concluded, but a few things were established:

1. There was no record of any sacristan named Downie, or Dauney, or Daunie, or any of the other variations on his name.

2. There was no indication in any of the University records or the various histories of Aberdeen about the event, not even a mild allusion.

3. The first mention of the tale in print turned out to be in the crisply titled *Things in general: being delineations of persons, places, scenes, circumstances, situations, and occurrences in the Metropolis and other parts of Britain with an autobiographic sketch in Lumine and a notice touching Edinburgh*, written by Laurence Langshank in 1824.

4. Langshank was the *nom-de-plume* of Robert Mudie (1777-1842), a prolific newspaper editor and author from Dundee.

5. Mudie was best mates with Sandy Bannerman (Sir Alexander Bannerman, M.P.), an Aberdeen character noted for his abilities as a raconteur and his liking for a bit of a laugh.

6. Some of the characters and situations in Mudie's account of Downie's death turn up, prototype-like, in some of Mudie's earlier works.

7. An almost exact duplicate of the Downie story appeared in 1793 in *The Bee, or Literary Weekly Intelligencer*, a periodical edited by Dr James Anderson, an Aberdeenshire-based agricultural reformer and intellectual. In this version, Frederick the Great punishes a recalcitrant general with a mock trial and execution, only the officer is 'reprieved' at the last minute, and lives.

The widespread (but not undisputed) view was that Bannerman and Mudie cooked up the Downie story based on the episode in *The Bee*, and Bannerman was recounting the dramatic tale at various drink-fuelled dinners in Aberdeen for a few years before Mudie published it in a relatively obscure book in London in 1824. This accounts for the speedy popularity of the story – once you've heard it (perhaps at a convivial dinner) you just have to tell someone else.

In a variation on the story, one not found in Mudie's original version, the panicked students swore each other to secrecy and buried the body in an unmarked grave before dawn. Several of the correspondents to *Notes and Queries* recalled visiting a green mound near Kittybrewster called Downie's Howe, and pointed out the name was shown on a map of 1789. Could, then, the story be true, an eighteenth-century murder mystery? Again, nothing can be certain, but it seems Downie's Howe and 'Downie's Slaughter' are two unconnected elements, only sharing a name. There was at least one prominent Aberdonian named Downie, and various parts of the landscape were named after him; this may have been another one. George Walker, who first made the connection between Downie, Mudie and Bannerman in his 1897 classic *Aberdeen Awa'*, investigated further in 1902 and found that an entire folklore had grown up about Downie's Howe. Bones were said to have been dug up, identified as human and reburied (uncorroborated); the owners of the land were said to have a legal duty to preserve the mound (untrue); and various men said their grandfathers knew the story from their pre-1800 days (uncertain, possibly the result of one generation gulling a younger one, or improperly-remembered conversations from many decades ago).

Downie's Slaughter had become a floating legend, sucking in existing and new features as it went. For example, one former student remembered being told that the reason the gowns worn by students at King's College had no collars while those of their rivals at Marischal College were decorated with velvet collars, was that the King's collar was removed as a collective punishment for the killing of Downie. Once again, this is entirely baseless, but as a raw undergraduate the man believed it.

As to the obelisk, it was entirely unconnected with Downie, being built as a folly by Alexander Leslie on his estate at ASHGROVE in the eighteenth century. It outlasted its eighteenth-century companion follies, and as the area became populated and then industrialised, the prominent structure, so different to everything else around it, seemed the natural home of the Downie legend. When the obelisk was finally removed in 1926, to be re-erected in Old Aberdeen, the legend came along for the ride.

To finish with, a contemporary urban legend that has as much running power as Downie's. Stop me if you've heard this one before:

A student spends his entire grant within a fortnight. To keep himself alive, he cooks a great wodge of porridge, stores it in a drawer, and for every single meal he simply cuts off a chunk and fries it up. He does this for a long, long time – and then gets admitted to hospital. With scurvy.

In Rodney Dale's *Book of Urban Legend*, this tale is set specifically in Aberdeen University, and a quick check online turns up Aberdeen as one of the more common locations cited in the various retellings. However, the urban legends website snopes.com has found variations of this basic story attached to dozens of campuses throughout Britain, Canada and America, with the vitamin-free diet item variously described as porridge, macaroni, ramen, hot dogs or even beer and crisps. On the other hand, as Snopes reported, there is a documented case of a Nigerian man who contracted scurvy in 1967 because he ate no fresh food or vegetables while studying in London, and another (unlocated) case from 2003 of a student contracting scurvy through eating nothing but junk food.

'I cannot tell how the truth may be; I say the tale as t'was said to me.'

BIBLIOGRAPHY

PSAS = Proceedings of the Society of Antiquaries of Scotland.

HISTORY, ARCHAEOLOGY AND GENERAL

Anon. 'The last Speech and dying declaration of James Henderson' (1790) Broadside in National Library of Scotland, shelfmark: 6.365(104)

Anon. 'A New Way of Raising the Wind!' (1829) Broadside in National Library of Scotland, shelfmark: Ry.III.a.6(047)

Anon. 'Murder' (1830) Broadside in National Library of Scotland, shelfmark: F.3.a.13(55)

Anon. 'The Only True Account' (1830) Broadside in National Library of Scotland, shelfmark: F.3.a.13(54)

Anon. 'Burking Shop Destroyed' (1831) Broadside in National Library of Scotland, shelfmark: F.3.a.13(6)

Anon. 'The Life of Calcraft' (1868) Broadside in National Library of Scotland, shelfmark: L.C.Fol.73(132)

Aberdeen City Council Archaeology Unit *East Kirk of St Nicholas Project 2006 Initial Report* 2nd edition (Aberdeen City Council; Aberdeen, 2008)

Adams, Norman *Scotland's Chronicles of Blood* (Robert Hale; London, 1996)
———— *Scottish Bodysnatchers: True Accounts* (Goblinshead; Musselburgh, 2002)
———— *Blood and Granite: True Crime from Aberdeen* (Black & White Publishing; Edinburgh, 2003)
———— *Hangman's Brae: True Crime and Punishment in Aberdeen and the North-East* (Black & White Publishing; Edinburgh, 2005)

Allardyce, Ann D. *The Goodwife at Home: Footdee in the 18th Century* (William Smith & Sons; Aberdeen, 1918)

Anderson, William *Rhymes, Reveries, and Reminiscences* (John Finlayson; Aberdeen, 1851)

Bain, Ebenezer *Merchant and Craft Guilds: A History of the Aberdeen Incorporated Trades* (J. & J.P. Edmond & Spark; Aberdeen, 1887)

Balfour, Bernard Maitland 'No Mean Aberdonians – Some Aberdeen Entrepreneurs' in John S. Smith and David Stevenson (eds) *Aberdeen in the Nineteenth Century: The Making of the Modern City* (Aberdeen University Press; Aberdeen, 1988)

Barrett, Michael *A Calendar of Scottish Saints* (The Abbey Press; Fort Augustus, 1919)

Blakhal, Gilbert *A Breiffe Narration of the Services Done to Three Noble Ladyes* (The Spalding Club; Aberdeen, 1844)

Brogden, W.A. *Aberdeen: An Illustrated Architectural Guide* (RIAS; Edinburgh, 1988)

Brogden, William 'Aberdeen's Architecture – from Classic to Caledonian' in John S. Smith and David Stevenson (eds.) *Aberdeen in the Nineteenth Century: The Making of the Modern City* (Aberdeen University Press; Aberdeen, 1988)

Brown, Chris *The Battle for Aberdeen 1644* (Tempus; Stroud, 2002)

Bruce, James *Lives of Eminent Men of Aberdeen* (D. Chalmers & Co.; Aberdeen, 1841)

——————— *The Black Kalendar of Aberdeen* (James Strachan; Aberdeen, 1843)

Bruce-Briggs, B. 'Peter Williamson: faker' in *Northern Scotland* 24 (2004), University of Aberdeen Centre for Scottish Studies

Buchanan, William *Glimpses of Olden Days in Aberdeen* (printed for the author at the Free Press Office; Aberdeen, 1870)

Byron, Lord George Gordon *Don Juan* (Penguin; Harmondsworth, 2004 – first published 1823)

Catling, Christopher 'The Archaeology of Leprosy and the Black Death' in *Current Archaeology* No. 236, November 2009

Chalmers, Mark 'The architecture of Pirie and Clyne' online at www.aberdeenarchitects.org

Coldham, Peter Wilson *Emigrants in Chains: A Social History of Forced Emigration to the Americas of Felons, Destitute Children, Political and Religious Non-Conformists, Vagabonds, Beggars and Other Undesirables, 1607-1776* (Genealogical Publishing Company; Baltimore, 1994)

Cooney, Neil *Medieval Aberdeen* (Aberdeen Town & County History Society; Aberdeen, n.d.)

Croly, Chris *Aberdeen's Castle* (Aberdeen City Council; Aberdeen, 2007)

——————— 'Aberdeen's Stones of Time' in *Leopard Magazine* December 2007

——————— *Aberdeen's March Stones Trail* (Aberdeen City Council; Aberdeen, n.d.)

Cruickshank, James 'Newhills Cross, Aberdeenshire' in *PSAS*, Vol. 60 (1926)

Defoe, Daniel *A Tour Thro' the Whole Island of Great Britain* (Penguin; Harmondsworth, 2005 – first published 1724-1726)

Douglas, Francis *A General Description of the East Coast of Scotland* (printed for the author; Paisley, 1782)

Edwards, John *Maritime Aberdeen* (Tempus; Stroud, 2004)

Eeles, Francis C. *King's College Chapel Aberdeen: Its Fittings, Ornaments and Ceremonial in the Sixteenth Century* (Oliver and Boyd; Edinburgh and London, 1956)

Eyre-Todd, George *Byways of Scottish Story* (William J. Hay; Edinburgh, 1930)

Fawcett, Richard *Scottish Cathedrals* (B.T. Batsford/Historic Scotland; London, 1997)

Fraser, G.M. *Historical Aberdeen: The Green and its Story* (William Smith; Aberdeen, 1904)

——————— *The Lone Shieling, or, The authorship of the 'Canadian Boat Song', with Other Literary and Historical Sketches* (William Smith & Sons, The Bon-Accord Press; Aberdeen, 1908)

Geddes, Jane (ed.) *King's College Chapel, Aberdeen, 1500-2000* (Northern Universities Press; Leeds, 2000)

Gibb, Andrew 'Notice of the Memorial Brass of Dr Duncan Liddel, and of the Tombstone of Sir Paul Menzies of Kinmundy, in Saint Nicholas Church, Aberdeen' In *PSAS*, Vol. 11 (1874-1876)

Harper, Norman *First Daily: A 250-year Celebration of the Press and Journal* (Aberdeen Journals; Aberdeen, 1997)

Harrower, Rachel Blanche 'Principal 'Rory' Macleod and His Posterity' in *The Aberdeen University Review* Vol. IX (1921-22) (No. 25 November, 1921)

Henderson, John A. *History of the Parish of Banchory-Devenick* (D. Wyllie & Son; Aberdeen, 1890)

——————— *Annals of Lower Deeside, Being a Topographical, Proprietary, Ecclesiastical, and Antiquarian History of Durris, Drumoak, and Culter* (D. Wyllie & Son; Aberdeen, 1892)

Jervise, Andrew 'Notices and Examples of Inscriptions on Old Castles and Town Houses in the North-East of Scotland' in *PSAS*, Vol. 4 (1860-1862)

——————— *Inscriptions From the Shields or Panels of the Incorporated Trades in The Trinity Hall, Aberdeen* (Lewis Smith; Aberdeen, 1863)

——————— *Epitaphs and Inscriptions from Burial Grounds and Old Buildings in the North East of Scotland* (David Douglas; Edinburgh, 1879)

Keith, Alexander *A Thousand Years of Aberdeen* (Aberdeen University Press; Aberdeen, 1972)

Kennedy, William *Annals of Aberdeen* (A. Brown & Co.; Aberdeen; W. Blackwood; Edinburgh; and Longman, Hurst, Rees, Orme and Brown; London, 1818)

Laurence Langshank (= Robert Mudie) *Things in General: Being Delineations of Persons, Places, Scenes, Circumstances, Situations, and Occurrences in the Metropolis and Other Parts of Britain* (Smith Elder and Co.; London, 1825)

Littlejohn, David (ed.) *Records of the Sheriff Court of Aberdeenshire Volume II: Records, 1598-1649* (Aberdeen University Press; Aberdeen, 1906)

Livingstone, Sheila *Confess and Be Hanged: Scottish Crime & Punishment Through the Ages* (Birlinn; Edinburgh, 2000)

Love, Dane *Scottish Kirkyards* (Robert Hale; London, 1989)

Lyons, A.W. 'Further Notes on Tempera-Painting in Scotland, and Other Discoveries at Delgaty Castle' in *PSAS*, Vol. 44 (1909-10)

MacAulay, John M. *Seal-Folk and Ocean Paddlers* (White Horse Press; Cambridge, 1998)

McDonnell, Frances *Aberdeen Obituaries 1748-1770* (Frances McDonnell; St Andrews, 1996)

Mackenzie, Norman 'When the Crematorium was a Hotbed of Rumour' in *Leopard Magazine* August 2006

MacLean, Neil N. *Life at a Northern University* (The Rosemount Press; Aberdeen, 1906 – first published 1874)

Maidment, James *Scotish Ballads and Songs* (Thomas George Stevenson; Edinburgh 1859)

Mann, Alison 'Mary Jameson's Tapestries' in *Leopard Magazine* October 2007

Marren, Peter *Grampian Battlefields: The Historic Battles of North East Scotland from AD 84 to 1745* (Mercat Press; Edinburgh, 1998)

Meldrum, Edward 'Sir George Skene's House in The Guestrow, Aberdeen – Its History and Architecture' in *PSAS*, Vol. 92 (1958-59)

——————— 'Benholm's Tower, Nether Kirkgate, Aberdeen' in *PSAS*, Vol. 95 (1961-62)

Miller, David G. *Aberdeen A Heritage Remembered: Buildings Loved, Loathed or Lost* (Aberdeen Town & County History Society; Aberdeen, 2009)

Milne, John *Topographical, Antiquarian, and Historical Papers on the City of Aberdeen* (Aberdeen Journal Office; Aberdeen, 1911)

Ministers of The Respective Parishes, *New Statistical Account of Scotland*, Vol. 12 (Aberdeen City of Aberdeen) and 14 (Inverness) (William Blackwood; Edinburgh and London, 1845)

Moir, Alexander L. *Genealogy and Collateral Lines, with Historical Notes* (the author; Lowell, Massachusetts, 1913)

Morgan, Diane *Lost Aberdeen: The Outskirts* (Birlinn; Edinburgh, 2007)

——————— *The Granite Mile: The Story of Aberdeen's Union Street* (Black & White Publishing; Edinburgh, 2008)

Morkill, J.W. 'Notice of a Human Hand and Forearm, Pierced with Nail Holes, and a Basket-Hilted Sword, Formerly Preserved in the Family of Graham of Woodhall, Yorkshire, as Relics of James, First Marquis of Montrose' in *PSAS*, Vol. 31 (1896-97)

Munro, Alexander Macdonald (ed.) *Records of Old Aberdeen*, Volume I: 1157-1891; Volume II: 1498-1903 (The Spalding Club/Aberdeen University Press; Aberdeen, 1909)

Nicol, William *History of the Old Bridge of Don or Balgownie Brig and its Surrounding Neighbourhood* (W. Nicol; Aberdeen, 1851)

North East Museums Partnership *Crime & Punishment Trails in Aberdeen & Stonehaven* (North East Museums Partnership; Aberdeen, n.d.)

Ogilvie, Thomas White *The Book of Saint Fittick* (Bon-Accord Press; Aberdeen, 1901)

Orem, William *A Description of the Chanonry, Cathedral, and King's College of Old Aberdeen, in the years 1724 and 1725* (J. Chalmers and Co.; Aberdeen, 1791)

Power, Matthew A. *The Protomartyr of Scotland, Father Francis of Aberdeen: A Glimpse of the Scottish Reformation 1559* (Sands & Co.; London and Edinburgh, 1914)

Rettie, James *Aberdeen 150 Years Ago* (EP Publishing; Wakefield, 1972 – first published in 1868 as Aberdeen Fifty Years Ago)

Ritchie, James 'An Account of the Watch-Houses, Mortsafes, and Public Vaults in Aberdeenshire Churchyards, formerly used for the Protection of the Dead from the Resurrectionists' in *PSAS*, Vol. 46 (1911-12)

————— 'Relics of the Body-Snatchers: Supplementary Notes on Mortsafe Tackle, Mortsafes, Watch-Houses, and Public Vaults, mostly in Aberdeenshire' in *PSAS*, Vol. 55 (1920-21)

Roberts, Revd David 'Three Bogus Trinitarian Pictures' in *The Innes Review* Vol. XI (1960)

Scott, Hew *Fasti Ecclesiæ Scoticanæ: The Succession of Ministers in the Church of Scotland from the Reformation*, Volume VI Synods of Aberdeen and of Moray (Oliver and Boyd; Edinburgh, 1926)

Scottish Notes and Queries Vol. VII June 1893 to May 1894 (D. Wyllie & Son; Aberdeen, 1894)

Scottish Notes and Queries: Second Series Vol. IV July, 1902, to June, 1903 (A. Brown & Co.; Aberdeen, 1903)

Seager, Delia 'Quakerism in the North-East of Scotland: Enthusiasm, Apology and Persecution' (paper presented to the conference 'After Columba, After Calvin' at the University of Aberdeen on 18 October 1997)

Shepherd, Ian *Aberdeen and North-East Scotland* (HMSO; Edinburgh, 1996)

Sinclair, Sir John, Ian R. Grant, Donald J. Withrington (eds.) *Statistical Account of Scotland 1791-1799*. Vol. XXX (EP Publishing; Wakefield, 1982)

Skelton, Douglas *Devil's Gallop: Trips into Scotland's Dark and Bloody Past* (Mainstream Publishing; Edinburgh and London, 2001)

Smith, Robert *The Granite City: A History of Aberdeen* (John Donald Publishers; Edinburgh, 1989)

————— *25 Walks In and Around Aberdeen* (HMSO; Edinburgh, 1995)

————— *The Hidden City: The Story of Aberdeen and its People* (John Donald; Edinburgh, 1999)

————— *Aberdeen Curiosities* (John Donald; Edinburgh, 2002)

————— *Grampian Curiosities* (Birlinn; Edinburgh, 2005)

Spalding, John *The History of the Troubles and Memorable Transactions in Scotland, from the Year 1624 to 1645* (T. Evans; London, 1792)

Stevenson, Robert Louis *Essays of Travel* (Chatto & Windus; London, 1905)

Stones, J.A. *A Tale of Two Burghs: The Archaeology of Old and New Aberdeen* (Aberdeen Art Gallery & Museums; Aberdeen, 1987)

Stuart, John (ed.) *The Miscellany of the Spalding Club* Vols I and II (The Spalding Club; Aberdeen, 1841)

————— *Extracts from the Council Register of the Burgh of Aberdeen 1570-1625* Vol. 2 (The Spalding Club; Aberdeen, 1843)

————— *Selections from the Records of the Kirk Session, Presbytery, and Synod of Aberdeen* (The Spalding Club; Aberdeen, 1846)

Thom, Walter *The History of Aberdeen* (Alex. Stevenson; Aberdeen, 1811)

Thomson, Albert A. *From Hungary to Holburn Street* (Aberdeen Shoemakers' Incorporation; Aberdeen, n.d.)

Todd, Margo *The Culture of Protestantism in Early Modern Scotland* (Yale University Press; New Haven, 2002)

Walker, George *Aberdeen Awa': Sketches of its Men, Manners, and Customs as Delineated in Brown's Book-Stall, 1892-4* (A. Brown & Co.; Aberdeen, 1897)

Watt, Archibald *Highways and Byways Round Kincardine* (Gourdas House; Aberdeen, 1985)

Watt, William *A History of Aberdeen and Banff* (William Blackwood & Sons; Edinburgh and London, 1900)

Webster, Jack *Jack Webster's Aberdeen* (Birlinn; Edinburgh, 2007)

Williamson, Peter *French and Indian Cruelty Exemplified, in the Life, and Various Vicissitudes of Fortune, of Peter Williamson: Who was Carried off from Aberdeen in his Infancy, and Sold for a Slave in Pennsylvania* (printed for, and sold by J. Stewart; Edinburgh, 1787)

Wilson, Robert *An Historical Account and Delineation of Aberdeen* (James Johnston; Aberdeen, 1822)

Winfield, Arthur 'Aberdeen past and future laid bare' in *Leopard Magazine* August 2009

Wylie, J.A. *History of the Scottish Nation* Vol. I (Hamilton, Adams, & Co.; London, and Andrew Elliot; Edinburgh, 1886)

Wyness, Fenton *City By the Grey North Sea: Aberdeen* (Alex P. Reid & Son; Aberdeen, 1965)

————— *Royal Valley: The story of the Aberdeenshire Dee* (Alex P. Reid & Son; Aberdeen, 1968)

————— *Aberdeen: Century of Change* (Impulse Books; Aberdeen, 1971)

————— *Spots from the Leopard: Short Stories of Aberdeen and the North-East* (Impulse Books; Aberdeen, 1971)

————— *More Spots from the Leopard* (Impulse Books; Aberdeen, 1973)

Wyness, Lys *A Brief History of The Seven Incorporated Trades of Aberdeen* (Aberdeen Town & County History Society; Aberdeen, 2009)

Yates, George C. 'Acoustic Jars' in William Andrews (ed.) *Antiquities and Curiosities of the Church* (William Andrews & Co.; London, 1897)

Yeoman, Peter *Medieval Scotland* (B.T. Batsford/Historic Scotland; London, 1995)

————— *Pilgrimage in Medieval Scotland* (B.T. Batsford/Historic Scotland; London, 1999)

MYSTERIOUSNESS

Anon. 'Strange and Wonderfull Apparitions' (1719) Broadside in National Library of Scotland, shelfmark: Ry.III.c.36(049)

Abercrombie, John *Inquiries Concerning the Intellectual Powers and the Investigation of Truth* (Waugh and Innes; Edinburgh, John Murray; Edinburgh, and Whittaker & Co.; London, 1835)

Adams, Norman *Haunted Scotland* (Mainstream Publishing; Edinburgh, 1998)

Allen, Greg Dawson 'The Pursuit of Witches' in *Leopard Magazine* October 2002

Balfour, Bernard Maitland *Secrets, Stories, Skeletons and Stones* (Cranstone House Publishing; Aberdeen, 1993)

Banks, M.M. 'Fishermen's Fears, Gipsies and Suttee' in *Folklore*, Vol. 45, No. 1 (March 1934)

Booth, J. Mackenzie 'Case of So-Called 'Spontaneous Combustion'' in *British Medical Journal* 21 April 1888

Bord, Janet and Colin Bord *Modern Mysteries of Britain* (Grafton Books; London, 1987)

Bougard, Michel *La Chronique des OVNI* (J.-P. Delarge; Paris, 1977)

Brand, John *Observations on Popular Antiquities: Chiefly Illustrating The Origin of our Vulgar Customs, Ceremonies and Superstitions* (F.C. and J. Rivington et al; London, 1813)

Cade, Maxwell C. and Delphine Davis *The Taming of the Thunderbolts: The Science and Superstition of Ball Lightning* (Abelard-Schuman; London and New York, 1969)

Chambers, Robert *Popular Rhymes of Scotland* (W.&R. Chambers; London and Edinburgh, 1870)

————— *The Book of Days; A Miscellany of Popular Antiquities in Connection with the Calendar, Including Anecdote, Biography, & History, Curiosities of Literature and Oddities of Human Life and Character* (W.&R. Chambers; London and Edinburgh, 1888)

Cutten, George Barton *Three Thousand Years of Mental Healing* (Charles Scribner & Sons; New York, 1911)

Dale, Rodney *Book of Urban Legend* (Wordsworth Editions; Ware, 2000)

Dalyell, John Graham *The Darker Superstitions of Scotland: Illustrated From History and Practice* (Waugh and Innes; Edinburgh, 1834)

Fort, Charles *Wild Talents* (John Brown Publishing; London, 1998 – first published 1932)

Gilchrist, Roberta 'Magic for the Dead? The Archaeology of Magic in Later Medieval Burials' in *Medieval Archaeology*, No. 52, 2008

Goodare, Julian 'The Aberdeenshire witchcraft panic of 1597' in *Northern Scotland*, No. 21 (2001)
————— 'The Scottish Witchcraft Panic of 1597' in Goodare, Julian (ed.) *The Scottish Witch-Hunt in Context* (Manchester University Press; Manchester & New York, 2002)

Goss, Michael 'Strange and Wonderful News …' in Steve Moore (ed.) *Fortean Studies* Vol. 1 (John Brown Publishing; London, 1994)

Grant, James *The Mysteries of All Nations: Rise and Progress of Superstition, Laws Against and Trials of Witches, Ancient and Modern Delusions Together With Strange Customs, Fables, and Tales* (W. Paterson; Edinburgh And Simpkin, Marshall, & Co.; London, 1880)

Gregor, Walter *Notes on the Folk-Lore of the North-East of Scotland* (Folk-Lore Society; London, 1881)

Guthrie, E.J. *Old Scottish Customs, Local and General* (Hamilton, Adams & Co.; London, and Thomas D. Mortson, Glasgow; 1885)

Halliday, Ron *UFO Scotland* (B&W Publishing; Edinburgh, 1998)

Hobbs, Sandy 'The Titanic Headline' in *Foaftale News: Newsletter of the International Society for Contemporary Legend Research* No. 61, April 2005

Lindley, Charles, Viscount Halifax *Lord Halifax's Ghost Book* (Geoffrey Bles; London, 1953 – first published 1936)

Love, Dane *Scottish Spectres* (Robert Hale; London, 2001)

Lowell, J. Russell 'Sir Thomas Browne and his Religio Medici. Our most Imaginative Mind Since Shakespeare' in *The Aberdeen University Review* Vol. IX (1921-22)

McAldowie, Alex M. 'Personal Experiences in Witchcraft' in *Folklore*, Vol. 7, No. 3 (September, 1896)

Mackinlay, J.M. *Folklore of Scottish Lochs and Springs* (William Hodge; Glasgow, 1893)

McPherson, J.M. *Primitive Beliefs in the North-East of Scotland* (Longmans, Green & Co.; London, 1929)

Maxwell-Stuart, P.G. *Satan's Conspiracy: Magic and Witchcraft in Sixteenth-Century Scotland* (Tuckwell Press; East Linton, 2001)

Milne, Graeme *The Haunted North: Paranormal Tales from Aberdeen and the North East* (Cauliay Publishing; Aberdeen, 2008)

Pickup, Gilly 'John Anderson: The Wizard of the North' in *Leopard Magazine* September 2005

Rorie, David 'Notes' in *Folklore*, Vol. 49, No. 1 (March, 1938)

Rust, James *Druidism Exhumed* (Edmonston & Douglas; Edinburgh. 1871)

Times, John *Eccentricities of the Animal Creation* (Seeley, Jackson and Halliday; London, 1869)

Walsh, William J. *The Apparitions and Shrines of Heaven's Bright Queen, in Legend, Poetry and History, From the Earliest Ages to the Present Time* (T.J. Carey; New York, 1904)

Wilson, Richard *Scotland's Unsolved Mysteries of the Twentieth Century* (Robert Hale; London, 1989)

FICTION

Clarke, Susanna *The Ladies of Grace Adieu and other Stories* (Bloomsbury; London, 2006)

MacBride, Stuart *Flesh House* (HarperCollins; London, 2008)

JOURNALS, NEWSPAPERS AND MAGAZINES

Auld Toon News (Old Aberdeen Community Council) Issue 9, September 2009
Blackwood's Edinburgh Magazine, No. 1, April 1817
Daily Telegraph 4 December 1998; 30 November 2000
Edinburgh Topographical, Traditional and Antiquarian Magazine September 1848
Evening Express 11 July 1973; 14 April 2009; 14 August 2009
Herald 7 August 2003
Huddersfield Daily Examiner 18 February 1993
Independent 7 August 2002
London Magazine, or, Gentleman's Monthly Intelligencer Vol. 35, 1766
London Medical and Physical Journal Vol. 46, 1821
Mail on Sunday 27 December 1998
The News No. 9 April 1975
News of the World 16 April 2000
Press & Journal 9 December 1931; 1 March 1933; 11 November 1963; 21 March 1989; 4 June 2004; 2 August 2006
Sunday Mirror 13 August 2006
The Times 7 April 2006

WEBSITES

Aberdeen Town and County History Society: www.aberdeenhistory.org.uk
The Cathedral Church of St Machar: www.stmachar.com
Church of St John the Evangelist: www.st-johns-aberdeen.org
East of Scotland Paranormal: www.esparanormal.org.uk
Grampian Police Museum: www.grampian.police.uk
Grand Lodge of Antient Free and Accepted Masons of Scotland (Lodge Aberdeen No. 1 Ter): http://aberdeenno1ter.com
Marischal Museum Virtual Museum: www.abdn.ac.uk/virtualmuseum
The Modern Antiquarian: www.themodernantiquarian.com
Royal Commission on Ancient and Historical Monuments in Scotland (Canmore): www.rcahms.gov.uk
Snopes Urban Legends: www.snopes.com
Survey of Scottish Witchcraft: www.shc.ed.ac.uk/Research/witches
St Nicholas Kirk: www.kirk-of-st-nicholas.org.uk
St. Peter's Catholic Church: www.stpetersaberdeen.org.uk/
UFO Casebook: www.ufocasebook.com
UFOInfo: www.ufoinfo.com
Water UFO Research: www.waterufo.net
Zoology Museum: www.abdn.ac.uk/~nhi708

INDEX